Colonial and Postcolonial Discourse in the Novels of Yŏm Sang-Sŏp, Chinua Achebe and Salman Rushdie

COMPARATIVE CULTURES AND LITERATURES

Daniel Walden
General Editor

Vol. 9

PETER LANG
New York • Washington, D.C./Baltimore • Bern
Frankfurt am Main • Berlin • Brussels • Vienna • Oxford

Soonsik Kim

Colonial and Postcolonial Discourse in the Novels of Yŏm Sang-Sŏp, Chinua Achebe and Salman Rushdie

PETER LANG
New York • Washington, D.C./Baltimore • Bern
Frankfurt am Main • Berlin • Brussels • Vienna • Oxford

Library of Congress Cataloging-in-Publication Data
Kim, Soonsik.
Colonial and postcolonial discourse in the novels of Yŏm Sang-sŏp,
Chinua Achebe and Salman Rushdie / Soonsik Kim.
p. cm. — (Comparative cultures and literatures; vol. 9)
Includes bibliographical references and index.
1. Literature, Comparative—History and criticism. 2. Imperialism
in literature. 3. Colonies in literature. 4. Decolonization
in literature. 5. Yŏm, Sang-sŏp, 1897–1963—Criticism and
interpretation. 6. Achebe, Chinua—Criticism and interpretation.
7. Rushdie, Salman—Criticism and interpretation.
I. Title. II. Series.
PN871.K56   809.3'9358—dc20   96-1863
ISBN 0-8204-3112-5
ISSN 1070-955X

Bibliographic information published by **Die Deutsche Bibliothek**.
Die Deutsche Bibliothek lists this publication in the "Deutsche
Nationalbibliografie"; detailed bibliographic data is available
on the Internet at http://dnb.ddb.de/.

The paper in this book meets the guidelines for permanence and durability
of the Committee on Production Guidelines for Book Longevity
of the Council of Library Resources.

© 2004 Peter Lang Publishing, Inc., New York
275 Seventh Avenue, 28th Floor, New York, NY 10001
www.peterlangusa.com

All rights reserved.
Reprint or reproduction, even partially, in all forms such as microfilm,
xerography, microfiche, microcard, and offset strictly prohibited.

Printed in Germany

Contents

Chapter One: Introduction 1
    Colonial Discourse 2
    Postcolonial Discourse and Shaping a Perspective 6
    General Background of the Three Writers' Worlds 11
    The Three Authors' Works...15

Chapter Two: Yŏm Sang-sŏp and Colonial Reality........................21
    Yŏm Sang-sŏp and Modern Korean Literature 21
    Psychological Topography of the Colonized: A Study of
        Yŏm's Short 'Trilogy" and *Mansejŏn* 36
    Three Generations: A Synthetic Vision in the Split World..............58

**Chapter Three: Chinua Achebe and the Creation of
        an African Discourse in English**....................................71
    Chinua Achebe and Modern African Literature 71
    Things Fall Apart: Disintegration of Tradition 87
    Arrow of God: Is It Ulu's?..99
    No Longer at Ease: African Corruption
        as the Second Coming 109

**Chapter Four: "Pickling" History in Rushdie's
        Works**..121
    Rushdie's Literary World...121
    Midnight's Children: Children of History 125
    Shame: The Origin of Violence 149
    Apocalyptic Visions 173

Chapter Five: Conclusion 179

Notes 185

Bibliography 197

Index 209

Chapter One

Introduction

This is a study of colonial and post-colonial discourse in the twentieth century through a close examination of works by three writers who deal with colonial experiences. These writers are, Yŏm Sang-sŏp a Korean, Chinua Achebe a Nigerian and Salman Rushdie an Indo-Pakistani origin British. At first glance, the grouping of these authors may seem odd because their cultural, historical, political backgrounds differ widely from each other. Yet, a certain universal experience binds them closely, namely, the nineteenth and early twentieth century global experience of imperialism and its consequences.

This study of the three authors explores colonial discourse and its counter discourse, postcolonial discourse, in order to understand how deeply colonial experiences affect each author's thought and aesthetic work. By questioning the validity of becoming an unfairly constructed object of inferiority and of bias, each author deals with the issue of his personal and cultural identity, particularly as a colonized subject. The fact that these authors come from varied cultural, traditional and historical backgrounds cannot be allowed to obscure another equally salient fact: each is the Other in colonial discourse. Each responds to the effects of colonization.

In approaching the relationship between ideology and literature in general and colonial/postcolonial discourse, I am indebted to scholars like Terry Eagleton, Frederic Jameson, Raymond Williams, Gayatri Chakravorty Spivak, and Edward Said. Terry Eagleton views literature as "complex historical articulation" whose forms and narrative modes reflect contemporary social, economic, ideological and political conditions. Accepting this view for this study of selected literary works dealing with colonial experiences, I will analyze how colonial experiences create various conflicts culturally, economically, psychologically, and aesthetically. During the imperial era, socio-political power structures reflected hegemonic struggles between the colonizer and the colonized. It may seem fair to approach colonial discourse from both perspectives. However, literary studies on the colonizer's view of the Other, or "the myth of the Other," are numerous. My study focuses on counter perspectives, on the perspectives of the colonized. This study thus marks a significant transition in the critical attention of the Third World subject from a mere representation in western discourse to a subjective matter constituted by its own textual voices.

Colonial Discourse

Colonial discourse is not simply an abstract term for how one perceives the Other.[1] It indicates more specific attitudes which, though they originated earlier, were significantly shaped by imperial expansion of the West during the nineteenth and early twentieth century. The sociopolitical and economic aggression of the West during the imperial era produced a body of "biased" knowledge—whether systematically constructed or not—which was dedicated to increasing the West's dominance over the rest of the world.

As noted above, the colonial and postcolonial discourse reflects a power structure in relationships of "We" versus "the Other." Edward Said's *Orientalism*, for instance, illustrates how such power structures are imbedded in academia. According to him, the idea of "Orientalism" cannot be viewed just as well-structured lies or myths of the Other. As a sign of Western power over "the Orient," such discourse reflects varying degrees of hegemony based on a considerable material and academic investment in a system of knowledge designed to "interpret"—hence judge—the Other. In his *Blank Darkness: Africanist Discourse in French*, comparing Europe's attitude toward Africa with Said's view of "Orientalism," Christopher L. Miller remarks that "Africanist discourse is at the least an *unhappy* Orientalism."[2] If the Orient is the Other to the West, Africa is the Other's other. He finds that one of the notable characteristics in Africanist discourse is Europe's projection of *nullity* into Africa.

The theory of Social Darwinism of the last century also attempted, in a systematic and scientific way, to prove that the fittest and strongest race, in this case, the white, was superior to other races. However, it should be acknowledged that Social Darwinism, Africanisme or Orientalism was built upon subjective view which often led to biased inaccuracy and distortion in so far as it had been supported and influenced by a one-sided dogmatic ideology.

In a cultural study, the Other should not be treated as an inert object for scientific research as if it were merely a natural object. Yet the West approached the Other with the same dominating attitude as it had towards Nature. The very idea of the West versus the Other is rooted in a Eurocentric world view; indeed "Orient" and "Occident" are concepts which reflect the western tendency to assert itself over and against non-western cultures. Even the term "non-western," by its very negativity, suggests definition by negative qualities. If the term colonial discourse presupposes a binary opposition of power between two different cultural entities as such, there is no doubt that colonial discourse had been dominated by the discourse of the West about or on Non-western culture expressing differences and similarities one way or the other.

Early stages of colonial discourse in a broad sense are usually documentary accounts of cultural contacts, satisfying one's curiosity on other exotic lands and their people. The idea of the "Noble Savage" is an example of white men's psychological and romantic projection of their cultural dissatisfaction onto the Other. And yet, implied is the notion of progress, that is, civilized versus primitive. Nevertheless early (self-centered) accounts of the west about the Other were relatively based on mutual respect. Montaigne's essay "On Cannibals," for example, has deep sentiments of respect and wonder towards "primitive" cultures. Despite the numerous descriptions of savage (barbaric) customs and primitive dwelling conditions he had heard from other, Montaigne's wise reflexivity places emphasis ultimately on the Other's cultural merits found in the metaphysical realm not in the material world. He used the Other and their positive Otherness to warn demoralization of his own civilization.

By the end of the nineteenth century, the remoteness of the Other in the early colonial discourse had been replaced by realistic necessities of economic and political interests, which brought the massive and systematic exploitation of non-whites along with strong racial biases. The romantic projection to the Other found in the eighteenth and early nineteenth century literature was replaced by wide-spread debasement and dehumanization of non-white races. Thus, racial consciousness or curiosity of earlier contact with the Other changed into serious "racism."

Colonial discourse reflects not only contemporary ideology but also sociopolitical situations. The narrative voice in literary works about the Other usually carries a negative judgment about them, and it perpetuates the West's superiority complex and the Other's inferiority complex. The ideology of imperialism or colonialism is actually cultural discourse which rationalizes inequality as it systematically distorts and devalues the Other and the Other's culture.

In creating a false conception of the Other, colonial discourse reveals the truth about power structures. The West has been the voice of the powerful. The political dominance all over the globe might be a kind of infallible evidence for supremacy of the western civilization during the period of imperialism. Imperialist rhetoric of the time served as an important tool to exploit and manipulate the Other through psychological dominance as well as political and military dominance. Literary works contributed to the perpetuation of such colonial or imperial attitudes.

Kipling's works on India captured readers' attention through glorious adventure tales in an exotic land and literally mesmerized them with his story-telling skill. Only a few alert readers detected hidden structures of imperialism in his romantic fantasy tales. The essence of the hidden structures might be mythification of the imperial powers. Through tales of adventurous white men in an exotic land of the East, Kipling glorified colonialists and the British Empire. He set up the ideal, and yet unmistakably romantic, images of the colonial officers engaged in the so-called "building of the Empire." Kipling's literary works thus fulfill the idea of "White man's burden" to enlighten less civilized people. Nevertheless, Kipling's short stories on India deal with fear of the Other and of the dangers in immersing oneself as a white man into the native culture. He consciously denies the charms and attractiveness in the native culture through his characters' speeches. When Kipling's characters fall in love either with Indian culture or with Indian women, they are condemned. In *Kim*, negative images of India thus mingle with exotic colors and vigor of Indian life. On the surface level of the narrative, Kim fulfills his spiritual and political goals. Beneath the surface, however, is a racism which didactically reinforces contemporary attitudes like Social Darwinism.

The later stage of colonial literature seems to be characterized by doubt and suspicion of imperial rhetoric. Kiplingian myths of Empire and imperialism were later questioned by many authors, such as E. M. Forster, Joseph Conrad and George Orwell. True colonial realities hidden behind the glorious mask of ideological rhetoric were eventually revealed in literary works by these writers' indirect quest for truth. Through the depiction of various difficulties facing colonial officers, they started to question the meaning of colonial life (existence) trying to see the Other as truthfully as possible. The colonials' sense of the noble mission of "building the Empire," which had been the backbone of imperialism, becomes a questionable subject to themselves, while they face the Other. The discrepancies existing between the ideology and the colonial reality shook the conscience of the western mind. Writers who experienced the colonial reality saw cracks in imperialism and its system. Despite the fact that they approached this delicate subject of colonialism cautiously, their works challenged the existing imperialistic value system.

Conrad eloquently and precisely wrote about the sickening aspects of imperial practice in the colony in his *Heart of Darkness*. Marlow, the narrator, speaks:

> Mind, none of us would feel exactly like this. What saves us is efficiency—the devotion to efficiency. But these chaps were not much account really. They were no colonists, their administration was merely a squeeze, and nothing more, I suspect. They were conquerors, and for that you want only brute force—nothing to boast of, when you have it, since your strength is just an accident arising from the weakness of others. They grabbed what they could get for the sake of what was to be got. It was just robbery with violence, aggravated murder on a great scale, and men going at it blind—as is very proper for those who tackle a darkness. The conquest of the earth, which mostly means the taking away from those who have a different complexion or slightly flatter noses than ourselves, is not a pretty thin when you look into it too much. What redeems it is the idea only. An idea at the back of it, not a sentimental pretence but an idea; and an unselfish belief in the idea—something you can set up, and bow down before, and offer a sacrifice to . . . .[3]

Prior to talk about his experience in the Congo, Marlow expresses his dismayed realization of discrepancies existing in colonialism as an ideological practice. Here, he (or Conrad himself) accurately expresses how the ideology, imperialism, functions to redeem the West's guilt in colonial practices. The conquest of the earth is actually robbery and massacre on a massive scale. By putting the ugly truth of practicing imperialism into words, he clearly shows discrepancies between the colonial reality and the sublimated ideology. When Marlow lies to Kurtz's Intended, Conrad individualized or privatized the ramification of Europe's Imperial lie. That is, the author brings out the ramification of the Imperial lie on a personal level. Imperialism affected every corner of the globe and every aspect of the society. It altered our perspectives irrevocably.

Postcolonial Discourse and Shaping a Perspective

The publication of *The Empire Writes Back: Theory and Practice in Post-Colonial Literatures* (1989) by Bill Ashcroft and others reflects the rising interest in postcolonial and Third World literatures. This book provides a theoretical background, various approaches to postcolonial discourse and models of postcolonial literary criticism. Though I started research on my subject long before this book's publication, I found that it approached Third World literatures in the postcolonial era in ways to similar to mine. My study of Yŏm, Achebe and Rushdie, however, not only exemplifies how to approach colonial and postcolonial discourse but it illustrates differences and similarities from a more consistently comparative perspective. Moreover, it goes beyond the Anglophonic focus of *The Empire Writes Back* and other related books on the postcolonial issues.

As I mentioned earlier, Marxist literary perspectives influenced me the most in viewing literature as time-bound reflections of ideology. In the aesthetic analysis of narrative discourse, along with other literary theories, the structuralist's treatment of languages and stories helped me to objectify different discourses even when the literary works come from different sociocultural backgrounds, as in this case of the three authors.

A basis knowledge of imperialism is necessary in the study of the twentieth century literature. There are many book on the subject, the most famous possibly being Lenin's *Imperialism: The Highest Stage of Capitalism*. Yet of all the studies, Hanna Arendt's *The Origins of Totalitarianism* seems one of the most useful. By approaching the subject through its sociopolitical and economic dimensions, her *Imperialism* (Part Two of *The Origins of Totalitarianism*) provides an insightful analysis of Europe's embrace of the ideology as a sociopolitical apparatus to serve its political and economic needs. Her book also provides links between Europe's bureaucracy and racism in the practice of imperialism.

As for the psychological and sociological ramifications of colonialism, works by Albert Memmi and Frantz Fanon have become indispensable in the study of imperialism in the postcolonial era. Memmi and Fanon not only analyzed fabrics of colonization but also treated the decolonization process in terms of their human dimensions, paying attention to both the former colonizer and the formerly colonized. From the perspective of the colonized, Frantz Fanon presented the most convincing analysis of the psychological and sociological consequences of colonization in his two most famous and important books, *Black Skin, White Masks* and *The Wretched of the Earth.*

Albert Memmi's *The Colonizer and the Colonized* provides various portraits of two basic actors of imperialist drama: the colonizer and the colonized. Thus, by presenting a detailed analysis of the human participants in colonialism, he shows clear discrepancies between myth and fact about the colonizer and the colonized. In this book, Memmi suggests that, in order to be "whole and free" human beings, members of each group have to cease to exist as categories or "types."

O. Mannoni's *Prospero and Caliban: The Psychology of Colonization* explains the colonial situation as an encounter of two different types of mentality: the colonizer as suffering from a desire for perfection and the colonized as having an intrinsic dependency complex. When these two different types meet each other, one becomes dominant and the other dependent. Thus, such a relationship becomes that of mast and slave. According to Mannoni, when the native's need for dependence is satisfied, he is no longer bothered by an inferiority complex. The native's dependency complex excludes his sense of gratitude as if a child does not feel any gratitude toward his parents until he has a certain degree of independence. It seems obvious that Mannoni's approach is racially and culturally biased. Above all, it does not sound convincing when he takes for granted that the native's (colonized) so-called dependence complex precedes colonialism. In his *Black Skin, White Masks*, however, Fanon criticized Mannoni's approach to colonial relationships. Fanon particularly rejects Mannoni's view of the dependency complex of the colonized as intrinsic. Fanon urges blacks to cast off the imposed inferiority complex. Instead of trying to become "white," they should act to change unjust social structures and values, the real sources of their conflicts.[4]

Racism or race consciousness is an important issue in colonial discourse. One's skin color has become a primary signifier to imply one's cultural, economical and sociopolitical being, including the projection of oneself as the Other. Among many studies on racism in literature, *"Race," Writing, and Difference* contains essays by a number of scholars on the subject. Henry Louis Gates, Jr., the editor of the book, states that "race has become a trope of ultimate, irreducible difference between cultures, linguistic groups, or adherents of specific belief systems which—more often than not—also have fundamentally opposed economic terests."[5] Gates has devoted his academic life to works by Afro-American writers. In *Figures in Black: Words, Signs, and the "Racial" Self*, for example, he analyzes figuration in narrative mode in Afro-American writers' works and how it signifies the "racial self." In a literary world dominated by the "white" male tradition, it is interesting to see how writers from marginalized backgrounds express their feelings and identities by using existing literary modes and media.

In gender discourse, it is obvious that men have considered woman as the Other, just as the West has considered non-west as the Other. Women are men's mirror image, as the Other is the West's. Gayatri Chakravorty Spivak combines feminism with the postcolonial approach to imperialism. Starting from her keen knowledge of "high" literary theories of deconstruction, of French intellectuals like Jacque Derrida and Michel Foucault, along with combinations of Marxist perspectives, she is concerned to debunk the innate imperialistic mode within Western discourse by analyzing the question of representation of the third world subject.

Her deconstructive way of pointing out the problematized issues of the subaltern in western intellectuals' discourse may actually help the West to become aware of the "real" existence of the subaltern. By naming all the marginalized and oppressed the subaltern, Spivak calls for the active role of subaltern historiography. She is also concerned with the question of shifting from subject-constitution to object-formation and vice versa. Having the two ways of representation, *Vertretung* and *Darstellung*, in her mind, it seems, she tries to create a voice for the muted subaltern, especially for the female subaltern. As an intellectual woman of Indian origin, she recognizes the "third-world" woman's plight, caught between patriarchal tradition and modernization under the "white" imperial system. Such a condition is worse than to remain as a silent nothingness. The "third-world" women are doubly marginalized by the patriarchal tradition and by "white" imperialism.

In the postcolonial era, one's choice of language in the ex-colonies can be a cultural, political statement. European languages as media to carry so-called "civilization" to dark areas have become official languages in most of the ex-colonies. Ironically, many ex-colonies, fearing the fragmentation caused by allowing their many native languages officially to flourish, have used former colonial languages as instruments of national unification. European languages remain, however, a major reminder of European colonial legacy. Struggling to have their own independent identity, ex-colonies are still divided on issues of abrogation and appropriation of the imported languages. Such issues touch writers even more poignantly. For instance, its evidences can be found in African literature. Some writers like Chinua Achebe and Wole Soynka of Nigeria choose to write in English, whereas a Kenyan writer, Ngugi wa Thiong'o, denounces it.

Ngugi wa Thiong'o is one of the most outspoken advocates of African literature in native African languages. Both his works and his life reflect his keen political awareness of anti-colonialism and decolonization. His position on the language issue in African literature differs from Achebe's, and it is discussed in detail in chapter two. Ngugi considers English and other western literatures to have played an important role in the perpetuation of imperialism. He basically regards departments of western literatures in Africa's institutions of higher education as a colonial legacy which will ultimately destroy African minds and souls. In 1967, Ngugi became the first African member in the Department of English, at the University College, in Nairobi. The next year, he proposed the abolition of the Department of English and its replacement by the Department of African Literature and Languages. Instead, in 1970, the department was changed to Department of Literature (including sub-department of French-based studies), and a Department of Linguistics and African Languages was formed.[6] In his book, *Decolonising the Mind* (1986), the last book—he has stated—he would write in English, Ngugi expounds the necessity of using African languages for African literature as a way of decolonization.

However, writers who choose to write in English or French can reach metropolitan audiences beyond their own countrymen. Their works point to the emergence of cross-cultural hybrids. Though I can sympathize with Ngugi wa Thiong'o's total rejection of colonial languages as a means of decolonization, I also consider the appropriation of European languages to be a possible means of decolonization. The works by Chinua Achebe and Salman Rushdie in English are, for instance, examples of successful appropriations. Despite their connection to the colonial past, they exist separately from "English" English.

Salman Rushdie's article in *The Times*, printed in early eighties, mentioned the significance of emerging "Third World" literatures in English:

> And the English language, like many of the other bequests, is tainted by history as a result. Something of the unwashed odour of the *chamcha* lingers around its cadences. The language, like much else in the newly independent societies, needs to be decolonized, to be remade in other images, if those of us who use it from positions outside Anglo-Saxon culture are to be more than artistic Uncle Toms. And it's this endeavour that gives the new literatures of Africa, the Caribbean and India much of their present vitality and excitement.[7]

According to Rushdie, the *chamcha*, literally "a spoon," is used for referring "a sycophant" actually. His phrase, "the unwashed odour of the *chamcha*," means the successful blending of native cultures in English. These writers from different cultural backgrounds display a distinctive use of English to invoke their identities.

Both Achebe and Rushdie are able to present their own unique cultural scenes and flavors in their works by using English. In the study of each author's narrative discourse, I will deal with each writer's narrative technique as he attempts to achieve and present his cultural identity through the imported language. One of the most striking features in the two authors' narrative is the use of native words untranslated in the English text. This phenomenon seems a distinctive characteristics of postcolonial writing, as the authors of *The Empire Writes Back: Theory and Practice in Post-Colonial Literatures* explain:

> However, such uses of languages as untranslated words do have an important function in inscribing difference. They signify a certain cultural experience which they cannot hope to reproduce but whose difference is validated by the new situation. In this sense they are directly metonymic of that cultural difference which is imputed by the linguistic variation. In fact they are a specific form of metonymic figure: the synecdoche. The technique of such writing demonstrates how the dynamics of language change are consciously incorporated into the text. Where a source culture has certain functional effects on language use in the english text, the employment of specific techniques formalizes the cross-cultural character of the linguistic medium.[8]

The book uses the term, english, to separate "tainted" English of ex-colonies from "English" English. Untranslated words in English texts are metonymic figures to indicate cultural differences between Anglo-Saxon culture and other native (source) cultures. Such queer hybrids of discourse bridge two different worlds with unexpected success, as shown in the works by Achebe and Rushdie. Writers' ingenuity to bring out the essence of their cultures in English text adds varieties in English usage, and it also enriches both English and their own native cultures.

Asian countries have different literary traditions, as they have different scripts and languages as well. However, the experience of colonialism and influx of western ideas and cultures altered their own traditions. Under the grip of imperial power, it could have not been easy for a colonized country to preserve or to develop their native language. In the case of Korean literature under the Japanese Occupation from 1910 to 1945, the fact that Korean intellectuals including Yŏm Sang-sŏp at the time mainly used Korean script, *han'gŭl*, for writing signifies their conscious efforts to preserve the cultural heritage and the Korean soul. The Japanese colonial policy after the March First Independent Movement in 1919, allowed Koreans to use Korean language and script, though strict and harsh measures of Imperial censorship existed. During the last stage of the Japanese Occupation from late 1930s to the end of World War II, Japanese colonial rules did not permit Koreans to use their language. Even they forced Koreans to change their names to Japanese ones.

As Kim Tong-in wrote in his essays recalling the colonial experience, he and other writers thought that they had a sacred mission to preserve Korean identity by writing in Korean even under such harsh circumstances. Therefore, Kim said, writers like him endured harsh censorship in order to leave an important cultural asset to subsequent generations.[9] Strictly speaking, Yŏm Sang-sŏp did not experience the same degree of harsh censorship as Kim Tong-in did because he spent the late period of Japanese Rule in Manchuria and came back to Korea after independence. That fact does not reduce Yŏm's significance ad contribution to modern Korean literature. Korean literature today owes a debt of gratitude to such writers at that time. They led the way in the development of modern Korean literature.

General Background of the Three Writers' Worlds

Korea's historical and geographical situations played a significant part in differentiating its colonial experiences from other parts of the world and even from other Asian nations. Korea was annexed by Japan in 1910 and emancipated in 1945 with Japan's defeat in World War II. Japan was rapidly emerging as a world power after the Meiji Reformation and was trying to extend its power over neighboring Asian countries. To Japanese, the Korean peninsula had been traditionally the bridge to China. With the rise of militarism, Japan quickly became one of the world's major imperial powers. Japan won the Sino-Japanese War in 1894 and the Russo-Japanese War in 1904. Japan was soon after granted international permission to control Korea. The weakened Korean government signed the treaty in 1910, which allowed Japan to control over the nation. Formally, it did not appear to be a military conquest, though it was, as least by implication.

Culturally, Korea had a superiority complex and called Japanese savage. Korea and Japan were heavily influenced by Chinese culture. Both used

Chinese characters and accepted Chinese philosophy like Confucianism. Both also received Buddhism through China. Yet between the two nations under Chinese influence, Korea played the role of transmitter of Chinese culture to Japan. Proud Koreans found it difficult to accept the Japanese occupation of their country. Unable to impose their own cultural superiority in Korea, Japan used the cultural imperialism of the West. Japan's colonizing rhetoric was to show how far Japan had advanced in their westernization and modernization, and how much Korea benefited by Japanese Occupation. In recent history, Japan became the major transmitter of western technology and science to Korea. The reversed role affected both Korean and Japanese psyches as much as the relationship of colonized and colonizer did to each other.

Korea has a long literary tradition, and its traditional literary forms and genres are various and rich. Even fiction as a part of the prose tradition can be classified in various ways according to its length, the script used (Korean or Chinese), the author's social class, and audience. Beside the rich written tradition, there is also an oral literature transmitted from generation to generation such as ballads, legends, mask plays, puppet-show texts and *p'ansori* (story singling) text. Until the invention of Korean alphabet, *han'gŭl*, in 1443–44, literary activities were in Chinese characters. Even after the invention of *han'gŭl*, much of Korean literature was written in Chinese scripts except some popular literary forms. Only around the turn of this century did Korean intellectuals begin to explore the possibility of *han'gŭl* with the rise of nationalism. Literary works by Yŏm Sang-sŏp and his contemporaries belong to the "modern literary movement" not to the traditional literary heritages of Korea. Korean literary pioneers like Yi Kwang-su and Ch'oe Nam-sŏn paved the way for the modernizing of Korean literature in terms of sophisticated styles, employing new genres and using spoken languages. Modernizing Korean literature means in some ways certain Korean responses to the reception of western literary traditions. The fact that all such activities were done under the Japanese Occupation probably affected how Koreans view the West.

As Paek Nak-ch'ŏng, a literary critic, mentions, many Korean people still do not show much abhorrence to wearing western clothes. If the West had occupied Korea, he thinks, many Koreans would have shown stronger desire to insist on their traditional costume in their daily lives. Even today the Japanese colonial legacy influences literature education in Korea. As Japan welcomed and eagerly studied western literatures, the Japanese colonial education emphasized works by western authors such as Shakespeare, Goethe, Tolstoy, etc., more than *Manyoshu* and *The Tale of Genji* of the classical Japanese literature. Such west-oriented attitudes, Paek supposes, also have much to do with the Korean anxiety about how to read western literatures.[10] Yŏm Sang-sŏp's works display and signify many distinctive aspects of Korean colonial experiences.

Chinua Achebe is an African, more specifically a Nigerian writer. Africa is the second largest continent on Earth. European imperial powers destroyed most of its indigenous empires. By 1884 the European powers began to divide the continent, so that by 1920 most of Africa except Ethiopia, Liberia and the Union of South Africa was under colonial rule or protection. There are many distinctive cultures and various traditions according to geographic regions and their people. In general, however, Northern Africa has been fused with both Arabic and Islamic traditions and Sub-Saharan Africa has contained the most original and exotic cultures.

As far as African literature is concerned, there have been traditions of written literature in both Hausa and Arabic, however, they are limited to a smaller geographic area than oral traditions. Sub-Saharan Africa has rich and varied oral traditions filled with myths, folktales, proverbs, riddles, and magical spells. African oral tradition has a close link with music, so much of poetry is recited in musical form.

The historical and political contacts between Europe and Africa affected African literature deeply, not to mention other sociopolitical consequences. In twentieth century African literature, the relationship between oral and written traditions is one of the most complex issues along with the language debate on choices between European and native tongues. Modern African literature was born under the colonial educational systems imposed by imperialism. The twentieth century African literature adapted forms and models drawn from western literature. Yet modern African writers successfully transform the foreign elements into their own cultural traditions by blending their traditional heritages such as oral literature, indigenous customs and philosophies. In that sense, Achebe's works are considered as archetypes modern African literature written in English. Achebe transcends his Nigerian experiences and represents those of the whole of Africa. The analysis of his three novels here is also to show an African effort to bridge the two different worlds—Europe and Africa—and to create African's own voice in the twentieth century.

The racial distinctiveness of Africa made it easy for Europe to regard

Africans as savages or children and "backward" in their progress in civilization. White men thought they belonged to a more "advanced" race, and thus "whiteness" was metaphorically quite important in Europe's subjugation of Africa. Though skin color played a role in European attempts at subduing Asian nations, it did not play as large a role there as in Africa. It was recognized that Asian nations had long-standing "civilizations." In order to satisfy their political and economic needs, European imperialism in Asia thus relied primarily on political and military power backed by their advanced science and technology. In Asia, the rhetoric of imperialism supported and complemented military strength.

With the presence of British in India, English writers showed indifference to particularities of Indian culture, and instead, created a mystic and alluring atmosphere of unintelligibility of India and its culture. Kipling's discourse is an archetype of such an imperial attitude toward India.

Indian civilization is one of the oldest and richest in human history. It is also a cradle of some of the most profound philosophies and religions. The literary tradition of India is largely the tradition of Sanskrit literature. Its Vedic hymns, Hindu scriptures date back to the second millennium B.C. The Vedic age in Sanskrit literature is followed by the age of the great epics, the *Mahabharata* (War of the Descendants of Bharata) and the *Ramayana* (Story of Rama). India also has its own tradition of drama, which is in many ways different from Greek drama. *Shakuntala* by Kalidasa (5th century) is the best known Indian drama in the world. Hindu philosophy and its way of life dominate Indian minds. Hindu mythologies are still alive, coexisting with secular realities. Besides the literatures of Hinduism, India also has a rich Moslem literature, largely in Urdu, an Indian language written in an Arabic script.

With the increase of European interest in India, the knowledge of Indian literary traditions and works reached the West. The impact of Indian philosophy and literature was immense and made deep impressions on many western writers and on western literary movements. The Indian influence, for instance, may be seen in the writings Thomas Carlyle and S. T. Coleridge, and in the pantheism of Shelley and Wordsworth, and, in America, in the transcendentalists such as Emerson and Thoreau.

Though the British colonial government promoted the use of English for education and administration, native languages of India did not disappear as the British had intended. The confrontation of Indian intellectuals with western civilization resulted in a literary Renaissance, which generated literary activities in many Indian languages. In the early twentieth century Indian literature, this Renaissance produced Rabindranath Tagore who wrote in Bengali, representative of a Hindu view, and Mohammad Iqbal who wrote in Urdu and Persian, a spokesman for a Moslem view. As for the contemporary Indian scene, there are hundreds of authors writing in over a dozen languages, it will not be possible to mention them here. Among those writing in English, R. K. Narayan, Raja Rao, Mulk Raj Anand and G. V. Desani are among the more popular. Salman Rushdie belongs to the most recently emerging group of Indo-British writers. He depicts the Indo-British sensibility with western literary mode and creates a kind of magic realism. Rushdie's concerns are, however, deeply related to contemporary human condition in society and to an individual's relations to history in a broad sense. At the same time, Rushdie identifies himself with the cultural heritages of India. His works absorb both Hindu mythology and the Islamic sensibility of religion.

The Three Authors' Works

In chapter one, I deal with Yŏm Sang-sŏp and some of his early works representative of Korean colonial discourse. These works were written during the 1920s and early 1930s, when Korea was under Japanese occupation. There are several authors who depicted vividly the colonial reality of Korea. Why, then, choose Yŏm Sang-sŏp? I chose him because I think he is the writer who maintained the most a balance between aesthetic excellence and sociopolitical consciousness. His contribution to modern Korean literature is monumental. The analysis of his works in chapter one includes that of the significance of Yŏm's contribution to modern Korean prose style and the psychological impact of being colonized. Yŏm is considered to have captured the contemporary colonial reality the best.

Even though Yŏm Sang-sŏp's works capture most accurately the sociopolitical atmosphere of the time, his colonial reality in fiction is mainly focused on the life of urban upper middle class and is captured with an intellectual's discriminative vision. His protagonists appear to be introverted spectators of life. They do not dedicate themselves to any political ideologies. Yŏm created, instead, several ideologically committed minor characters as a means to reflect sociopolitical moods in Korea. His main protagonists' apolitical stance parallels in some way Yŏm's own attitudes toward the actual ideological turmoil upsetting the equanimity of Korean intellectuals.

Korean society in 1920s was not immune from the impact of Russian Revolution in 1917. As socialism gained many supporters among Korean intellectuals, Korean society was polarized by two conflicting ideologies, namely west-oriented liberalism and Marxist socialism. Many writers inclined to the latter denounced "art for art's sake," and launched movements espousing "art for the people." Korea Artista Proleta Federatio, know as KAPF, was formed in 1925, and its members stressed "socialist realism." As a result, general artistic sensibility was lost by the promotion of ideological propaganda. KAPF members' works mainly depicted the miserable living conditions of proletariats in order to emphasize a kind of harsh realism. In 1926, Yang Chu-dong and other writers started a counter movement to return to Korean traditions and to enrich the Korean language.

In the midst of such ideological turmoil within the art community, it was remarkable that Yŏm maintained his neutral position as a sympathizer. He never committed himself to any of these movements. As a serious artist with a sense of mission for development of Korean modern literature, Yŏm seemed unable to remain satisfied with any literary movements associated with political ideologies. In his early essays written during this period, Yŏm often criticized the socialist movement in art. Ironically, Yŏm's apolitical attitudes actually helped him to achieve an aesthetic balance in his naturalistic realism. Not being involved with any sense of political mission, Yŏm could devote himself to recreate reality as is. He never regarded literature as a means to serve any other end. Thus, his early works mirror contemporary Korean society under Japanese Rule. Just as it may be said that European modernists escaped from the oppression of imperial politics by retreating to an abstract and unrealistic world in art, so too one may consider Yŏm's consciously apolitical stance to suggest the extremes of political polarization of Korean society at that time.

Major themes in Yŏm's works are also common issues in the other two writers' works. These are political tensions, racial tensions and language issues, as in the colonial experiences of the West versus the Other. Yet, figurations of such conflicts between the colonizer and the colonized in Yŏm's works differ from those of Achebe's and Rushdie's. Yŏm's works reflect the subtle differences in colonial experience through characterization and narrative mode including the inversion of Japan's colonial rhetoric. By being written during the Japanese Occupation, his works also deliver the immediacy of the colonial experience. In the Yŏm chapter, I also try to show

how Yŏm's works differ from the other two writers'.

I personally find the placement of Yŏm's works within the context of world literature, instead of considering him only within the context of Korean literature, very rewarding. Literary theory in western academic is Eurocentric because it was created from western cultural and literary traditions. Eurocentrism even dominates the theory of colonial and post-colonial discourse. However, if one studies colonial discourse in Yŏm's work, one has to modify or even abandon Eurocentric perspectives. Colonization in this case took place in two neighboring countries in Asia, Korea and Japan. The distinctiveness of such a relationship means that literary theory cannot be blindly and easily applied to it. One more factor to be borne in mind is that Yŏm wrote in Korean, his native language and not in the language of the colonizer. Henry Louis Gates, Jr. mentions the limitation of current literary theory in relation to the study of black literature.[11] For me, western literary theory is also marginal to the study of Korean literature. Like Gates, I also use literary theory as a "prism" to refract colors and patterns in texts, in this case both in English and Korean. Thus, by relating works by a major Korean writer like Yŏm Sang-sŏp to writers like Achebe and Rushdie, I try to shed a different light on the evaluation of his work.

In chapter two, I deal with Chinua Achebe and his three early novels; *Things Fall Apart* (1958), *No Longer at Ease* (1960) and *Arrow of God* (1964). This chapter seeks to reexamine Achebe's soul-searching literary exploration of African culture, tradition and history. In order to illuminate the Igbo people's colonial experience and its consequences, Achebe depicts changes in Igbo tradition and culture inflicted by the British colonial presence.

European colonial discourse on Africa was always condescending. Thus, Achebe's dignified and stately narrative voice shatters the European "myth" of the Other. His portrayal of Igbo people and culture is contrasted to that of Conrad's portrayal of the Congolese in *Heart of Darkness*. Achebe has successfully created a different kind of discourse on Africa. His works are among the first in English to present an authentic inside view of African culture and people, to the world outside of Africa.

In the introduction to the Achebe chapter, I try to show the problems and challenges that African literature has faced in postcolonial era. Among the most influential and famous African writers, Chinua Achebe and Ngugi wa Thiong'o differ in their opinions about the use of European languages in

African literature. Above all, the language issue is the most debated in African literature. Such a debate is a part of efforts that Africans try to free themselves from the stigmatized history and to establish their identity apart from former colonizer's influence.

In his early fiction, Achebe depicted the disintegration of traditional Igbo society of Nigeria as a consequence of British colonial incursions. This has come to represent the typical colonial experience of the whole of Africa. Since the publication of his first novel, *Things Fall Apart*, in 1958, Achebe has been considered as one of the most important writers in African literature. Charles R. Larson mentions Achebe's significance in African literature in that he has become "the most original African novelist writing in English." Achebe's influence has extended to a whole group of younger African novelists. His *Things Fall Apart*, Larson says, become recognized by African and non-African literary critics as "the first 'classic' in English from tropical Africa."[12]

As an archetype of African discourse in postcolonial era, Achebe's works display his artistic ingenuity. He uses untranlsated Igbo words to deliver distinctiveness of African culture and tradition. By inserting Igbo proverbs and folklores in proper places, he successfully blends African oral tradition with Western discourse.

I focus on Achebe's sociopolitical and historical consciousness reflected through characters or situations in the novels. Thus, I arrange my discussion of his novels by the sequence of temporal background rather than by the chronology of their publication. In that way, changes and conflicts in Igbo society caused by the contact with the West seem coherently presented. I therefore discuss *Things Fall Apart* (1958) first and his second novel, *No Longer at Ease* (1960), last, and *Arrow of God* (1964) second.

In chapter three, Salman Rushdie and his works are discussed. Just as Chinua Achebe and his works represent the African experience of colonial contact, Salman Rushdie and his works are closely tied to the history of the Indian subcontinent.

The question I asked about the inclusion of Yŏm Sang-sŏp also can be asked about Rushdie. Why him? I like Timothy Brennan's reply to a similar question in his *Salman Rushdie and the Third World*:

> For one thing, India—the largest and most important single colony in a long history of European greed—had not been given its due in the West's renewed interest in 'Third-World' literature. Beyond that, no one in the remarkable history of Indo-

English prose—a tradition that includes Nehru, Gandhi, Mulk Raj Anand, Kamala Markandaya and Raja Rao—had anything like Rushdie's success in popularizing the subcontinent for a Western public, although many of them tried. And there was also the point that Rushdie's story had as much to do with England as with India and Pakistan. Thus, the 'in-betweenness' of the cosmopolitan—a creature, as Rushdie puts it, of 'translation'—was not only essentially there in his person but theoretically accounted for on every page of his work.[13]

Even before the publication of *The Satanic Verses*, Rushdie was famous. In studying his two major works, *Midnight's Children* (1981) and *Shame* (1983), my main concern is to capture Rushdie's pessimistic sense of being "handcuffed to the history." In *Midnight's Children*, Rushdie tries to allegorize the history of Indian subcontinent through his narrator-protagonist, Saleem. His works include sociopolitical questions of centrality versus marginality, of migration or displacement. They also can be political satires about politics in both India and Pakistan, even in Britain. The analysis of the two novels in this chapter will show his concerns much more clearly. His *The Satanic Verses* includes religious fanaticism as a form of repression as well as all the subjects mentioned above for its major themes. Instead of analyzing his Islamic allusions in the work, I will discuss the religious elements in the novel as a signifier of his Indianness. At one of his interviews with India Today, Rushdie said that he considered *The Satanic Verses* as a part of trilogy along with his previous two novels, *Midnight's Children* and *Shame*.[14] If one follows the subject of migration and displacement as one of his main themes, he might conclude *The Satanic Verses* draws the subject to some kind of ending, and to one's surprise, a positive one.

Instead of bringing out open conflicts, Rushdie chooses to embed the colonial experience in Indian or Pakistani daily life and politics. For instance, when Rushdie talks about centrality versus marginality, he presupposes that the post-colonial world power still is subjugated to former imperial powers. When the colonial experience surfaces, it usually takes on metaphorically transformed features such as political oppression, shame, concerns for power. Such a narrative technique gives his works a reputation of magical realism.

Rushdie's unique narrative effectively combines the aesthetic sensibility both English literature and the Indian tradition. His text produces multiple layers of meanings and allusions. Rushdie depends on an eclectic collection of metaphors drawn from various religions and mythologies, phantasmagoric narratives and sociopolitical ideologies. Such a narrative discourse successfully preserves mythical and transhistorical realms still in an Indian psyche. Some critics already noted that Rushdie's narrative is like that of García Márquez, Laurence Stern or Günter Grass. Yet one can also consider that his fantastic tough in the narrative might be derived from Indian literary tradition found in the two most important epics of India, *Mahabharata* and *Ramayana*. Besides many allusions to Hindu mythology in his works, for instance, the narrative tone of *Shame* in a way resembles such transhistorical tone of the two epics. Rushdie's perspective on reality is thus a curious mixture of Western and Indian elements. He himself calls it "an angle-poised" perspective. Thus, certain magical qualities in his novels may derive from India's literary tradition or from Hinduism, while the poignant yet potent political satire may stem from western literary traditions. Besides, the influence of *Arabian Nights* is obvious throughout the narrative of Rushdie's novel. His works are true hybrids of the East and the West.

Victimized by imperialism, Asia, Africa and India have changed irrevocably. Even the genre my three authors have chosen—that of the novel—demonstrates the extent to which the West has exerted its influence on the non-western world. And yet the novel itself in these cultures has been transformed. It is no longer the property of writers like Cervantes, Fielding, Austin, Dickens, Balzac, Flaubert, or Tolstoy, to mention some pre-20th-century figures. This study focuses on three different "transformations" in light of a common historical experience: the global experiences of imperialism in the twentieth century.

Chapter Two

Yŏm Sang-sŏp and Colonial Reality

Yŏm Sang-sŏp and Modern Korean Literature

Yŏm Sang-sŏp (1897–1964), a dominant leading literary figure in modern Korean literature, introduced psychological analysis of characters and realistic depiction of ordinary life. The ordinary life he depicted is mainly about middle class urban dwellers. With his long, discursive narrative style and rich vocabulary, he contributed a great deal to the sophistication of modern Korean prose. He was also an active member of *P'yehŏ* (*Ruins* 1920), a literary magazine.[1] Even though the magazine did not last long, the impact of its existence was powerful enough to create a certain trend in contemporary literary movements along with its rival literary journal, *Ch'angjo* (*Creation* 1919). As a key member of the P'yehŏ group, Yŏm often debated literature and criticism with Kim Tong-in, who was the central figure of the Ch'angjo circle. Their literary dialogues, which sometimes concerned personal matters, actually enhanced the development of literature at that time. After the period of Yi Kwang-su and Ch'oe Nam-sŏn, Yŏm and Kim became the dominant literary figures of the time, exceeding the two literary predecessors and their achievements.

Yŏm Sang-sŏp's literary career began with the publication of a short story, "P'yobonsil ŭi Ch'ŏng'gaeguri" (A Green Frog in a Specimen Room), in the literary journal *Kaebyŏk* (*The Dawn* 1920) from August to October of 1921. The story is considered to be the first naturalist work in Korea. After the success of his first work he devoted his whole life to writing, except for several vocational excursions as a reporter, an editor or a teacher, each for relatively short periods of time. Compared with other writers of short-lived fame or devotion among their contemporaries, Yŏm's tenacious devotion to literature made him a very prolific writer. Throughout a career spanning more than forty years, he wrote over two hundred works, including twenty-eight novels, many short stories and critical essays. In his youth Yŏm studied in Japan and was familiar with the naturalism which was in its peak there around the 1910s and 1920s. After introducing naturalism, however, he maintained a realistic writing style as his own. His writing is more like a scientific documentation of contemporary life. Reading one of his fictional works gives readers today a chance to re-experience certain social and political changes in Korean history.

During Yŏm's lifetime, Korean society underwent tremendous changes in every aspect. Since he lived in Seoul near the Kyŏngbok palace, as a child Yŏm Sang-sŏp often witnessed the turmoil of the Late Yi Dynasty struggling for survival in the midst of the colonial powers. He grew up under the Japanese Occupation of Korea (1910–1945) and lived through the experience of Japanese Colonial Rule. After the liberation, Korean society was once again engulfed in a vortex of political and ideological struggles. Eventually when the Korean War (1950–1953) broke out, Yŏm joined the Navy. Having experienced turmoil and hardship, Yŏm's keen eyes never failed to observe daily life in the midst of social and political chaos. He grasped fleeting moments of ordinary life and with rich vocabulary preserved them in fictional form. His characters make us aware of what happens around us, as they are caught between the tides of great social changes and yet are able to care so much about the petty details of living.

In this chapter on Yŏm Sang-sŏp, I will focus on his early works mostly written in the 1920s and a monumental work of early modern Korean literature, *Samdae (Three Generations* 1931). Among several works written in the 1920s, "P'yobonsil ŭi Ch'ŏng'gaeguri (A Green Frog in a Specimen Room)," "Amya (Dark Night)," "Cheya (The New Year's Eve)" and *Mansejŏn (The Year before the March First Movement* 1922) will be discussed.[2] These works are particularly interesting, both because they present all the characteristics of the author's writing style and because they reveal the reality of Colonialism in Korea more vividly than any other works written at that time. By reading these works, the actual day-to-day problems of life are encountered, examined, exposed and challenged. Yŏm's poignantly depicted conflicts and problems are realistic enough to influence our perspectives concerning the past. Above all, these problems and conflicts are closely tied to the course of Imperialism and the transitional period of Korea facing the new tide of western civilization.

After the annexation of Korea by Japan in 1910, the major external elements affecting Korean writers were political situations and "indirect" contact with Western literature. The following statement by Suh Du-su sums up the literary trends at that time which were responding to the influx of new western "isms" already filtered through Japanese reception:

> Many "isms" in literature had been introduced into Korea from the West—in most cases through Korean students in Tokyo. In the West, literary tradition had spanned a long enough period of time for many schools of thought and writing to develop. Each new "ism" was in part a self-conscious resistance to the dominance of the old school or schools. Each school, however, usually to take the place of an older one. Fighting against old and trite techniques and modes of interpretation of human life was pursued by one school after the other. Young Korean men and women studying abroad were eager to select the most suitable elements from these different schools of literature; they were overwhelmed by the dazzling changes which were introduced to Japan from the West. Many of them were voracious in digesting foreign elements in such a way that they could mold their own works into a distinctive "Korean" tradition. It should be noted, moreover, that the majority of these works were full of something repulsive in substance, and gloomy in expression. The milieu in which they produce their works resulted in mush retrospective sentimentalism, the only free outlet for Koreans under Japanese domination.[3]

This kind of literary activity and self-expression was not possible until the first nation-wide independent movement, the *Samil Manse Undong* (The March First Movement) in 1919.[4] The March First Movement was the first major massive instance of Koreans showing their discontent and resistance against Japanese Rule since the annexation in 1910. This nation-wide movement was inspired by the Principles of Self-determination of People proclaimed by President Wilson in 1914. However, the *Manse Undong* ended in failure. The Japanese crushed it with cruel and harsh measures. The very failure of this movement altered Koreans' attitudes and perspectives toward the future. Optimism and hope for independence, which had been building gradually before the outbreak of the *Manse Undong*, turned into pessimism: the collective dream for emancipation was shattered with one blow.

The dominant mood in *mundan* (the literary circle) after the March First Movement was a melancholic morbid sentimentality and depression. Often it led to the expression of self-pity with a tone of morbid decadence both in literature and in writers' private lives. This change of mood also led to some changes in literary themes. The didactic literature of the pre-*manse undong* period gave way to a literature more concerned with aesthetic issues. It also brought a shift in literary themes. It shifted from the sociopolitical appeal of didacticism of enlightenment period of Yi Kwang-su and Ch'oe Nam-sŏn preceding the March First Movement to personal and emotional quest. Some writers also turned to historical novels, perhaps wishing to avoid the harsh censorship at that time. Koreanized Romanticism and Decadence were dominant, especially in poetry. The decadent trend of the time was, indeed, inevitable; it resulted from the uneasiness about their political and social surroundings after the failure of the independence movement and from the acquisition of knowledge about literary decadence in the West. Contemporary intellectuals were thus able to express their own personal frustration along with the colonized's agony and despair.

Even though the failure of the independence movement did not bring the nation's independence, it created some visible changes in Japanese colonial policy. The Japanese Government, alarmed by this massive resistance, changed its policy toward Korea from a Militaristic Approach (*Mudan Chŏngch'i*) to the so-called the Cultural Policy (*Munwha Chŏngch'i*). Under the new governor-general, Saito Makoto, the new policy allowed Koreans to have more educational institutions and more access to more various cultural activities than before. Yet the number of police increased substantially and the political activities by Koreans were strictly repressed. It is a well-known fact that the cultural policy of the Japanese was ultimately a tactic only to placate unsatisfied and angry Koreans. For a better understanding of this period, we should consider the social and historical significance of the movement and its outcome. In order to assess cultural activities after the Manse Undong, we need to consider them from positive as well as negative perspectives, though the latter seems to have been pervasive in sociopolitical study of the era. I agree with the following statement by a literary critic about Korean social conditions during the 1920s:

> When we recognize the cultural policy by the Japanese as an ultimate stratagem of deception, it doesn't mean that we should deny possible utilization of the policy for accelerating national independence movements and maximizing its benefit to Korean people. Actually many examples found in increased cultural and social activities such as independence movements (struggles), labor movements, peasant movements, and women's movements, etc. demonstrate such positive uses of the cultural policy after the 1920s. Several newspapers, magazines, and literary magazines were published, and many educational institutions were established. Through this process, vigorous activities in [artistic] creation and [academic] research brought progress in many areas of literature, art, religion and education, etc. The literary history of Korea after 1920s should be apprehended from this angle, because it basically means synthesizing two separate dimensions of [cultural] significances [at the time]: One is the succession of an anti-feudal spirit which flourished in the plebeian literature in the late Yi Dynasty; the other is the growth of anti-imperial and nationalistic awareness which opposed the Japanese Occupation of Korea.[5]

This critic's statement illustrates the effort to look at the problems of the colonial period positively and constructively; this dark period in Korean history had some positive aspects. This critic specially mentions Yŏm Sang-sŏp's *Samdae* (*Three Generations* 1931) as one of the best literary works written during the Japanese Occupation.[6]

In dealing with the colonial reality depicted in fiction, it should be noted that Yŏm Sang-sŏp's depiction of colonial reality, or historicizing of the period, differs from that of Rushdie and Achebe in its perspectives. Achebe knows colonial reality in its tradition, Rushdie as the past. Both of them try to re-create its reality with a sense of purpose and have a relative freedom to forge their creative imaginations concerning historical facts. The safe distance between the authors' present realities and their fictional realities may well allow them added creative freedom. A critical reification of one's ideas based on historical facts might require a sure sense of commitment and courage. When one does it to criticize the present openly, however, he might endanger his life. Rushdie's case is an obvious example. Rushdie deals with the past very successfully in *Midnight's Children* and *Shame*. Though he often criticizes contemporary Indian and Pakistani societies, he does so indirectly by using several ingenious literary devices. He also places himself at the safe distance of an expatriate. But in *The Satanic Verses*, his religious allegory has created a furor in the Muslim world and it is costing him dearly. He has had to give up his freedom and cannot live in public for fear of *fatwa* (a legal ruling that Salman Rushdie should be apostatized from Islam and be killed). He provoked such reactions against him by dealing Islam in a negative way, to the degree to offend the Moslem community around the world.

In Yŏm Sang-sŏp's case, he always risked punishment for what he wrote. The "Satanic Affair" Rushdie has been engaged in is an example of what might have happened to Yŏm in his day, although the focus and the nature of his case might well have been different. Yet an analogy between Yŏm and Rushdie can be drawn concerning repression and rigidity of each society. Yŏm wrote about his contemporary reality accurately and thoroughly with a reporter's eye. His subject, of course, was colonial realty under Japanese Occupation. Therefore, Yŏm's depiction of colonial reality has a much greater sense of immediacy than does Rushdie's or Achebe's. Yŏm Sang-sŏp, after all, was fully immersed in his society and was bound to its social conditions.

Since Yŏm Sang-sŏp's early works were written during a repressive time, we can detect his ever-present awareness of Japanese censorship in his narrative discourse. For instance, the author rarely gives his own judgment directly. Instead, he suggests the horror of living in the police state under the Japanese. By creating several men of ideas as minor characters and associating them with the ideological struggles of Koreans and the Japanese reaction to them, he is able to express his own opinions indirectly. Sometimes he intentionally trivializes the appearance of Japanese police which seems omni-present. As a mast of realistic description, he depicts the poverty-stricken living conditions of his characters with great accuracy and usually without revealing his own opinion. All these techniques might have been Yŏm's way of escaping the net of Japanese imperial censorship.

Yet it seems an ironical paradox that such a well-calculated authorial precaution so clearly reveals the oppressive reality. For instance, a casual presentation of a Korean student or an intellectual shadowed by Japanese detectives without any reason but being Korean as in *Mansejŏn* (*The Year before the March First Movement* 1922) must have been common at that time, for such scenes frequently appear in Yŏm's works. This kind of detail depicted casually with a contemporary perspective speaks loudly about the harsh, repressive conditions the colonized had to face in their daily life.

Therefore, when we read Yŏm's early works, we have to be able to read "unspoken" words, between the lines. Like the game of finding meanings in Lacanian writing, the true meanings or the actual causes of given problems are not mentioned directly at all. Thus only readers who have prior knowledge and understanding of the colonial period understand the meaning of the "unspoken" words and the intentional avoidance of direct language. As in Barthes' *S/Z*, which ponders the plural text through an analytical presentation of "Sarrasine" by Balzac where the word "castration" is never mentioned, here in studying Yŏm's works I will try to read "unspoken" words as accurately as possible and to explain why Yŏm, unlike Rushdie or Achebe, did not directly condemn Japanese Imperialism or any of their policies, but kept his views hidden. By demanding the reader's active participation in this respect, Yŏm Sang-sŏp's early works are not merely "readerly" texts: they are "writerly" in Barthes' term.

Besides the immediacy of colonial reality, we notice another very important element in Yŏm's works of that time, namely his ambivalent attitude toward Japan. His ambivalence seems rooted in his family background and what Japan stood for in his life.

As has Kim Yun-sik, an active critic of modern Korean literature, I have found biographical explanations for Yŏm's ambivalence toward Japan. Yŏm Sang-sŏp had an elder brother who had graduated from the Japanese Military Academy and had been promoted to major in the Japanese Army. For Yŏm, this brother was a source of pride and shame. On the one hand, the brother was a source of pride because of his success in life. Without this brother, Yŏm would not have been able to study in Japan and attend a formal junior high school and prestigious Keio University, which he could not finish likely due to financial difficulties. His brother's success under the Japanese, however, also caused him shame. It is a kind of paradoxical entrapment of an individual as a historical being. If Yŏm Sang-sŏp saw his brother's success from a Korean perspective, it represented a shameful assimilation of Japanese culture and collaboration with the Japanese policy over Korea. Being unusually stubborn and proud, Yŏm as a Korean intellectual might have refused him to accept his brother's success. For his own education and comforts in life, Yŏm owed much to this brother, but this indebtedness was a psychological burden. He might have been agonized by such an antinomic existence.

It seems obvious that Yŏm tried to distance himself from his brother as much as possible. The psychological burden of his "brother complex" is described only once in his autobiographical story, *Mansejŏn* (*The Year before the March First Movement* 1922). Its protagonist shows a similar ambivalence toward his brother's chameleon-like adaptability and success in life.

Yŏm was imprisoned for about three months for his anti-Japanese resistance. He tried to gather people for the declaration of Korean Independence in Osaka in 1919. As the representative of the Korean laborers in Osaka, he wrote the Declaration of Independence in response to the 2·8 Independence Proclamation by the Korean students in Tokyo and to the nation-wide independence movement in March of 1919. Kim Yun-sik suggests that the reason why Yŏm by himself tried to declare his won version of independence is that he wanted to compensate for his "brother complex" through some gesture of resistance against the Japanese Occupation of Korea.[7]

In this incident, however, it is interesting to see that Yŏm claimed to be a laborer. This, in fact, shows his interest in Socialism, which was popular among intellectuals at that time following the Russian Revolution of 1917. However, he was never deeply involved and made no commitment to that ideology nor did he contribute to the Proletarian literature which swept

Korea in the 1930s. Instead, he created "sympathizers," and through them he expressed his concerns about socialism.

In Yŏm's literary world, his ambivalence is evident in his narration and sense of characterization. No character is seen black or white. They are ambivalent mixtures of all elements in life. Yŏm's characters are more faithful to their own personal needs and desires, though they have limited choices in life under the Japanese colonial policies. Through his personal situations, Yŏm probably understood the dilemma of life which was reflected in his creation of characters. Later Yŏm's brother became a teacher of Osan School, which was known to be one of the most nationalistic institutions in Korea. The brother's chameleon-like sensitivity to the real world forced him to resign from the Japanese Army because he could not imagine his future as a colonized in the colonizer's military. Again he led Yŏm to become a teacher there, when Yŏm quit the Dong-A Daily. During the time of his Osan stay as a teacher, it seems Yŏm was not contented, either. He fictionalized his inner conflicts and dismayed reality hidden behind the reputation of the nationalistic school in "E Sŏnsaeng (Mr. E 1922)." As the critic Kim Yun-sik mentions, it might be true that Yŏm's devotion to literature saved him from a schizophrenic existence.[8]

Images of Japan and the Japanese are also treated with ambivalence in his works. To Yŏm, they are objects of hatred who are responsible for all miseries of the Koreans. At the same time, they are admirable for their advancement in Modernization or Westernization. Yŏm's protagonist cannot hide his envy toward Japan's achievements in modern history. He tries to emulate Japanese intellectuals and aspires to be a "modern man." Consequently, Yŏm's "love-hate relationship" with Japan is evident in his works.

Above all Yŏm was educated under the Japanese and he was taken away from Korean society to study in Japan. He spent the critical student years in Japan. Thus Japan existed in two separate domains in his life; one as the object of hatred and the other as the source of much desired modernity. Yŏm wrote later, regarding his early education and contact with literature:

> Though it was a very unfortunate *unmyŏng* [fate] that during that period [the period of Japanese Ruling] our education was done in the Japanese language, which was to receive Japanese culture, my personal situation was much more unfortunate because I spent the later period of my youth apart from Korean elements. For instance, before I appreciated *Ch'unhyangjŏn* (*The Story of Ch'unhyang*, a classic Korean story) as a literary work, I read Tokutomi Roka's *Hototogisu* (*The Cuckoo* 1898–99). As for Yi In-jik's *Ch'iaksan* (*The Ch'iak Mountain* 1908)[9], I just overheard my mother's reading while trying to hold back my tears; but for Ozaki Koyo's *Konjiki Yasha* (*The*

Golden Demon 1897–1903), I read it to my [Japanese] landlord and her daughter. All these were disgraceful and unfortunate experiences for a Korean and a writer just beginning his literary career. . . . Despite the fact that I'd never composed a *sijo*[10] before, I had written Japanese *waka*[11] in my youth. These facts are not things to be proud of.[12]

As a young apprentice in literature, one of the main sources of Yŏm's literary knowledge was the *Waseda Bungaku*. He called the journal "lecture notes for the self-educating student." From this monthly, he learned about the western literatures, literary theories and criticism translated into Japanese. In this essay, he frankly acknowledges the dualism in his literary world. He says his experiences are unfortunate, because it is tragic that a writer cannot develop his aesthetic sensibility based on his own cultural and literary heritage. Yet through his works, Yŏm himself showed literary maturity to transform his contacts both with Japanese and western literatures into one of his own creative Korean experiences. As a result, his early works witnessed the unique historical settings of the colonial period. For these reasons, he deserves to be called one of the most important writers in modern Korean literature.

Yŏm's ambivalence toward Japan is similar to that of Conrad toward Africa and European imperialism in *Heart of Darkness* (1899), which he during the height of Imperial practices based on his personal experiences in Belgium Congo. The work is so symbolic that the journey into the heart of Africa becomes almost a psychological journey into the heart of one's innermost self. Through literary metaphors, however, Conrad shows us the crack in the ideology of Imperialism, the evil of colonial reality hidden under the façade of the sublime rhetoric through his stark and yet impressionistic presentation of colonial reality in Congo. And yet the ending of the story blurs the whole issue of doubt concerning Imperialism, as Marlow the protagonist-narrator lies to Kurtz's Intended about Kurtz's real life and death. Marlow's lie is the lie of the Imperialist. It reflects, however, the dominant voice of contemporary society and its values. The facts that the narrator, Marlow, lies in the end, suggests that the Imperial lie seemed inevitable to Conrad, who himself faced the believers in Imperialist lies with his published story. Kurtz's fiancée represents the majority of gullible believers of imperialist lies. These believers were Conrad's intended audience. The whole moral issue of Imperialism Conrad opens up in the beginning of *Heart of Darkness* is closed with a sense of ambiguity. After all, his narrator, Marlow, realizes that "what redeems it [the ugly truth of the conquest of the earth] is the idea only."

The personal backgrounds and sociopolitical situations of both Conrad and Yŏm were similar. Both were expatriates: the former, culturally; the latter, politically. Both were somewhat assimilated in the culture of the oppressor.

Searching for a Form as a Means of Self-Expression

The *mundan* (the literary world) of the 1920s in Korea was formed around coterie magazines. It was a literary subculture through which writers were able to associate with one another both as social acquaintances and as artists. Each literary subculture formed an allegiance against other groups of writers and became a major source of gossip. Actually the strong rivalry between Kim Tong-in, the central figure of the *Ch'angjo*, and Yŏm Sang-sŏp of the *P'yehŏ* was based on this kind of partisanship among literary groups.

Yŏm's attitude toward literature was very serious and he tried hard to find a literary medium suitable to him. He tried poetry and didn't like it. He was right to stop, for, as Kim Yun-sik points out, the two poems he published in Japan are very good examples of Yŏm's lack of poetic sensibility. Yŏm himself, in autobiographical essays, remembers that he always seemed to have preferred fiction over poetry.

After coming back from Japan in 1920, Yŏm became a reporter for the *Tong-A Daily*, in which he published several columns demonstrating his interest in literature. More importantly, the job presented him with the opportunity to meet leading Japanese literary figures in person, such as Yanagi Muneyoshi and Shiga Naoya. Yŏm became committed to fiction-writing only gradually, however. Even after he became very active in his literary group, the P'yehŏ coterie, which was formed from February to April of 1920, Yŏm did not publish any major work of his own until his short story, "P'yobonsil ŭi Ch'ŏnggaeguri" in 1921. Yŏm recorded his agony of creation and personal frustration in his essay, "Chŏsu ha esŏ (Under the Ailanthus Tree)" in January, 1921. This essay is a bridge uniting his creativity to the form of fiction. This experimental writing enabled him to objectify his private world, and to use it create a fictional world. Only after publishing this essay could he write his first masterpiece revealing his internal turmoil through the protagonist called X.

The sincerity toward literature found in Yŏm's writing is similar to that of the Taisho literature of Japan. Taisho literature was dominated by the *Shirakaba* group (the White Birch). The leading figures of the *Shirakaba* group were Arishima Takeo and Shiga Naoya. Shiga Naoya's famous phrase, "Bun wa hito nari" (Writing is the person), epitomizes the viewpoint that a writer's character determines the quality of his literary output.[14] A work and its author are so closely related that one cannot be separated from the other. In order to write well, according to this belief, one has to strive constantly to be a better person as a Confucian sage would do in Confucian society. Shiga's works were among the best of contemporary prose fiction, especially his *Shishosetsu* (*watakushi shosetsu*, I-novel). This genre, which flourished during the Taisho period in Japan, was highly autobiographical. Thus its narrative tone is confessional and very sincere. The sincerity was achieved through the author's sincere approach to writing fiction. To the authors of this philosophy, writing might be a way of achieving a higher state of mind like the "Tao" of a Confucian sage.

Yŏm's attitude toward literature was similar to *Shirakabaha*'s (Shirakaba group). Yŏm tried to find a way of expressing "individualism" through writing. At the same time, like the Shishosetsu writers, he regarded a literary work and its author as identical. Yŏm saw writing a novel as a means of improving himself. He could not separate himself from the work he wrote. It is quite obvious in one of his early criticisms, "Yŏ ŭi P'yŏngjajŏk Kach'i rŭl Nonham e Tapham" (Replying to the argument on my worthiness as a critic),[15] that he cannot separate a work from its author's personality. For the same reason, according to him, a judge must find out the personal background of a criminal before he can judge him. Thus when one criticizes another's work, one cannot disregard the author's character reflected in the work. Yŏm wrote, "If one were to ask Dante, Goethe, Hugo, or Tolstoy to write in the vulgar form of the popular novella, would that not be unreasonable?"[16] In other words, the great writers have personalities equivalent to their masterpieces. This may or may not be true in reality. But having this philosophy toward the relationship between literature and the personality of its creator, Yŏm struggled to find a way of expressing himself. Exposing his private domain to the public for the greater cause of aesthetic formulation, Yŏm had to learn to balance the real and the fictional worlds in his writing.

Yŏm's first essay mentioned earlier, "Chŏsu ha esŏ" (Under the Ailanthus Tree) published in the second and the last issue of *P'yehŏ* in January 1921, foreshadows the first psychological and confessional writing in Korea. In this essay, Yŏm mentions why he cannot write and how much he is annoyed by the disharmonies inside the P'yehŏ circle. At that time, one of the founders of the group, Hwang Sŏk-wu, dismembered himself. Kim Ŏk, Kim T'an-sil and Kim Ch'an-yŏng disassociated themselves from the P'yehŏ and joined the Ch'angjo circle.[17] In the midst of the internal turmoil among the coteries, Yŏm suffered from his own personal frustration as an artist. Interestingly, Yŏm included the description of a nightmare in his first work. He frankly describes the masochistic pleasure he experiences while suffocation from a woman's grasp. His personal agonies resulting from the pressure to write and frustrated attempts are revealed in this dream. This dream appears in both fictional form and essay form. In the fictional world, the same dream indicates the protagonist's psyche as much as it reflects Yŏm's own in his essay. These almost identical descriptions of his dream indicate that Yŏm finally achieved the personal objectivity necessary to write about his own world and to fictionalize reality. After practicing ways to fictionalize his own life and emotions through this essay, Yŏm was finally able to write his first work, "P'yobonsil ŭi Ch'ŏnggaeguri." The essay finally became the stepping stone for launching his career as a writer by proving his confidence in dealing with the reality of human experiences, both psychological and historical, in the form of fiction. This mastery led him to write a whole new kind of fiction for Korea, namely confessional and psychological realism.

Confessional Narrative
Yŏm's early works are characterized by their confessional tone, which was an absolutely new way of telling a story at that time. It was in a way a big surprise to the literary world. When Yŏm's first work, "P'yobonsil ŭi Ch'ŏnggaeguri," was published, his literary rival Kim Tong-in called it "the advent of a new Hamlet." Kim was so surprised that, as he mentions in an essay, "I felt great uneasiness about Sang-sŏp's appearance, and yet I could not help but be awfully delighted by the advent of this new Hamlet."[18]

Yŏm is not just telling a story; his narrative in this first work contains stream of consciousness and psychological analysis of characters. And also the conscious narrative voice is constantly searching for a way of defining self/individual in relation to the whole society. Through Yŏm's writing, modern Korean literature truly acquired its "modernity" in the area of aesthetic sensibility.

The "modernity" in Korean literature after the *Kabokyŏngjang* (Kabo Reformation 1894) was characterized, most of all, by the fact that such a "modern" literary work was written in Korean script and in the vernacular style.[19] In the pre-modern period, the term "*sosŏl*" (literally small talk, novel) indicated the cultural displacement of prose style far from respectability. Unlike historiography and verse, *sosŏl* was regarded, under the strong influences of Confucian ethos, as a vulgar and lowly form of entertainment, especially suitable for women and children. Also the Korean script, the *han'gŭl*, used by women and commoners, was not appropriate for respectable literati. To literati, the *hanmun* (the Chinese script) was the medium of expression. Literate men used literary Chinese, though they could not even speak the language. In terms of writing, they were bilingual in some sense.

This kind of attitude, however, began to change by the late nineteenth century. Especially after Yi In-jik started a "new novel" written in pure Korean script and yet not totally without the style and the tone of old days' story-telling, the *sosŏl*, the *sinsosŏl* (new novel) became a very important form not only to entertain the public but also to educate and enlighten. Using the *han'gŭl* also began to imply a patriotic and nationalistic sentiment in the vortex of imperial power struggles involving Korea. It resulted from the cultural movements led by several nationalistic scholars and historians like Ju Si-Kyŏng and Shin Ch'ae-ho. With introduction of western novels to Korean intellectuals, the word, *sosŏl*, meant a new 'westernized' genre differed from the traditional "small talk." The social position of *sosŏlga* (a novel writer) had been established by that time as an intellectual educated under the modernized (westernized) education system.

Yŏm wrote with mixed scripts of Korean and *hanmun* (Chinese characters) in his early days, as the way the Japanese used *kanji* (Chinese characters) in their script. Especially his early short stories had many Chinese characters in the text. Yŏm Sang-sŏp's use of Korean and Chinese together in his early writings indicates his solipsistic isolation in his intellectual growth without having contact with the world of Korean literature on the peninsula (*mundan*). His isolation as a young writer in his twenties resulted in his writing works using many Chinese characters; meanwhile, other Korean writers were already using Korean script exclusively because by that time modern Korean prose style had achieved an expressive stability. Authors such as Yi Kwang-su, Choe Nam-sŏn and mostly Kim Tong-in had refined it sufficiently.

Yŏm even used *p'i* (*kare* in Japanese pronunciation) and *p'inyŏ* (*kanozo* in Japanese) for third person pronouns, which had been used in contemporary Japanese since the Meiji period, influenced by pronouns in

Western languages. This indicates the degree of Yŏm's isolation among Korean writers and at the same time it emphasizes his familiarity with Japanese language and its literature. Instead of using p'i and *p'inyŏ*, Korean writers were already using *kŭ* and *kŭnyŏ* for the third person pronouns. Sometimes some authors used *kwŏlcha* and *kwŏllyŏ*, too. According to Kim Tong-in, he and other members of the Ch'angjo struggled to invent new and convenient pronouns. Kim Tong-in says that he consciously dedicated himself to refining the modern Korean prose style. His conscious effort started as early as in 1918, even before the March First Movement. Kim mentions that it would have been very difficult and confusing for Korean writers after the March First Movement, unless he had not set the standard of prose style and adequate use of language.[20] Yŏm obviously was un aware of this and conveniently used *p'i* and *p'inyŏ* by merely changing the pronunciation of the Chinese letters into Korean pronunciation. According to Kim Yun-sik, Yŏm continued to use these pronominals until the spring of 1922. By the time he wrote "E Sŏnsaeng (Mr. E)" in September of 1922, he had begun to use *kŭ* and *kŭyŏja* instead of *p'i* and *p'inyŏ*.[21]

One notable characteristic in Yŏm's early works, is his use of the capital letters of the English alphabet for characters and sometimes for places. Yŏm used initials, such as X, E, P and Y, etcetera, without any apparent reason. Since the *mundan* (literary circle) at that time was such a closed society, he might have wanted to avoid the possible identification of his characters with his actual acquaintances. This tendency continued until around 1926. By the time "Nam Ch'ungsŏ" was written in 1927, his characters had full proper names.

In the study of Yŏm's works, especially his use of language, one cannot ignore his family background and lifestyle.[22] Such knowledge is important for understanding the nature of Yŏm's narrative and his command of the language. Also, his personal experiences in life are closely related to his works and to his value and philosophy as a writer.

Yŏm's family belonged to the *chung'in* class (middle class people), a class placed between the *yangban* aristocrats and the commoners or farmers. Placed in between, *chung'in*s were used to be sensitive to reality. The *chung'in*s were less confined to Confucian ethics than the *yangban* class and more financially secure than the commoners. Thus coming from this traditional background, Yŏm could sense all the major changes during the last period of the Yi dynasty and the influx of new ideas from the outside world. He was ready for modernity. Besides his middle class family background, the fact that he grew up in the capital, Seoul, had much to do with his realistic sensibility.

And for his rich vocabulary, it can be attributed to the fact that his family was native to Seoul. Seoul Korean spoken by middle class people was considered the standard and still is. So his family background and origin gave him great advantages as a writer, especially when compared to other contemporary writers such as Kim Tong-in. Though the latter was already famous and established as a writer, his use of Korean could not match Yŏm's in terms of vocabulary and style. Kim was aware of his limitations. Since Kim's was an aristocratic family from P'yŏng'an province, located on the northwest side of the peninsula, he grew up in relative isolation and in pampered surroundings. His vocabulary and world view were limited to those of his social class, when compared to Yŏm's.

As for the relationship between his private world and literary world, Yŏm relied heavily on his personal experiences and surroundings for writing materials. Especially in his early days, some works were very autobiographical and/or were drawn from his acquaintances. Thus, in general, Yŏm is not considered to have the wild imagination or genius-like eccentricity to ignore common sense. He usually observed reality or his own surroundings carefully with, one might say, a reporter's eye. Many of his characters are drawn from real people he knew, and social backgrounds and his descriptions are more or less the real situations at that time. Actually he wrote several novels modeled after his acquaintances. For example, *Haebaragi (Sunflower* 1923), its title later being changed to *Sinhon'gi (Records of a Newly-wed* 1949), was based on the famous new woman, Na Hye-sŏk and her scandalous marriage.[23] Her life as a new woman was in every way new to the contemporary mores. Yŏm's early works discussed here seem mostly based on his experiences and inner thoughts.[24]

This kind of "plagiarism" of life in Yŏm's writing seems to originate from his philosophy of literature and his search for personal identity as a young man. I intend to deal with these issues in detail in the next sections of this chapter. Yŏm treated writing very seriously. To him, it was more than just creating stories to entertain. It led him to think about himself and how to live. Strict self-scrutiny and observation of reality perhaps led him to confessional narrative. Critics call his three early short stories a trilogy; "P'yobonsil ŭi Ch'ŏng'gaeguri (A Green Frog in a Specimen Room 1921)," "Amya (A Dark Night 1922)" and "Cheya (The New Year's Eve 1922)." The most distinctive characteristics of these works are, first, that their narrative tone is confessional and psychological and, second, that the protagonist of each story is educated and young like the author himself.

"P'yobonsil ŭi Ch'ŏng'gaeguri" seems to depict the author's psychological state of mind after returning to Korea from Japan. "Amya" is about a young man's agony at the crossroads of "love" and "art." The image of this young protagonist can represent an alter ego of the author himself. The third work, "Cheya," consists of a young woman's letter to her husband before her suicide on the eve of a new year. The descriptions of characters' psychological and situational dilemmas render such a mood as if the characters themselves confess directly to readers. In turn, it invites readers into the characters' inner psyche with a great sincerity, and that was not being done in Korea at the time.[25]

A Psychological Topography of the Colonized: A Study of Yŏm's Short "Trilogy" and *Mansejŏn*

Early works by Yŏm Sang-sŏp serve as the best means to measure conditions of life under the Japanese Occupation, especially immediately following the historic March First Movement in 1919. Among the contemporary writers, Yŏm was one of the few who wrote realistic novels. Employing the standard language of the middle class, Yŏm wrote about the world he knew and experienced, that is, the life of the urban middle class. In a sense, Yŏm's works are exemplary historical articulations which provide readers a realistic glimpse at colonial situations depicted mostly through the eyes of a young intellectual like the auth himself. The primary importance and significance of Yŏm's early works, which will be discussed here, can be found both in their literary achievements and in their historicity regarding the significance of the historical event, namely the March First Movement and its aftermath in Korean society.

The significance of the pivotal turning point in Korean history can be seen in *Mansejŏn* (The Year before the March First Movement 1923). As its title suggests, there is a dichotomous world of "before and after" divided by the Manse Movement. However, Yŏm's plot structure implies that Korea after the Manse was still the same dark and depressing world despite the claimed sweet-coated policy change by Japan. Yŏm penetrated through the "deceptive" division between the *Mudan T'ongch'i* (the Militaristic Rules) and the *Munwha T'ongch'i* (the Cultural Rules), and he depicted paradoxically the grim reality of Korea.

Yŏm's three early works, "P'yobonsil ŭi Ch'ŏng'gaeguri," "Amya" and "Cheya," marked the introduction of a new literary trend in the development of modern Korean literature. As discussed in the previous section, the psychological description of each protagonist is very personal and the narrative tone is confessional. Their dilemmas illustrate the typical agony of a young intellectual in the colonized country. All three protagonists are fictionalizations of the author himself and their experiences are the author's experiences in reality. The young protagonists' struggle to find the meaning of life or their own identity is aggravated by the fact that their country has been colonized. The lack of political and cultural autonomy makes it difficult for them to find the truth or the means to express it. Unlike the Japanese, the Korean writers had to go through much more restrictive censorship and suffered from severe economic and financial problems. They also had less access to printing media, which in turn aggravated their financial plight.

Yŏm's vision of life is grim and dark. His protagonists struggle to escape from their living conditions. All of them feel like living in a dungeon of doom with no way out, haunted by shadows of death. As young elites, protagonists of Yŏm's early works try to define their identity and to pursue personal ideals. They are, however, ultimately bewildered and shattered by reality. They realize that they have fallen into a trap, into the world of conflicts between modernity and tradition, the young and the old, and the colonizer and the colonized. Each of the protagonists seems to represent the young author facing the dilemma of life more complicated by the uncertain political situation of the nation.

Given the sense of despair and self-pity which leads intellectuals to indulge themselves in self-destructive activities, the most prevalent mood in the works of twenties was helplessness and frustration. Instead of expressing nationalism and aspiration for the nation's independence in a direct way, writers chose to put the message across indirectly and they turned their attention to individual's emotions rather than to didactic and enlightening themes. Critics usually ascribe the cause for such changes to the failure of the March First Movement, which shattered Nationalism and optimism at one blow. For instance, a pessimistic vision of life is reflected in Yŏm's very early works such as "P'yobonsil ŭi Ch'ŏng'gaeguri (A Green Frog in a Specimen Room 1921)" "Amya (A Dark Night 1921)," "Cheya (The New Year's Eve 1922)," "Chukŭm kwa kŭ Kŭrimja (Death and its Shadow 1923)" and *Mansejŏn* (The Year before the March First Movement 1923). In these works, the most dominant metaphors are of dark night and of the grave. Titles such as Amya, Cheya and Myoji (grave) reflect the dark and depressing visions of life in each work. All surroundings are desolate and sinister like a moonless night shadowed with images of death.

As the young author himself seeks solutions in life, his characters' lives are plagued by the shadow of pessimism and frustration. And yet this kind of confusion gradually gives way to cautious optimism. This kind of growing process coincides with Yŏm's personal maturation as a man and artist of a colonized country. The image of each frustrated and agonized protagonist in his trilogy finally comes to grips with his own identity through a psychological journey in *Mansejŏn*.

"P'yobonsil ŭi Ch'ŏng'gaeguri": A Morbid and Unrealized Dream for Freedom

In "P'yobonsil ŭi Ch'ŏng'gaeguri," the protagonist X identifies his situation with that of "a frog" for an anatomic experiment: "Meanwhile, either I lie down during the night or sit calmly during the day, what adheres deadly to my mind and inundates my nerves with cruelty is an image of a frog for vivisection with its four legs pinned down on the plank" (*YSC* 9:11). This image ultimately symbolizes the confined life without any freedom for either politics or self-realization. Interestingly the frog in X's mind is not dead, but is pinned down and helplessly suffering from the Japanese biology teacher's hand which is poking its internal organs one by one. This image bothers X so much that he develops an anxiety neurosis. At the same time, he hears other parts of himself encouraging him to escape from his suffocating room, which symbolizes his confined situation. He knows that he does not even have the courage to kill himself. As a spectator of life, he seems indecisive on any matter. Only with his friends' company can he leave his claustrophobic room.

He decides to travel to the north.[26] At P'yŏngyang, he encounters a madman with long hair. The image of the insane man reminds him of another madman whom he saw in Tokyo. He envies their care-free life style. He says that "real happiness lies (can be found) in such a kind of life" (*YSC* 9:15). That kind of life epitomized in the image of a madman seems to represent a life-style of freedom without caring about what others think or without any responsibility in life. X, with one foot in reality and the other in romantic escapism, projects his longing for freedom onto the image of a madman. His desperate attempt to escape from reality brings him face-to-face with a madman named Kim Ch'ang-ŏk. Kim is no other than the protagonist's alter-ego, whose sanity has been destroyed by colonial reality.

The narrative structure of the story is clearly divided into two kinds. Except for chapters six to eight, the narrative is focused on the prime protagonist X's psychological and emotional state of mind. Therefore, the tone is more philosophical and confessional. When the narrative is focused on X, there is not much action. The narrative contains a stream of consciousness which is a very "modern" characteristic of fictional narratives. Shocked by this new technique of story-telling, Yŏm's literary rival, Kim Tong-in called it "the advent of New Hamlet." Kim's phrase of "new Hamlet" is quite relevant when we see the protagonist's introspective brooding over the meaning of life. Hamlet as a character has become identified with the humor of melancholy, and with a complex, subtle, and almost paralyzing sensitivity to the imponderable ironies and mysteries of life. And yet, the source of X's agony and pain is rather obscure in comparison with Shakespeare's Hamlet, who is driven mostly by revenge. A probable reason for X might be the suffocating reality of colonized situations which preclude all possibilities of self-realization, including proper ways of self-expression. The sociopolitical mood in Korea must have been very different from that of Japan, where the author was immersed in a relatively rich and diverse culture. Both the sense of helplessness evoked in the image of a frog and X's limited living sphere signified with his suffocating small room indicate the repressive confinement Yŏm faced in terms of limited access to ways or means of living.

When the narrator tells the story about Kim Ch'ang-ŏk, the narrative tone is totally different. The segment on Kim is more like a story-within-a-story. It does not contain much psychological topography of the character, but describes only the symptoms of his mental malaise. The narrative tone is one of traditional story-telling, where actions or plots are more emphasized. Readers are told the whole life story of this madman from his birth to the present encounter. This fascinating life story, however, reveals a very significant sociopolitical truth, namely, the colonial experiences. The madman's plight might have happened to X. The madman had been an intellectual in the colonized Korea just like the protagonist X. His experiences in life can be shared by all educated men at that time.

In most of Yŏm's works, there are characters whose lives are affected by the Japanese police search for "*chuŭija* (-ismist)," which Japan often used as an excuse for the crush of any independence movement or nationalism. Here the *chuŭija* specifically refers to a socialist. Instead of using the word, *sahoechuŭija,* to refer socialists, Yŏm merely uses such incomplete word. Perhaps it was to avoid Japanese imperial censorship.

The madman, Kim, is also one of the victims of those round-ups for "chuŭija." The narrator describes all kinds of personal experiences which had actually occurred to Kim. Almost all of them are unfortunate ones. The narrator focuses on Kim's family life and emphasizes the death of his wife. After a second marriage, Kim, having overcome his sorrow, is about to receive an honorable award for his ten-year service as a teacher. But he is imprisoned for reasons not given in the text. The narrator only describes it as being "due to an unexpected event" (*YSC* 9:33). Yet there is a short cryptic and yet suggestive sentence, which explains why Kim is imprisoned: "About the time when his daughter was born, the Bible on his desk was substituted with lecture notes from the department of politics and economics of a certain university in Tokyo" (*YSC* 9:32). This sentence suggests Kim's ideological involvement with dominant ideologies of the time. But this information seems trivialized intentionally by the narrative voice, which superficially emphasizes and elaborates on Kim's family situations.

Only careful readers can catch a glimpse of its meaning and significance to the text; the restrained voice of anti-colonialism. The lecture notes might have contained Marxism or socialism, which had been considered a subversive ideology both in Korea and in Japan at the time. The Japanese imperial government repressed it, because in Japan it might weaken the governmental control over intellectuals who threatened to disrupt Japan's militarism, and because in Korea it threatened Japan's colonial power by awakening Koreans' nationalism through analogy between the oppressive and exploitative relations in colonizer versus colonized and in bourgeois versus proletariat.

After his release, Kim becomes mad or pretends to be mad. His "preaching" is full of significant admonitions concerning contemporary social issues. He builds a three-story house with a little money and few materials. In a real sense, it cannot be called a house. Yet in Kim's deranged dreaming eyes and mind, the house represents the actual embodiment of his self-realization and idealism. When Kim speaks to his visitors, his talk reveals his intellectualism and critical viewpoints.

With a comical touch and twist, Kim disguises his hatred for Japan. Such anti-Japanese ideas are expressed indirectly through the ideological medium of westernization. Even before X meets Kim Ch'ang-ŏk, he is irritated by the erosion of capitalism, one signifier of Japanese colonialism. When X and his friend climb up to the Ŭlmiltae (the Ŭlmil Pavilion), expecting to witness the glory of the Korean past, the first object to catch X's eyes is a commercial ad from a tailor for western suits posted to one of the benched around the place (*YSC* 9:16). This subtle irony is again expressed through the madman Kim. Kim casually mentions to the visitors how he tried to emulate the science and technology of the west by building the house more efficiently than the Westerners (*YSC* 9:26). He also criticizes the intellectuals who prefer a foreign language over the Korean language and script.

The narrator clearly shows that Kim is a megalomaniac who thinks he can contribute to peace on earth. So the title of his imaginary organization is *Tongsŏ Ch'inmokhoe* (the Council for Peach between the East and the West). The cause of his insanity on surface is his personal misery. Yet Kim as a madman primarily is concerned about big issues like peace between two hemispheres, colonialism, the World War I, Korean nationalism and even patriotic criticism on Korean snobbism, etc. Every issue he touches on has a certain truth to it. Only the protagonist, X, is able to see the tragic implications in the destruction of such an intelligent man's sanity. X ambiguously presents the fact that the direct cause of Kim's madness is Japanese colonialism. The paradox or irony seen through Kim's life and ideas is created by his madness. What happened to him is so probable that it might have been actual reality itself. Any yet the probability is blurred by the fact that Kim is an insane megalomaniac. In his madness, critical ideas such as anti-Imperialism or promotion of world peach become almost farcical through the comical touch and twist in narrative tone, which mainly represents rational and sane views. Yet X's empathy toward Kim delivers the hidden implications in Kim's life.

Among all the characters, only the protagonist X sees through the truth hidden under the mask of madness. Or maybe he projects his own desire on to the madman. He identifies with him. Suddenly Kim becomes the alter ego of X. Yet the narrative tone in the section on X's perspectives is pessimistic and dark, filled with images of death. When X is finally told that the madman disappears after burning down the house, he is very much disappointed. The news brings different reactions from X and his friend, Y. Y takes Kim's disappearance as a kind of spiritual denunciation. Yet X deplores the reality which does not allow even "the great philosopher" like Kim living in his own "fantastic" realm to live with absolute freedom: Kim's realm of madness is not enough for self-realization. X's realization that even in the realm of madness one cannot experience true freedom in this colonized country, Korea, comes to him so suddenly that he equates the colonial reality with death. Only after X sees the place for the traditional corpse carrier decorated with colorful phoenix during his short excursion, does he reach a kind of certain spiritual enlightenment: Only death can free the mortals (*YSC* 9:47).

Yŏm makes it clear that the suffocating life under Japanese occupation does not allow people to have an optimistic vision of life. The only vision the protagonist of "A Green Frog" can have is either of a frog with his abdomen helplessly exposed or of an insane megalomaniac dreaming of achievements and contributions for "global peace."

"Amya": Wanderings of the Confuesed Mind

The young man in "Amya" is lost. He isolates himself from people and becomes critical and cynical about things that are important to others. He does not want to belong to a worldly society (*YSC* 9:56).

The situations and problems the protagonist "X" faces are not clear except that his personal dilemma in life comes from the personally conflictive choice between "love" and "art" (*YSC* 9:52). He loathes everything without apparent reason and is overwhelmed by boredom (*ennui*) and sense of absurdity. His mind is preoccupied with abstract and abstruse questions. To him, the reality others experience is felt as an alien domain or as surreal. He is living in his death; his vision is as dark as night and his reality is cocooned like a vault for a corpse (*YSC* 9:57). X's agony seems very superficial and arbitrary, however, his mental sufferings are exact symptoms related to more fundamental problems rooted in political ambiguity and uncertainty of his youth in the colonized nation.

It seems there is no hope or future. There are two images in the story summing up X's perception of reality. First, the image of a bear confined in a cage symbolizes X's situation in life (*YSC* 9:48). Like the bear, he has no alternative but to be confined. He neither feels that he is living his own life nor that he belongs to the world (*YSC* 9:53). Like the bear in the cage, he feels that he is merely surviving. The second important image is drawn from a crippled boy he encounters on the street. The protagonist, X, pities the boy who is trying to fly a kite. Being crippled, the boy cannot run fast enough to do it. Yet he tries again and again. Looking at him, X identifies his situation with the boy's. No matter how hard he tries to overcome obstacles and to achieve his goal, unfortunate circumstances simply do not allow him to. As the crippled boy cannot run fast enough to fly a kite, X also cannot achieve self-realization under oppression such as colonial rule. To symbolize this suffocating situation, Yŏm Sang-sŏp uses the metaphor of the grave. This motif is again reified in the *Mansejŏn*, written in 1923, two years after this work. With the sudden revelation that this world is a grave (*YSC* 9:53), the protagonist becomes more cynical about all human affairs, about, for example, marriage and death. He mentions that marriage is just "a public announcement of one's adulterous decision" (*YSC* 9:53). Since as a youth he is pushed to get married by his mother, he becomes extremely sensitive about the issue.

The protagonist finds comfort in reading *Birth Pangs* by Arishima Takeo. Deeply touched by the book, this sensitive young man cries and admits that he's never before experienced this kind of pure emotional overflow (*YSC* 9:56). This passage moves the critic, Kim Yun-sik, to argue that Yŏm was influenced heavily by the authors of the *Shirakabaha* such as Arishima Takeo and Shiga Naoya, and that without their works he would not be an author.[27] As I mentioned in the previous chapter, this kind of blanket statement belittles Yŏm's literary achievement, making it into only an imitation of Arishima Takeo's *Birth Pangs*. Yŏm was creative enough to conjure the unique situation of Korea into his fictional world and characters. Kim Yun-sik also mentions that this work is a personal record of Yŏm's own experiences.[28] Considering Yŏm's serious attitudes toward literature and creative process, it is possible that Yŏm was suffering from his own awareness of his own limitation as a writer at that time. The metaphor of a crippled boy trying to fly a kite can be taken as a metaphor for a novelist who is trying to find to express himself.

Though the ending is somewhat ambiguous, even the most literal-minded reader can detect Yŏm's sense of optimism. The author himself wrote his own criticism on the work in the preface of *Kyŏnuwha* (1923), which is the first publication of the short trilogy in one volume: "A young man who idealizes art criticizes the others' insincerity and has already experienced tiredness and ennui. At the same time, he laughs at his own weakness as a mortal being. And yet he shows some efforts to look forward, with uncertain hope" (*YSC* 9:422). As the author mentions, the protagonist shows caution and limited anticipation toward the future indicated in the final passage; "while heeding his steps on uncertain ground, he struts along the long and wide Kwangwhamun Taepyŏng street, which seems stretched out endlessly"(*YSC* 9:58).

"Cheya": A Victim's Vision of Life

Life seems even harsher for a "new woman." Choe Chŏng-in in "Cheya" is defeated by traditional morality and ethics, and suicide is the only alternative left to her. The whole story is Chŏng-in's confession to her personal life and her philosophy. Her avant-garde lifestyle represents modernity, westernization and freedom, yet it is thoroughly ridiculed and condemned by contemporary society.

Chŏng-in is a "new woman" who tries to live her life according to her belief. She was educated and became a teacher. Yet she believes in "free love" as a way to achieve true "equality" with men and "emancipation" from the traditional suppressive norms governing women. Besides her numerous affairs before the marriage to her present husband, she had a serious relationship with E and got pregnant. The man did not take the relationship seriously, meanwhile Chŏng-in's parents were arranging the marriage to the present husband. Seventy-five days after her marriage, however, she was separated because of her pregnancy. In the midst of confusion, she receives a letter from the husband on Christmas Eve, saying that he would forgive her. The letter of forgiveness causes her to think about many things. She reminisces her past. Instead of going back to him, she decides to kill herself. So on the last night of the year (1921), she commits suicide to justify her flamboyant lifestyle and to not deliver an illegitimate child. She realizes that her avant-garde lifestyle has not changed anything in the society and that she has been the victim of the conflicting ideology of patriarchy and feminism.

The whole story consists of Chŏng-in's letter, in which she not only explains, justifies and defends herself but also accuses her husband and society in general. When she talks about her promiscuity, she partly traces the reason back through her genealogy. At the same time, she questions many conventions and traditions regarding women. She asks, for instance, what chastity and feminine virtues are. She also urges other women to actively respond to societal injustice and inequality.

Chŏng-in partly blames her family background for not being a conventionally chase woman. According to her confession, Chŏng-in herself is an illegitimate child born of an illicit love affair. Her grandfather still has two concubines, one of whom is her age. She grew up with her mother whose lifestyle was far from the tradition of virtue and chastity. She says that she has inherited such undesirable tendencies. It sounds, however, as if she uses her intelligence and education to satisfy her sexuality. By attributing her lack of traditional virtue to her family's lifestyle, she only takes partial blame for what happened to her and on her. Instead of committing herself fully to a "free love" based on her philosophy and conviction, she acknowledges that she has let her biological tendency and lack of "proper" education take where she is, that is, the place of the "new woman."

There is no doubt that Chŏng-in behaves the most outspoken feminist of her time. Her insight into the problems of women shown throughout the letter to her husband is so accurate that her observations and thoughts on women's issues are relevant to readers today, decades after they were written. The following is her address entitled "A Fight of Sexes," for a lecture meeting by "new women," where she is attracted to Mr. E.

> The men and women of today will achieve true harmony between them, only after they experience a period of struggle between the two sexes. Not only is it required of woman, but to man it is also a necessary process of training him about the gender issue. However, complete equality between man and woman presumes equal rights and responsibilities in both mental and material matters. Even among the women who talk about the problems of woman in the world, there are some who only focus on the ideological issues and neglect the important material matters. It is a very serious contradiction. While woman is trying to emancipate herself from the slave state of today, she is financially dependent on man. It is as silly as giving the key to one's room to the enemy and blaming him for not setting him free. Thus it inevitably leads to the issue of jobs for women. At the same time, it also leads to the question of woman's role and responsibility at home, and to the question of how woman can get a job. However, such problems are issues we can discuss within a day. . . . Thus the most urgent issue is the education of woman. In order to achieve woman's independence, the education issue which is as important as the job issue should be preceded. Therefore, we as the awakened comrades will debate and pursue the issue fundamentally and at the same time, we feel the pressure of responsibility and obligation to strike the first in the fight between the sexes. (*YSC* 9:77–78)

Here she expresses her thoughts on the woman's issue very clearly, and she claims to be a leader. Her understanding of the issue is accurate and ahead of her time. But how were her ideas received and how much did they really influence Korean society?

Chŏng-in later realizes that at the meeting she got attention only because she was a woman, not because she was respected and admired for her knowledge. She accuses society in general:

> Actually the audience was all male, despite the fact that it was a lecture meeting on and by women. The Korean society, so to speak, is an unheard-of strange place where men work on women's issue and women work on men's. Nevertheless, what is this phenomenon that so called all of lecture meetings eventually turn into a kind of testing place for music school entrance? Alas, we are born in this kind of society. It

seems to me that contemporary society is also not much different from the mere expansion of our home. (*YSC* 9:78–79)

Chŏng-in writes to her husband about how she used to think about the idea of "chastity." She says that the society is basically unjust because: "the so-called fetters or trammels of virtue and morality reign only over delicate women. A brocade of eulogy such as the virtue of chastity and the sublimity of constancy hides the provision that a woman should spend her whole life in slavish service and sacrifice to a man. Moreover, rules of morality are unjustly harsh only to a woman (*YSC* 9:74)." She continues:

> What is chastity? Is it men's fulfillment of possessive desire by imposing it upon women under the condition of guaranteed livelihood? Or is it a desire to fulfill a so-called cultivated men's noble taste? If one wants exclusive possession of a woman to such a degree, why doesn't he make a female statue to look at or buy several flowerpots? Then doesn't that make it simple and reduce the worry of robbery? . . . Is a woman a commodity to deal and to pay for fun and cosmetics? If that's the case, it is too inhumane and foul even for trade, isn't it? Then when a woman enjoys herself the praise and pride of being called a chaste woman, it is also a weird hobby or taste. It is also an ignorant behavior to abuse human nature too much. (*YSC* 9:74–75)

Here Chŏng-in makes her position clear that a woman has as much right to pursue pleasure as a man does. But the society which allows men the pursuit of pleasure, she argues, imposes a strict moral code on women. She also accuses women of contributing to the perpetuation of this kind of patriarchal tyranny by submitting to an unequal standard (*YSC* 9:76). She quotes the Bible (Mathews 5:28) that no one is innocent: "That whosover looketh on a woman to lust after her hath committed adultery with her already in his heart." Yet she goes further by saying that "when there arises a passionate attachment or liking between a man and a woman, isn't it possible to allow and accept the emotion to take over under the condition of mutual agreement? (*YSC* 9:76)"

Chŏng-in makes a distinction, however, between "forced" and "voluntary" constancy. She admits that voluntary chastity is a true virtue, and it is considered a manifestation of one's individuality based on free choice. To keep one's chastity out of love and devotion is a woman's duty toward herself. It is a fulfillment of her moral commitment. Chŏng-in, however, chooses a different path to fulfill her duty toward herself. Instead of keeping her chastity, she chooses free love based on her true feelings toward men, without caring whether it means promiscuity or not. When she talks about a woman's duty toward herself, it echoes Nora's speech in the end of Act III of *A Doll's House* by Henrik Ibsen (1828–1906).[29]

By the time she writes her final letter, however, she admits that she has been selling her body for her own survival and education, despite her belief that one's chastity is not a commodity (*YSC* 9:77). She blames men, including her husband. She asks him in the second part of the letter to admit that he vainly flaunts having an educated and modern "new woman (*sinyŏsŏng*)" as a wife.

Chŏng-in is a victim of her society. Even though she tries to escape from conventional norms by expressing her flamboyant personality, she is trapped in a moral dilemma. There simply is no means available for finding an escape from the judgment of traditional patriarchal moral scrutiny. As a "new woman," she is treated merely as a sexual object. Society is not ready for an avant-garde woman like her and considers her an object of curiosity or gossip. Thus a woman like Chŏng-in has to fight two enemies: unfavorable conditions under the loss of national autonomy and the patriarchal system which oppresses and conditions woman under man's authority. She has to be forever subservient.

Chŏng-in seems to be defeated by society and by men. Yet her inquiry into various issues concerning the relationship of the sexes and society in general enlighten the reader. Chŏng-in's critical ideas about women and society seem not much different from the author's own ideas. Evidence of this can be found in Yŏm's essay and this short story. In the essay, "For the Ultimate Virtue," Yŏm says that Nora's act of abandoning her roles as a mother and a wife can be an ultimate virtue, because to be a whole human being is a self-reformation which requires courage (*YSC* 12:44–45).

Chŏng-in's death can be both defeat and transcendence. The final awareness brought by the letter of forgiveness from her husband allows her to achieve her final resolution—death. She realizes that her fight for women's equality has been futile. She is used and ridiculed as an object of social mockery. Even if she goes back to her husband, it only means that she would have to carry the stigma of adultery throughout her life as Hester does "A" in *Scarlet Letter*, and she would have to obey him as the price of being exonerated by his generous pardon. To her, death is preferable.

The time setting of her death is very symbolic. The word "cheya" [in the lunar calendar] renders an image of a dark, cold, desolate moonless night. Such a sky invokes a sinister feeling rather than optimistic anticipation of the New Year. It effectively foreshadows Chŏng-in's death. The image associates her failure in life and her imminent death with metaphorical darkness.

A sense of helplessness and despair, which Yŏm's protagonists express through melancholy and sentimentality, is well visualized through the images of a frog pinned down for an anatomy class ("A Green Frog in a Specimen Room" 1921), a black bear in the cage and a crippled child trying to fly a kite ("Dark Night" 1921). Each protagonist is either given no opportunity to fulfill his life or is defeated by 'snobbish' society. Yŏm effectively juxtaposes their frustrated situations, which might possibly be typical for an educated youth in the colonized country, with symbolic images.

Among such conditions of inescapable morass of confusion and despair, Yŏm manages to show a dim and yet optimistic beam of hope using the same method of creating images and narrative tones. Such a moment of epiphany can be found in each work; a moment of sudden enlightenment by the protagonist in "A Frog" in the end, the young man in "Dark Night" showing a gesture of looking forward to embracing an uncertain future and the admirable and determinate choice for death by a young woman in "New Year's Eve." All of them are eager to find the meaning of life and solutions for their mental and physical anguish.

Above all the ultimate moment of revelation comes in *Mansejŏn*, originally titled Myoji [Grave]. By changing its title from a symbolic one, Myoji, to Mansejŏn [The Year before the March First Movement], Yŏm *historicized* and *politicized* the work.

Mansejŏn: *A Psychological Journey of the Colonized*
The word "Manse" refers the historical event of March 1919, which is called the *Samil Manse Undong* in Korean. The March First Movement was a major nation-wide independence movement after the Japanese occupation in 1910. This became a sharp turning point in Korean literature as well as in politics. The movement brought some visible changes in Japanese colonial policy. There seemed to have been underlying assumption by Yŏm that the contemporary social circumstances had improved, especially when compared to those of previous years of the movement. Despite the fact that the work reveals negative aspects of life and thus indirectly accuses Japanese colonial policy, Yŏm might have been able to escape from the severe censorship by suggesting some improvement in reality and hope for the future. He maybe intended to witness the miserable and bleak days by depicting various aspects of life through the eyes of a young student like the

artist himself. This might explain why Yŏm changed its title. Among Yŏm's numerous works, this is regarded as one of the best exemplary historical articulations in modern Korean literature. Its fictional world is put into the context of history. It is linked in historical time and space, that is, the reality of Korean society right before the March First Movement.

The novel opens with remarks about time and the circumstance of the narrator-protagonist, Yi In-wha. His point of view is retrospective. Most of the story is narrated through a flashback. The narrative voice successfully maintains its vividness, proximity of events and, above all, the narrator's mental states throughout the story. It begins:

> It was the winter of the year before the Manse took place in Chosŏn [Korea]. At that time something happened, which made me give up the final exam, already half-completed, and forced me to go back to Chosŏn all of a sudden. The reason was nothing but an urgent telegram I received telling me that my wife's illness had become very serious. She had been suffering from postpartum illness ever since that autumn. I can still visualize that moment vividly. When I left Tokyo, it was the second day of the exams. (*YSC* 1:11)

This opening paragraph reveals many things about the narrator himself and the structure of the story. It frames the structure of the story-telling, which makes it possible to control and limit the surface plot. By mentioning the *Manse Undong* in the first sentence, Yŏm historicizes the setting of the novel. The fictional world claims its link with the historical time and space, which serves readers as a mirror of the contemporary Korean society in the winter of 1918. As for his private life, we know that he is a Korean student studying abroad in Tokyo, is married, and has recently become a father. His wife is suffering from certain complication after a child birth.

Strange enough, however, we don't feel much of the narrator's emotion either toward his wife or his baby. The lack of feeling gives rise to another issue about his relationship with his wife and women in general. Caught between tradition and modernity, he married under the norms of tradition; he resists the forced way of life now with the raison d'être of a "modern" man. Before treating this issue further, we must say something about Yŏm's narrative technique in this novel.

The narrative technique of retrospection limits the scope of the whole story and controls its major plot. A sentence like "still I remember the moment vividly" leads the reader to anticipate the moment itself: the day of his departure from Tokyo. As in a movie, the camera eye shifts from the present to the past by vivifying scenes of the past gradually in overlapped pictures of the past and the present. The sentence connects two worlds by a smooth transition of time. The day of departure is the real beginning of the story as well as the journey itself both psychological and physical.

Yi sets out on his journey in the night somewhat reluctantly. This night journey from Japan, the colonizer, to Korea, the colonized, holds symbolic significance in reflecting a psychological topography of the colonized as well as a general vision of colonial reality. Yi discloses not only his personal problems but also the devastated living conditions of Koreans. This journey can be read as a symbolic odyssey, a search for his identity and the meaning of life, especially for a young man like him living in a transition period caught in the political dilemma and conflicts of value between the old and the new; tradition and modernity. This homeward journey is transcended its meaning to a symbolic odyssey by enabling Yi to achieve self-realization and embracing his identity.

The journey toward Korea is a journey to the center of his own being, making him face reality directly. In many aspects, Yi's journey is similar to Marlow's into the "Heart of Darkness," in Joseph Conrad's *Heart of Darkness*. Yi's journey, like Marlow's, is shadowed with images of death. It seems like a journey to the end of night and leading to "the grave yard." To him, living in Korea is like living inside a tomb. The circumstances are devoid of life and hope. He can smell the deterioration and decay. And yet he comes to realize that this country is where he belongs. He identifies his own being with his nation's suffocation.

His wife's illness foreshadows the presence of death from the beginning of the story. And also the image of night signifies death in its bleakness and darkness. Yi's discussion with a passenger in a train about the issue on public cemetery, his elder brother's involvement in a lawsuit for an ancestral graveyard, family concerns for his wife's funeral and burial site even before her death, etc., all these incidents remind him of death and nauseate him. Nevertheless, as his journey proceeds, these issues become his reality. They surround him naturally, just as the encroaching evening darkness eventually swallows the whole world.

During Yi's journey, he is constantly reminded of his national identity by the Japanese police. At every station, he is checked by the police and his luggage is searched thoroughly. Only because he is Korean, he has to go through a series of humiliating processes of Japanese police searches and investigations. He tries to ease the pressure from this political harassment by calling it cynically a "routine wrangle causing him a severe headache" (*YSC* 1:34). Somewhat intimidated by the presence of police, he succumbs to the power of authority and follows them like "a docile cow entering the butchery" (*YSC* 1:43). The narrator-protagonist tries to restrain his emotions and remain indifferent and calm. However, the narrative voice in the description of scenes with the police is filled with anger and self-pity, sometimes with self-mockery. It shows the internalization of the narrator-protagonist's anger, frustration and humiliation. After he goes through all the police harassments, he cannot hold his tears back. The moment of his crying prefigures his ultimate self-realization, which comes later at the Taejŏn station.

While he is struggling to keep his dignity by internalizing his anger and humiliation, another significant incident resuscitates his patriotism. He happens to overhear shocking conversations between two Japanese passengers. One who calls himself a labor recruiter is explaining his methods of "recruiting" *yobo*[30] to the other Japanese proudly:

> Actually it is very easy thing to do, you know. . . . After establishing a contact with companies in Home Islands, you just gather yobo, you know, in other words, Chosŏn coolies. Laborers. After all, you recruit them most easily in southern Kyŏngsang Province. (*YSC* 1:38)

The other man doubts whether Chosŏn coolies are civilized enough to do industry work. Their conversation reflects the pervading contempt for Koreans among Japanese. The former answers:

> I don't care whether they can do factory work or not. Anyway, yobos are very submissive and willing to do any hard chores. Above all, they are destitute. That is the ideal condition exactly suitable for our purposes. Of course, at first you need to wheedle them; they can get paid well: all work is so easy. . . . Once they agree to go, then they are like rats in the trap. Not to mention hard work and underpayment. Even if they starve to death, they cannot do anything. Ha, ha, ha. (*YSC* 1:39–40)

Yi finally realizes that all the poor Korean workers are deceived by such "thief-vagrant-swindlers" and sold to factories in Japan know as "Hell on earth." Most shocking thing to hear is their apparent contempt for Koreans. Even these lowly Japanese, whom he would probably despise for their occupational, educational and economic background, dehumanize Koreans. According to their conversation, Koreans are sub-human, at best similar to tamed domestic animals, and yet, slightly better than native Taiwanese.

Dehumanized Koreans become easy prey for economic exploitation. During the course of their conversation, the two Japanese also express their contended agreement with the advantageous and superior political position in the colony, which they attribute to the harsh "effective" ruling methods of the Governor General Terauchi.

Yi hardly can believe what he has heard. Even though he is not an ardent fighter for independence, he cannot control his desire for national independence. He confesses to readers that, until experiencing this kind of physical and psychological abuse and humiliation, he used to forget his nationality and the need for national independence. Now he concludes that a spirit of resistance and animosity is only natural. One's need for vengeance is ironically nurtured by the other's severe oppression (*YSC* 1:39). One might speculate on Yŏm's hidden comment on the outbreak of the *Manse Undong* through his alter-ego, Yi. It seems as if he is indirectly saying that the Samil Undong is inevitable, considering the extent of Japan's harsh ruling methods which benefit only the colonizer.

When his ship arrives at Pusan port, Yi's initial feeling is one of relief. To him Pusan stands for not only "the best harbor" but also "the most important gate of Chosŏn." Overwhelmed by emotion, he remarks further: "In fact, Pusan represents the whole of Chosŏn. Microcosm of Chosŏn, the symbol of Chosŏn. Oh, glorious Pusan! (*YSC* 1:52)." Interestingly, his opinion of Pusan reflects a significant change in Korean's world view after the annexation by Japan. Before Japan's rise as one of the Imperial powers, Korea considered its relationship with China as primary in foreign affairs. Thus Inch'ŏn played an important role in connecting the two nations besides land routes to the north. After the annexation in 1910, however, Japan became not only the political center of the world of Koreans and the source of everything but also its connection to the outside world. Yi's remarks on Pusan reflect this change of perspective and also the extent of Japan's colonization of Korean mind.

As soon as Yi becomes aware of the actual changes which have taken place in Pusan, however, his initial feeling and positive view of the city are shattered. Due to an increased number of Japanese settlers, he is not able to find even one Korean restaurant except many two-story Japanese style *yŏkwan* (inns). The term *yŏkwan* literally means an inn, however, it actually means a brothel for prostitution. Besides, the downtown of Pusan has been literally colonized and turned into a Japanese town. He has to give up his desire to eat *kimch'i* (Korean cabbage pickle) and to use a spoon. In Pusan, people try to imitate the new lifestyle introduced by the Japanese.

Under the Japanese colonial rules, there was a systematic exploitation of women: one way was by absorbing the labor force into various factories, the other was by establishing a systematic public prostitution. All these were possible with the advent of capitalism strongly backed by Japanese Imperial militaristic rules. Under Korean traditional social system, courtesans were usually for officials. After the Japanese rules, public prostitution was allowed and established suitable structures. Thus ordinary men were able to enjoy *kisaeng* (courtesans) openly in one of *yŏkwan* or *yukwak* (pleasure houses). This kind of male behavior was easily absorbed and accepted by the strongly polygamous and patriarchal Korean tradition. Yŏm Sang-sŏp describes several scenes and suggests that such kind of changes in life brought moral degradation. It is, in a way, an indirect way condemning the Japanese colonial rule and the capitalistic exploitation of Korea.

The protagonist again ponders upon what it means to be a Korean under Japanese Rule. Even a young courtesan or waitress he encounters at a restaurant in Pusan, wants to be identified as a Japanese, despite the fact that her Japanese father has abandoned her. Yi decides not to blame her for denying her Korean mother, since he knows that among Koreans some pretend to be Japanese even when speaking obvious Korean-accented Japanese or sometimes broken Japanese. Among Korean bureaucrats was a despicable and repugnant type of people who abused their own people more harshly than Japanese did (*YSC* 1:81).

Having witnessed social changes in Pusan, Yi associates haunting images of death with the vanishing of Korean tradition and spirit. Pusan is literally "colonized" by Japanese settlers. He ponders Koreans' whereabouts and the fate of this "pitiful white-clad race." He realizes that the Japanese policy of modernization is just a tool to exploit Koreans. Modernization for Korea means only the denigration of traditional values and the imitation of new lifestyle. Koreans pay too high a price for their curiosity for the new. Losing their land or selling other properties, they have to migrate to the north. Yi calls them "a group of losers." The more Japanese settle and become prosperous backed by the colonial policy, the more Koreans have to leave their hometowns and become destitute. As he gets closer to home, it becomes clear that the metaphoric darkness of night, death and grave all become symbols of the colonial reality of Korea.

The changes in Pusan illustrate the changes the whole nation has gone through under the Japanese Rule. The evidence of social change a Kimch'ŏn echoes that at Pusan. In Kimch'ŏn, Yi's elder brother lives a prosperous life using his chameleon-like adaptation ability. Yi is nauseated by his brother's way of life: a concubine, a close relationship with local Japanese, and the obvious enjoyment of material success. And yet he himself is wise enough not to express his displeasure openly. Ironically, his brother has supported him financially in his studies. Yi In-wha's relationship with this brother parallels Yŏm's relationship with his own brother.

As a man of intellect, Yi also scrutinizes and criticizes the Koreans' fault for allowing these hellish miseries. It is, however, very interesting to compare Yi's self-criticism with the Japanese version. According to his observation, Koreans do not have any positive qualities to show to foreigners: They are lazy; they drink excessively and smoke heavily; they spend time only in futile arguments such as family relationships and concerns for their clans; they have neither vision for the future nor any scientific knowledge. Thus the longer the Japanese stay in Korea, the more contempt the have for Koreans (*YSC* 1:57). This self-criticism shows some degree of internalization of the Japanese Imperial rhetoric. It coincides with the colonizer's "myth" of Imperialism. As Japan indulged in her pride as one of the major colonial powers along with other Western nations, she considered Korea an inferior, unable to do anything without her help. The conversation mentioned earlier between the two Japanese on the ferry is a good example of Imperial contempt for the colonized. It illustrates a sharp contrast to a point made by Meiji politicians, Saigo and Okubo, in regard to Korean's attitude toward Japanese.[31] The "intolerable arrogance" of Korean's toward Japan which bothered those political bureaucrats seems to have disappeared and been replaced by the inferiority complex as show in Yŏm's works.

All these examples taken from this story speak about colonial reality in Korea. Kang Tong-jin's *Ilche ŭi Han'guk Chimnyak Chŏngchaek Sa* (*History of Japanese Imperial Policies in Invading Kore*a 1980) shows that Japanese policy were very carefully orchestrated the systematic degradation of Korean people, their tradition and history. After the March First Movement, the Japanese employed various means to achieve the goal—the continuation of the colonial rule by demoralizing Korean independent spirit—such as distortion of Koran history, creation of the negative "myth" about Korean characteristics and its distribution throughout the glorification of Japanese Imperial power, etc.[32].

Frantz Fanon mentions in *The Wretched of the Eart*h that the relationship between the colonizer and the colonized is like that between master and slave. In order to maintain that relationship, the colonizer has to dehumanize the colonized by using force and violence until he turns into an animal. Japanese administration had the same approach to ruling Korea until the outbreak of the March First Movement. According to F. Baldwin's *The March First Movement*, the Japanese considered Korean people to be an inferior, incompetent, unruly race whose only possible salvation lay in becoming like the Japanese. "Backward and disorganized, Korea had forfeited its right to national independence and had been politically obliterated by annexation in 1910. The Governor General [Terauchi] considered Koreans totally incapable of organizing a coherent, sustained independence movement."[33] This one aspect of their blind "myth" about Koreans shows their over-confidence and low regard for Koreans, which was shattered by the March First Movement.

In *Mansejŏn*, the negative views about Koreans and their living conditions are given an ultimate epiphany. The nightmarish vision Yi In-wha has at Taejŏn station leads to his ultimate awakening to colonial reality. It strikes him suddenly and upsets his romantic views of life. Yi has held somewhat objective views by distancing himself from the bleak surroundings and even from his emotions, until he experiences this revelation. He realizes that he has been inside a metaphorical grave like anyone else in Korea. The moment of insight comes right after a horrifying scene of the arrest of a peddler. The author mystifies him somehow by hinting his real identity as a fighter for Korean independence in disguise. And his arrest by the Japanese police reassures such a suspicion. The fact that the enigmatic peddler sells *kats* (traditional top hats for men) may symbolize his patriotism. Before the peddler's arrest, he and the protagonist engage in a series of discussions about contemporary issues like the public cemetery and modernization. His arrest makes Yi feel the political tension in Korea as a living nightmare.

It is past midnight, when the train stops at Taejŏn station. Outside it is very cold and snowing. On the platform, Yi experiences a nightmarish vision somewhat like a Joycean epiphany. Among several Koreans chained and guarded by Japanese policemen, there is a young woman carrying a baby strapped to her back. The child, not knowing its mother's miserable situation, sleeps. When Yi meets her eyes looking at him blankly, he is shocked by the scene and its implications. The woman doesn't show any of the shame or shyness which would be expected in a traditional situation; she seems rather absent minded. Her empty expression indicates the seriousness of her plight. The woman's situation and her poverty-stricken shabby look epitomize Korean living conditions. Yi is overwhelmed by his mixed feelings of compassion, anger and frustration. He mumbles to himself out of anger: "Is this life? Damn death on everything" (*YSC* 1:83).

The inside of the train is gloomy and foggy, filled with smoke and soot from the stove. Overwhelmed by disillusionment and frustration, Yi feels like he is sitting inside a huge coffin "infested with pests and maggots" (*YSC* 1:83). Even the subtle cosmetic fragrance of a nearby courtesan turns into a rotten smell of death and desperation. All of these accumulated and recurring images of death finally culminate at the moment of his wife's death.

Consequently this journey provides Yi with an opportunity to grow out of his suffocating surroundings. At first he considered his marriage as the invisible fetters of tradition. His wife epitomized the traditional values from which he had tried to escape, whereas Chŏng-ja (Shizuko) would be an ideal woman of his choice. Chŏng-ja is a Japanese girl working in a restaurant. Since she is smart and has the ambition to continue her education, Yi treats her differently from other waitresses. Before he proceeds to his homeward journey, Yi meets Chŏng-ja and flirts with her. Chŏng-ja seems to take the relationship with him rather seriously. In his *Yŏm Sang-sŏp Yŏn'gu*, Kim Yun-sik mentions that, according to Cho Yŏng-am, Chŏng-ja (Shizuko) was modeled after the real person, P'um-ja (Shinako), for whom Yŏm once had deep feelings.[34]

In Yŏm's many other works, women are accurately observed and characterized. At the same time, they represent certain types of women from various social and educational backgrounds. Also Yŏm shows us social and individual problems due to industrialization and the advent of capitalism through his portrayal of female characters in "Cheya" (New Year's Eve 1921), *Haebaragi* (sunflowers 1923), *Sarang kwa Choe* (*Love and Sin* 1928), *Yisim* (*Two Minds* 1929), etc. Yŏm's understanding of women's lives and dilemmas seems deep when compared to that of other contemporary male authors such as Kim Tong-in. Yet his portrayals of female characters clearly indicate his conservative moral stand on women's issues.

His wife's death enables Yi to reconsider his marriage and to redefine his relationship with his wife other than a "fetter" of tradition. Even if he does not have passionate love for her, he understands the significance of marriage and its lessons. Her death appears futile at first, suggesting that a woman's life victimized by tradition and contemporary social conditions. Yet, her death awakens Yi about her role and mission in life. Yi feels a strong responsibility as a father and a man. Her death also symbolizes the defeat of traditional values which will soon to give way to the new.

Yi experiences a psychological and symbolic rebirth through her death. Their son is a strong symbolic manifestation of rebirth or regeneration in the never-ending life cycle. Yi also comes to terms with his relationship with Chŏng-ja. He writes to her:

> Even though she [wife] died, I cannot consider her as really dead. . . . Because she teaches me very important lessons of life, that is self-reliance. . . . Even if her body returns to the Earth, through her teaching, it seems, she's remarried to me in a spiritual sense. Besides, she left my only seed in this world. . . . I feel a strong responsibility and obligation to raise him well. (*YSC* 1:105)

In this letter, it is clear that instead of denying tradition, he embraces it by remaining faithful to his wife and committing himself to being a good father. He also politely refuses Chŏng-ja's request to meet her again. He tries instead to transcend their relationship by classifying it as a past Platonic love. He denies his previous passion for her. He says to Chŏng-ja in the letter that "I realized that I have a duty to myself to work out my own salvation (*YSC* 1:105). Again, here is echoed the same message of "the Ultimate virtue," which Yŏm through his literary heroine, Chŏng-in in "Cheya," identifies with Nora's awakening.

It is interesting to note differences between the 1924 edition of *Mansejŏn* published by Koryŏ Kongsa and the 1948 edition published by Susŏnsa in which the letter to Chŏng-ja has a totally different tone and explains the need to end their relationship in a different way. In the 1948 edition, the protagonist, Yi clearly states that the difference of their nationalities hinders their being together. He asks her, "Have you ever heard of a nation where an elementary school teacher carries a saber to the classroom?"[35] When there is no need to worry about Japanese censorship, Yŏm obviously tries to express his anti-Japanese feeling more strongly. In the name of nationalism, he tries to escape from the relationship with a former waitress whom he once considered an object of pleasure. In this edition, in an effort to explicitly express his anti-Japanese sentiments, Yŏm lost some of the aesthetic balance of the earlier edition.

Anyhow, the protagonist has solved his own dilemma of love. By recognizing his role as a man and father, he also transforms himself from a romantic, idealistic youth into a mature and responsible man. He accepts and faces the reality, and attains a positive attitude toward the life. He decides to go back to Japan to finish his study. All these positive decisions indicate his self-realization based upon his wholesome identity as a Korean. He frees himself from the stigma of being a colonized. As Marlow learns his lesson from the journey to Africa in *Heart of Darkness*, Yi finally grows through his experiences and achieves the psychological triumph and personal maturity, which offer a promising future.

Three Generations: A Synthetic Vision in the Split World

Yŏm Sang-sŏp pioneered the genre of the long novel by writing many such novels early his career, while his contemporaries were mainly producing short stories. After publishing *Mansejŏn* in 1924, Yŏm serialized almost a novel a year in one of the major daily newspapers at the time in addition publishing numerous short stories and essays. He literally paved the way for other novelists. During the 1930s, other historically conscious realistic novels were published, such as *Tak'nyu* (*Mud Stream* 1937) and *T'aepyŏng Ch'ŏnha* (*Peaceful World* 1938) by Ch'ae Man-sik, and *Taeha* (*A Big River* 1939) by Kim Nam-ch'ŏn.

Yŏm's *Samdae* (*Three Generations* 1931) was serialized in the daily newspaper, *Chosŏn Ilbo* (Chosŏn Daily), from January 1st to September 29th in 1931. Most critics in Korea today generally agree that it is the best novel written during the colonial period. The thoroughly depicts the daily life of upper middle class people in Korea under Japanese Occupation. Yŏm's realistic portrayals of characters, including minor characters, reflect his excellent ability to depict the essence of daily life and what it meant in that particular historical context.

As its title suggests, the main pathos of *Samdae* is derived from the conflicts and contrasts among three generations. Besides the stereotypical generation-gaps among characters, the novel also includes ideological conflicts between conservatism and radical Marxism, which started to become poignant issues in Korean consciousness. The story is told from the perspective of the youngest generation. Its main protagonist, Cho Tŏk-ki, has an opportunity to examine himself and face reality when he visits home from Japan where he studies. The way he understands his relationships with his grandfather and with his father ultimately leads him to synthesize two different worlds, as he reaches maturity. The tension between what his grandfather stands for as a thesis and what his father stands for as a antithesis creates typically agonistic situations in the transitional period of Korean history. Both the "grandfather's" firm-rooted and rigid code of tradition and "the father's" shallow imitation of foreign ideas and westernization, prefigure the schizophrenic circumstances of the next generation like Tŏk-ki. Thus, thematically, the story focuses on how to find "the middle way" in life; thus middle way will eventually become the key to finding self-identity. Through various characters, Yŏm asks such questions and shows at least how the protagonist makes his own choices in life and deals with reality wisely, balancing his entrusted responsibilities and his own choices in life.

Besides presenting a diachronic slice of life through three generations of the Cho family, Yŏm also deals with a synchronic dimension of reality through Tŏk-ki and his friends. The title of the first chapter is "Tu Ch'in'gu" (Two Friends). It is very significant in many ways. Yŏm shows obvious sensitivity to the ideological fights going on at that time between Marxism (Socialism) and Conservatism (Nationalism). Each of the two friends represents a different ideology which dominated the conscience of the contemporary intelligentsia.

As the narrator calls them, Tŏk-ki is a "bourgeois" and Pyŏng-wha a "Marx boy." Both of them come from established and comfortable middle class families. Yet Pyŏng-wha becomes a serious "Marx boy," who denounces his own father and lives in poverty-stricken conditions, while Tŏk-ki still dwells in the comfortable environment of the upper middle class. The narrator explains the nature of their friendship:

> Even though they meet once or twice a year only during vacation, these two young men talk to each other with sarcasm every time, as if to compete for a spiteful tongue. Yet they have never been really angry toward each other. In junior high school, they were smart enough to compete for the top until their graduation, and they grew up in similar family circumstances. Therefore their deep understanding and empathy toward each other could not be easily abandoned, even their young and green friendship.
> There are no differences in their intelligence and logical reasoning, but Tŏk-ki is the son of the rich and his complexion gives a comfortable and mild aura in its lucidity; Pyŏng-wha gives an air of stubbornness, of not bending to others, an impression which mostly comes from his dark and brazen face. (*YSC* 4:13–14)

The contrasting lifestyles of the two friends show the actual impact of such ideological conflicts within the intellectual milieu. Along with this kind of ideological struggle among Koreans, Yŏm reveals aspects of moral corruption which accompanied the advent of capitalism. The lifestyles depicted through the characters such as Tŏk-ki's grandfather and father illustrate how deep and serious is the immorality caused by a greed for "money" regardless of the generation gap.

Tŏk-ki, who belongs to the youngest generation, is literally torn between his grandfather and his father. At the same time he tries to reconcile the ideological differences he finds in his many friends. As mentioned earlier, his best friend, Pyŏng-wha, is a medium to expose the dominant ideology of socialism.

The narrator of the story unravels intricate social structures by following Tŏk-ki's movements and identifying Tŏk-ki's perspectives as his own. Thus, information about each character comes from the Tŏk-ki-like narrator's objective observations. Each chapter, especially in the beginning, has its own significance and plays a very important role in the story's plot development.

In the first chapter, entitled "Tu Ch'in'gu" (Two Friends), readers meet Tŏk-ki's best friend, Pyŏng-wha, a serious Marxist. Then the second chapter is about Tŏk-ki's previous female classmate, Hong Kyŏng-ae. Tŏk-ki meets her unexpectedly at a café where his friend Pyŏng-wha often goes. She was once Tŏk-ki Tŏk-ki's father's mistress and now is a "bar-girl." Tŏk-ki, disturbed greatly by the sight of her drinking, smoking, and even flirting with other customers, cannot help blaming his father who, because he abandoned her, is responsible for her change (*YSC* 4:20–21). He also wonders about his half-sister, born out of the relationship between his father and Hong Kyŏng-ae.

In the third chapter, readers are led into more detailed and intricate situations of the Cho family. Here, the relationships among the female characters in the household are introduced. The relationship between Tŏk-ki's young grandmother and his mother creates very awkward situations, which aggravate the male conflicts among the three generations. The detailed family situations and the tensions among the family members are well captured in their treatment of the sacrificial rite for the deceased matriarch, Tŏk-ki's real grandmother: The present young grandmother, who has to show some concern about the preparation for the sacrificial ceremony on behalf of the former wife, is in an awkward position. Tŏk-ki's mother is also tense since she has difficulty dealing with the mother-in-law who is younger than herself. Besides, she feels that she has been pushed aside by this unrespectable mother-in-law. She either avoids dealing with her directly or obviously shows her condescension. Thus, Tŏk-ki's wife plays a role similar to her husband. She is placed between the tensions generated from the step-grandmother-in-law and the mother-in-law.

All associations of the proletarian friend, Pyŏng-wha, are also thoroughly examined by the narrator. The fourth and fifth chapters introduce another important female character, P'il-sun, a daughter of Pyŏng-wha's landlord. The descriptions of the poverty-stricken household and its occupants are a very important part of Yŏm's realism. P'il-sun supports the whole family by working at a factory. Her father was once involved in the national independence movement, and for this he was imprisoned and tortured severely and is till suffering from the aftermath. Being a Marxist, Pyŏng-wha is unable to pay his rent. With his Marxist ideology, he has influence on P'il-sun. Later P'il-sun is torn between the ideologies of Pyŏng-wha and Tŏk-ki. The life of a factory worker is represented through P'il-sun. A new form of female exploitation in the industrialized capitalistic society is reified, and yet the issue of exploitation under the Japanese is blurred by Yŏm's conservative and petit bourgeoisie angle on life in general.

After introducing the characters and situations, the narrator establishes basic personal and social conflicts. Tŏk-ki gets interested in P'il-sun and is sympathetic toward her living condition. He tries to help her and is willing to support her education. As a young man he is attracted to P'il-sun's innocent beauty, and as a man of wealth he feels some kind of moral obligation to take care of the family of a national independence fighter. Yet, as a married man, he checks himself and scrutinizes his own intentions.

Tŏk-ki's encounter with P'il-sun echoes his father's involvement with Hong Kyŏng-ae, who is also a daughter of an active nationalist. Hong Kyŏng-ae's father asked Tŏk-ki's father to take care of his wife and daughter after his death. Though, at first, Tŏk-ki's father, Sang-hun, did not intend to possess the daughter, their frequent contact with regard to financial matters led them to develop a personal relationship. Tŏk-ki fears being like his own father, especially in his emotional attachment to P'il-sun. He comes to understand his father's involvement with Hong Kyŏng-ae. Tŏk-ki realizes that his father's motive to take care of Hong Kyŏng-ae's parents was, at first, based on pure sympathy and a sense of moral obligation, for he himself feels the same way toward P'il-sun's family.

As a general picture of the society is drawn from the Cho clan's daily life and concerns, the main occupation of each generation can be a measurement of colonial reality. Following are surveys of each generation's characteristics in the Chos.

The grandfather's primary concern is to keep the family prosperous and to continue the family line. In order to fulfill such patriarchal duties, he cares about "money" and the family name the most. To him, keeping the ancestral shrine means more than just performing ancestral sacrifices. Buying the social title, Ŭi-kwan, he joined the *yangban* (aristocrat) class. Besides contributing a tremendous amount of money to compile the rewritten *chokbo* (a genealogy), he had bought even a *yangban*'s tomb and spent fortune for its reconstruction to show it off as one of his ancestors (*YSC* 4:81–82). He distorts the traditional concept of ancestor worship. Swarms of people are attracted to his household in order to take advantage of Cho Ŭi-kwan's vanity for family name. Among them, his second wife and a distant relative, Cho Ch'ang-hun, are main intriguers to exploit Cho Ŭi-kwan's vanity for family name. All the business concerning the *chokbo* and the false ancestral tomb are actually their ideas. Filled with greed, they try to dull the old man's wits so that they can carve out a much bigger piece of the old man's money.

Cho Ŭi-kwan's marriage is based purely on his desire to provide the family line with satisfying sons of his own, unlike the one he has right now. Thus, he marries a relatively young woman called "Suwŏn Chip"(a woman from Suwŏn), who is even younger than his own daughter-in-law. With her, so far, he has a daughter, who is younger than his great-grandson. As a man of seventy, he is dreaming of having a son if he lives to be eighty-five (*YSC* 4:80).

Cho Sang-hun, the son of Cho Ŭi-kwan and the father of Cho Tŏk-ki, is the opposite of his own father. He has had a westernized education and has even been to the United States of America for two years. When he was young, he was very ambitious and tried to reform society. He involved himself in social education and became a Christian. Yet, his transformation is so shallow that his fundamental self is not much different from that of his own father. His lust for women seems to be inherited from his father. He is continuously involved in affairs with young women. He once had a mistress, Hong Kyŏng-ae, who is his son's classmate. Though a daughter was born out of this relationship, Sang-hun literally abandoned them after providing them with a house and some money. Presently he often visits pleasure houses and is developing a new interest in a young "new woman," Kim Ŭi-kyŏng. He detests his own wife. During the day, he behaves as a pious religious leader and educator; in the evening he drinks beer and plays majong like a vulgarian. His split life is a reflection of his own self. He probably adopted a new lifestyle as an attempt to reform the feudal and patriarchal society, followed by his idealistic visions inspired by a newly acquired western knowledge and religion. Now he is lost and his idealism is tarnished.

Cho Sang-hun's series of idealistic attempts to "modernize" society bring about a serious estrangement from his own father and the rest of his family. His position in the family becomes very awkward. Socially and emotionally he is lost and unable to find his proper place. The rejection by his own father is disastrous for his sense of security. Cho Ŭi-kwan fears that this son's Christianity would prevent him from properly serving his spirit after his death. Christians at that time usually did not observe the tradition of ancestral sacrifice, which they as monotheists considered a form of serving another god. The grandfather, embodying traditional values, cannot accept this converted son, so he denies him the possibility of being the chief inheritor of the family fortune. As a reaction to such a stubborn and traditional father, Sang-hun equally detests his father's snobbism. He looks down upon his father's obsession with embellishing the family name and observing unnecessary rituals (*YSC* 4:80–81).

Instead of assuming responsibilities in life, Sang-hun escapes from all of them and loses his way. His son, Tŏk-ki, is the only one who can see his father's and grandfather's true nature. Tŏk-ki sees his father as a social victim of a transitional society. Instead of accusing his father for being a Christian and a hypocritical modernist, Tŏk-ki understands him in terms of both historical context and individual conditions:

> He [Tŏk-ki] does not think that his father is free of any fault, but he is not an unusual hypocrite or a bastard, either. If one measures each individual in the world, he can find only one penny's worth of difference or fault in each of them not even a dollar's worth. And yet approximately twenty or thirty years ago when he [the father] was struggling to get out of the old feudal society as a young man of a new generation, like any young man at that time, he tried to become a young noble-minded patriot. In trying to be so, naturally such people got together in the Church, since they were not allow to pursue any political careers. There they genuflected under a church altar, and it became the beginning of their religious life. (*YSC* 4:35)

Here Tŏk-ki understands the inevitability of the sociopolitical circumstances of the colonized, and explains the nature of his father's being a shallow Christian. Tŏk-ki thinks that his father's position in the family and even in society is a most unstable and agonizing one (*YSC* 4:36). His deep understanding of his father shows his compassion toward everyone, yet throughout the story he tries very hard not to follow his father's path.

Disappointed by this westernized son, the grandfather expects a great deal from his grandson, and plans to entrust to him what he considers to be the most sacred and important role, namely, the keeper of the family fortune and the ancestral shrine. Tŏk-ki feels his grandfather's expectation as an inescapable burden, and it puts him in a very awkward position toward his father, who occasionally tries to exert his parental authority. Tŏk-ki's solution to this conflict ultimately leads to a desirable and idealistic "middle way" as seen through the author's perspective.

When Tŏk-ki's grandfather is about to die, the story takes a dramatic turn. All the members in the Cho clan are interested in their own share of the dying man's fortune. Tŏk-ki reluctantly returns from Japan in order to attend to his grandfather, and the young step-grandmother feels tense. The step-grandmother, Suwŏn Chip, conspires to obtain the keys to the safe where her husband stores all documents on property along with his will. Before his death, however, the grandfather hands over the most important keys to his grandson, Tŏk-ki:

> The grandfather, even after asking his wife, Suwŏn Chip, to go out, told him [Tŏk-ki] to open a small safe close to his bedside and take out the bundle of keys. He entrusted the keys to Tŏk-ki and instructed him as such.
> "Is there any reason for me [Tŏk-ki] to take them already? I think I should go back [to Japan] when your condition improves! Besides, how can I take them before father?
> For Tŏk-ki, it was so in regard to the order of things. Furthermore he could not take charge of a household without finishing his studies. (*YSC* 4:253)

However, the grandfather insists:

> "Which is more important, your studies or your family? If things did not matter without you, that's another story. However, think about the future of this household after my death, even if you're too young. Give up the idea of graduation or other such things, and keep the keys. Your whole life depends on the keys and so do the family's fortune. You have to keep the ancestral shrine while taking care of the keys. What I entrust to you upon my death are the shrine and the keys—there are only these two. Besides [asking] these two, there's no need for a will or anything else. The reason why I have had you study so far is for you to keep these two and to take care of them well. If you study, abandoning these two, it would be like holding a funeral without a corpse." (*YSC* 4:254)

The bundle of keys to the safe symbolizes Cho Ŭi-kwan's whole life and his philosophy; keeping the tradition of ancestral worship and social status, including money. The old man has tried always to keep such values, regardless of moral corruption. Again his money becomes the most important motif for testing the moral degradation of the Chos.

As revealed in the conversation between the two men, Tŏk-ki is at first reluctant to take full responsibility for the family fortune. Such a responsibility entrusted to him as a grown-up provides Tŏk-ki a new perspective on life and a new revelation on human relationships. He has a chance to open the main safe in his grandfather's room, after discovering that someone else in the family has attempted to open it. Finally Tŏk-ki witnesses each family member's share meticulously divided by the grandfather with instructions and conditions of when and how it will be available to the share holder (*YSC* 4:266–68). He notices that the will was written only ten days previously, when the grandfather was very sick. When he imagines his grandfather's difficulties in writing such a thoughtful will for the sake of the Cho family during his serious illness, Tŏk-ki is so touched by this image of him that he nearly weeps (*YSC* 4:268).

Upon witnessing his grandfather's will, Tŏk-ki questions his ability to fulfill his grandfather's expectation of him to be a good keeper of the family shrine, though he thinks he can be a good guardian of the safe (*YSC* 4:268). This becomes a central question of the story, along with the way Tŏk-ki deals with the people around him: Tŏk-ki's values in life, his awareness of the importance of money, his way of dealing with men and women as a man of power in the family, his friendship with Marxists, etc.

Tŏk-ki, as a sympathizer, is involved in a series of police inspections to arrest Socialists and Independence activists. His friend, Pyŏng-wha's world is a window to such underground organizations. Among the members of such organizations, Pyŏng-wha's position is not on the extreme left when compared to that of a minor character, Chang Hun. After being imprisoned, Chang Hun chooses suicide rather than reveal member secrets to the Japanese police. Since Hong Kyŏng-ae and Pyŏng-wha are actively involved in underground actions, both of them are also imprisoned. P'il-sun's father suffers further from this incident, and his health rapidly deteriorates. In the midst of this, Tŏk-ki is summoned by the police under the suspicion of providing finances to underground socialistic independence movements through Pyŏng-wha's connection. Behaving wisely and respectfully, Tŏk-ki clears himself of the accusation. Yet his father, isolated and feeling powerless without money, attempts to get some money without Tŏk-ki's permission and to elope with Kim Ŭi-kyŏng, is disgraced and put in jail. Tŏk-ki, to avoid hurting his father's feeling and dignity, does not charge him.

Instead, he supports him, saying that the money his father has taken is not stolen but given by him. Handling all the stressful situations wisely, Tŏk-ki proves his abilities to take care of family fortune and to lead the family.

Later, Tŏk-ki ponders upon the meaning of his experiences since his grandfather's death:

> As a person who did not even graduate from high school, he [Tŏk-ki] took over the responsibilities for two or three households. Moreover, if he took care of P'il-sun and her mother, it might be impertinent. Yet he thought maybe such was life.
>
> Thanks to his grandfather, because of his inherited fortune, he became unnecessarily busy and was recognized by everybody. If Cho Tŏk-ki had not have money, who on earth would trust such a naïve academic like him and ask the favor of taking care of one's spouse and children, when one faces death?
>
> Wŏn-sam once remarked, "Is ancestry more important? [No,] money is more precious!" When he thought about it, he was right. When P'il-sun's father asked him to take care of things after his death, he might have been talking about money, not about becoming his future son-in-law. (*YSC* 4:416–17)

Tŏk-ki is asked to take care of P'il-sun and her mother by her father. Before assuming such a responsibility, he ponders upon his own motive in becoming involved with the family. As mentioned earlier, this situation makes him think about the relationship between his father and Hong Kyŏng-ae. He concludes, however, that he should accept this responsibility out of moral obligation not his feeling toward P'il-sun (*YSC* 4:417–18). For the same reason, he also resolves to take care of his half-sister.

Tŏk-ki grows out of his life's experiences and is ready to deal with reality in a mature fashion. He takes account of all the good and the bad in his grandfather's and father's values. By taking the responsibilities as a keeper of the family safe and shrine, Tŏk-ki inherits traditional Confucian values and internalizes them as his own. Though being able to criticize his father, he is cautious not to make the same mistakes as his father did in the course of modernization. Through Tŏk-ki in *Samdae*, Yŏm attempts to show how harmony in such a divided society is possible. Tŏk-ki's education and his mature personality assure the picture of a promising future.[36]

As for the ideological line of the main protagonist, interestingly, Tŏk-ki does not stand for conservatism only. He is a mixture of both the ideologies of conservative nationalism and of socialism. He is a "sympathizer." Tŏk-ki's stand on this issue is Yŏm's own. Yŏm Sang-sŏp understood both sides very well, however, he could not commit himself wholeheartedly to either of them. Instead of following the law of black and white, he created a character aware of gray areas.

Tŏk-ki's letter to Pyŏng-wha illustrates his ideology very clearly. He writes:

> Caught in the fervor of [class] struggle, or instead, rather habitual petty emotions, you imprisoned your big body inside of the fervor and fastened a lock. It is very piteous to me. . . . Do you think it is right even when you treat me with such emotions generated from the class struggle? (*YSC* 4:181)

Tŏk-ki criticizes Pyŏng-wha's ideological rigidity and pleads with him to be more humane:

> The [class] struggle is not the only medium for conquest. Embraces and influence are also as effective as shrapnel for overthrow. If a fight is straightforward and military, embraces and influence will be useful for conscription and for prisoners of war. The methods of embraces and influence are as positive as a fight and direct confrontation. (*YSC* 4:182)

In the letter, Tŏk-ki also mentions about Pyŏng-wha's influence on P'il-sun. Tŏk-ki opposes Pyŏng-wha's opinion about P'il-sun's future, which includes her going to Russia to study Marxism. Tŏk-ki says that if Pyŏng-wha really loved her like a sister, he should not impose his ideology or philosophy upon her. If he does, it would be out of selfish impulses and a disregard for her own existence (*YSC* 4:185). Tŏk-ki is sympathetic to the poor and socialists like Pyŏng-wha; however, he does not rely on socialism in approaching or facing such a depressing reality. He looks at poverty and human suffering from the perspective of humanism. Though his moral values are conventional, his attitude toward socialism is based on a deep understanding of society and human nature. Tŏk-ki's viewpoint is almost identical with Yŏm's own on this subject.

As the story unfolds, the balance in the plot structure is well maintained between the male plot and the female plot. The male sphere is juxtaposed with the female sphere in the story. The conflicts among three generations are not exceptional among the female characters: the tensions between Tŏk-ki's step-grandmother, mother and his wife in the family situations echo exactly the male relationships. The parallelism extends; the grandfather's second marriage to a young woman foreshadows Tŏk-ki's father's extramarital relationship with young women, Hong Kyŏng-ae and Kim Ŭi-kyŏng, and finally Tŏk-ki's affectionate feeling toward a young girl of his sister's age, P'il-sun. Through this kind of symmetrical plot development, Yŏm analyzes the nature of intricate family relationships, role divisions by gender, and the meaning of tradition and modernization along with their impact on daily life. Yŏm presents readers with an individual's place in the three-dimensional coordinates on the axes of historical, social and sexual contexts. In *Samdae*, the sense of the continuation of life or one's historicity found in one's relationship with others is presented through daily scenes full of pretty concerns, yet the author never loses the thread of the important question, namely, the meaning of life under colonized circumstances.

The scope of colonial reality presented in *Samdae* and other works by Yŏm is in a way limited because he mainly focuses on the upper-middle class. In his works, bourgeois life is central; the poor and the miserable, mainly, oppressed working class and farmers, are marginalized. Readers see only a glimpse of them rather than a full exposure of their life and thus have difficulty empathizing with them. In this respect, the fact Yŏm's realistic description of colonial reality is partial. Considering the fact that the majority of the population was workers and farmers living in the countryside at that time, the relatively luxurious life depicted in Yŏm's works is not exactly representative of colonial reality. Korea was not yet industrialized, so the presentation of urban life is not representing the whole Korea under Japanese Rule.

Yŏm did not deal with rural life, as other class-conscious contemporary writers did. Consequently, his world is filled with modern aspects of life more than anyone's, such as instillation of capitalistic values and use of modern appliances and gadgets in daily life. The characters' obsession with money in *Samdae*, as mentioned earlier, for example, indicates a significant value change along with the incursion of capitalism in Korean society. Tensions and conflicts are aroused through modern media, such as telegram, telephone and a safe. Thus one can measure the extent of the incursion of modern technology in daily life. In fact, the journey in *Mansejŏn* most effectively utilizes the modernized aspects in Korea: traveling by train and ship. Introduction of locomotive was the ultimate symbol for Japanese in westernization of Korea. For their colonial rhetoric, Japanese used railroad to tell how well they modernized Korea and how much Koreans were benefited by the Japanese Rule. By depicting modern and new aspects in life, Yŏm unconsciously tells readers the extent of changes caused by Japanese colonial rule after the March First Movement.

The scope of reality depicted in his works is panoramic, seen from an intellectual's perspective. Yŏm was truthful to his own reality, the life of the urban middle class, which is surely a depiction of colonial life.

Yŏm Sang-sŏp's early works portray the individual's struggle to grasp the meaning of life under an uncertain political and national identity. His characters provide us with vivid images of reality at that time and enable contemporary readers to re-experience colonial life. Along with other major writers and poets, Yŏm utilized the most advantageous situations resulting from the March First Movement, the change in colonial policy allowing limited freedom of expression. With continuous devotions to fiction using the standard colloquial language, Yŏm helped early modern Korean literature to reach its full maturity.

His maturity as a writer parallels the development of modern Korean literature, since his *Samdae* is generally considered to be the best literary tapestry of contemporary fictional and realistic worlds. Its protagonist is no longer lost in the world of ideas and questions. He understands the nature of all conflicts and resolves them in terms of reality not in terms of wishful thinking. His world synthesizes two conflicting worlds: his grandfather's traditionalism and his father's modernism with its antithetic westernization.

During the 1920s, intellectuals turned their frustration (due to the failure of the March First Movement) into a creative force in every field with publication of various literary coterie magazines. All the achievement in literature during 1920s could not have been possible if not for the nationwide independence movement, the March First Movement. In addition to being timeless examinations of life, Yŏm's works have been witness to Korean colonial history. Yŏm's world is not mixed with the epic world in the Bakhtinian sense. His fictional world is the immediate reality of Yŏm's own, and therefore, it creates "the zone of maximal contact with the present and with contemporary reality." It makes Yŏm a great realist and novelist. While living such a chaotic transitional time, Yŏm had employed a remarkably modern concept of novel. Considering the shortness of time to acquire a sense of western aesthetics and to translate it into a Korean one, Yŏm's works are good evidence of the extraordinary leap in the development of Korean modern literature.

Chapter Three

Chinua Achebe and the Creation of an African Discourse in English

Chinua Achebe and Modern African Literature

The Nigerian writer Chinua Achebe is probably the best-known among contemporary African writers, along with his country's Nobel laureate of 1986, Wole Soyinka (b. 1934). His first work, *Things Fall Apart* (1958), is the most widely read novel by an African writer. This work brilliantly illustrates the intricate cultural fabric of African society prior to contact with white culture and its religion.

Achebe was born in Ogidi, widely known as Biafra, Nigeria, in November 1930. He had his first lessons in Igbo.[1] When he was about eight, he began to learn English like Oduche in *Arrow of God* (1964). At about fourteen, he was chosen for the Government College at Umuahia. Shortly before his eighteenth birthday, he matriculated at the new University College, Ibadan, to study medicine. At Ibadan, he changed his major to literature. After he took his University of London degree, awarded at University College, Ibadan, an affiliate of University of London, he began his career in the Nigerian Broadcasting Corporation. At the same time he wrote two novels, *Things Fall Apart* (1958) and *No Longer at Ease* (1960). Twelve years after he joined the Nigerian Broadcasting Corporation, he resigned in order to devote himself to his literary career.

Achebe's first novel, *Things Fall Apart*, provides tremendous insight for non-Africans, or even for Africans, into traditional African culture and people: traditional village life full of all sorts of people, some admirable and vivacious, others despicable; tribal society with its norms and traditions; contact with whites and Christianity and its tragic consequences. The title comes from Yeats's poem, "The Second Coming," in which the poet expresses his view on the course of history and Christianity. By giving such a title to his first novel, Achebe makes clear his view on history. He is dealing with the disintegration of tradition and the coming of a new era.

If his first novel is a tragedy about the downfall of a traditional hero, Okonkwo, Achebe's second novel, *No Longer at Ease*, is about the downfall of Okonkwo's grandson, Obi Okonkwo. The title is taken from a line in T. S. Eliot's "The Journey of the Magi." As a modern magus, Obi Okonkwo is unable to identify himself either with western values and education or with traditional African values. Instead he lets himself drift on the stream of social corruption and materialism. In consequence, he has to face his own social downfall. Through this novel, Achebe criticizes not only the whites and their colonial rule over Africa for bringing confusion and chaos of values but he also criticizes the new generation of Africans, like Obi Okonkwo, who traded in their traditional values and sense of ethics for superficial material gains.

Achebe's third novel, *Arrow of God* (1964), goes back in time and is set in Umuaro just after the death of Okonkwo of Umuofia in *Things Fall Apart*. The novel gives clearer pictures with inside perspectives about what happens after the incursion of the whites and Christianity. The hero of the story is Ezeulu, the Chief Priest of Ulu and gods of the six villages of Umuaro. He plays power games between his tribal rivals and the British colonialists. When he exerts his power as the Chief Priest upon his own people by ordering them to postpone the yam harvest, instead of strengthening his authority and traditional values, the action brings about an increase in converts to Christianity and the eventual destruction of the traditional way of life. The rigidity of African tradition, in other words, causes its own destruction by its inability to adapt to new values like Christianity.

In *A Man of the People* (1966), Achebe illustrates more clearly the contemporary problems of the post-colonial era. By dealing with the corruption of Nigerians in the government, instead of blaming the whites, he directly attacks Nigerians. In this novel, Africans finally seem to dominate African scenes. As Achebe mentions, ". . . still I do hope that the great African novel will not be about a disreputable European,"[2] and he intentionally bids farewell to Africans' obsession with whites and Europe. Achebe's most recent book, *Anthills of the Savannah* (1987), reveals more about the problems of contemporary African society and its politics through the depiction of three characters' lives.

Achebe's literary world asks and reveals the most poignant problems and issues contemporary Africans face. Regarding Achebe's main concerns reflected in his works, a critic, Abiola Irele, has stated the following:

The immediate subject of Chinua Achebe's novels is the tragic consequences of the African encounter with Europe—this is a theme he has made inimitably his own. His novels deals with the social and psychological conflicts created by the incursion of the white man and his culture into the hitherto self-contained world of African society, and the disarray in the African consciousness that has followed.[3]

But Achebe's major themes are not limited to the conflicts between the African and the white. By creating an African voice or discourse, Achebe reaches beyond the African audience. Though one cannot deny that his use of English as a medium helps his works reach a wide audience outside Africa at the beginning, it is his artistic genius which makes him deserve being called one of the best writers in the world.

African Literature and Its Language

Numerous controversies still exist about the tradition of African literature. In the introduction of *The African Assertion: A Critical Anthology of African Literature*, its editor, Austin J. Shelton, provides a cursory definition of African literature as follows:

1. The most typically African literature is vernacular, that in the tribal language.
2. Non-vernacular African literature is a result of the contact between African and European. . . .
3. African literature arises from and mirrors the African community and the historical experiences of Africa. . . .
4. African literature is therefore "committed" and is seldom an expression of art for art's sake.[4]

Interestingly, this definition suggests clearly that African literature should be political or is inevitably political. It sounds biased to say that African literature cannot be an expression of art for art's sake, while in other literatures it can be. If one views literature or even other forms of art from a Marxist perspective, however, one cannot escape from the claim that any literature in any style is "political." However, in this case, the fourth point cited above explains or represents the unique African condition or aesthetic perspective, as Achebe expresses in the beginning of "Africa and Her Writers:" "*Art for art's sake is just another piece of deodorized dog shit.*"[5]

In 1967, in his study, *Africa in Modern Literature*, Martin Tucker divided African writers into four categories:

1. The Westerner or other non-African writer who utilizes the subject matter of Africa in a language not native to the African continent.

2. The African writer, black, or white, who utilizes the subject matter of Africa in a language native to the African continent.
3. The African writer who utilizes subject matter other than Africa, but who writes in a language native to the African continent.
4. The African writer who utilizes the subject matter of Africa, but who writes in a Western Language that has, by custom, become part of the African means of communication.[6]

Using these categories, Tucker cites a few representative writers in a number of languages: in English (Chinua Achebe, Joyce Cary, Cyprian Ekwensi, Graham Green, Ernest Hemingway, Langston Hughes, Wole Soyinka); in French (Bernard Dadié, Birago Diop, David Diop, André Gide, Joseph Kessel, Jean Lartéguy, Jean Malonga, Ferdinand Oyono, Jean-Joseph Rabéarivelo); in German (Kurt Heuser, Janheinz Jahn); in Danish (Johannes Buchholtz); in native African languages (David Cranmer Theko Bereng, Thomas Mofolo, Samuel Yosia Ntara); in the English of South Africans (Nadine Gordimer, Sarah Gertrude Millin, Alan Paton); and in Afrikaans (Nuthall Fula, Ernst van Heerden).[7] This characterization of an African writer seems too broad; for instance, it sounds odd to include Hemingway among African writers.

In a conference held in Makerere, Kampala, Uganda, in 1962, according to Achebe, there were discussions that Conrad's *Heart of Darkness* qualifies as African literature while Graham Greene's *Heart of the Matter* fails because it could have been set anywhere outside Africa.[8] Achebe expressed his doubts on this judgment and yet he seemed to take it as a metaphor for indicating the difficulty of defining African literature as expressed in his essay, "The African Writer and the English Language," in 1964. Ten years later, Achebe presented his own definition of African literature and African novelists with a firm voice:

> The first is that the African novel has to be about Africa. A pretty severe restriction, I am told. But Africa is not only a geographical expression, it is also a metaphysical landscape—it is, in fact, a view of the world and of the whole cosmos perceived from a particular position. This is as close to the brink of chaos as I dare proceed. As for who an African novelist is, it is partly a matter of passports, of individual volition, and particularly of seeing from that perspective I have just touched with the timidity of a snail's horn. Being an African, like being a Jew, carries certain penalties—as well as benefits, of course. But perhaps more penalties than benefits. Ben Gurion once said: *If somebody wants to be a Jew, that's enough for me.* We could say the same for being an African. So it is futile to argue whether Conrad's *Heart of Darkness* is African literature.[9]

Even though Conrad wrote about Africa, Achebe does not consider him as an African writer. It is because Conrad remained a European. The same reasoning is applied to Joyce Cary. Though his *Mister Johnson* has African characters and is set in Africa, the whole perspective of Cary's work is European and the story, addressed to a European audience, appeals to their taste.[10]

About all kinds of attempts to define African literature, Achebe takes a position of "leave it alone": let African literature define itself in action, instead of limiting its scope by such precocious attempts. He explains this view well in "Thoughts on the African Novel." For further information about the development of African literature, M. Keith Booker's brief historical survey of the African novel helps readers understand. It provides the complex historical and cultural weavings in African novel.[11]

In defining of African literature, what language a writer chooses to write in becomes a very poignant issue. To some, European languages merely represent a colonial legacy; to others, they are excellent means of uniting all African souls and of adding variety to African literature. Eldred Jones remarks that "the most obvious sign of the influence of Europe on African literature is in the language of African literature."[12] The use of European languages by African writers does not function in a simple manner because it carries a colonial legacy. Thus some critics and authors believe that European languages in African literature are still contaminated with their colonial roles, carriers of "civilizations" to the "jungle." Thus, the African writer is stigmatized by his use of the colonizer's language. Lloyd W. Brown comments precisely on this issue:

> The ex-colonial writer is consistently ambivalent towards the metropolitan tongue. On the one hand, it is the historical tool with which his colonial status was shaped and the indigenous traditions of his "jungle" distorted. And, on the other hand, this alien tongue is the useful *lingua franca* through which he reaches his discrete readership in Europe and Africa.
> But above all, English, French, or Portuguese is the old colonial badge which simultaneously recalls the exclusivism of Prospero the colonist, and gives voice to Caliban's cultural revolution. The ex-colonial transforms the cultural "burden" of the mother country's language into the means of expressing a sense of human identity, and of liberating his modes of self-perception.[13]

However, Eldred Jones also comments that "it has been shown by several African authors that a work can be written in a European language and still convey something of the African experience in artistic form."[14] He continues about the use of adopted languages by African writers:

> The African writer need not therefore be dominated by the language of his adoption, though it is perfectly possible that he may be. It is possible that with the adoption of his new language he may become mesmerized by the material in it and quite unconsciously reflect ideas and attitudes not really his own. This, of course, really means that a person who is so mesmerized cannot be a really successful artist. For the true artist learns from all he meets but distils it in his own imagination and makes something new and original out of it. This should be the aim of the African writer. To be faithful to his own imagination, whatever language and whatever medium he happens to be using.[15]

Since the 1950s, the decolonization process in African literature and culture has been remarkable. Besides the attempt at defining African literature, including the language issue, the struggle for its liberation from Eurocentricism has been another on-going concern. Confidence in such liberation is voiced by many writers through their numerous works. Among them, a Kenyan writer, Ngugi wa Thiong'o (b.1938), attracts world-wide attention for his works and his "decolonizing" voice.

According to Carol Sicherman's book, *Ngugi wa Thiong'o: The Making of a Rebel*, Obiajunua (Obi) Wali's controversial and provoking article in 1962 stirred Ngugi's doubt about continuing to write in English. Wali's article was presented at the Conference of African Writers of English Expression at Makerere in June 1962, and the next year it was published in *Transition*. Wali's article raised the same language issue in African literature, which affected many African writers writing in European languages. The following is an excerpt from his article:

> What I am advocating here is not easy, for it entails a good deal of hard work and hard thinking, and what is more, a necessary casting overboard of hardened debris of the overblown ego. It would force some 'leading' critics to go in for the hard school of African linguistic studies, a knowledge of some of the important African languages, before generalizing and formulating all kinds of philosophical and literary theories. Literature in Africa would then become the serious business that all literature truly is, reaching to the people for whom it is meant, and creating a true culture of the African peoples that would not rely on slogans and propaganda, nor on patronage of doubtful intentions.
>
> The basic distinction between French and German literature, for instance, is that one is written in French, and the other in German. All the other distinctions, whatever they be, are based on this fundamental fact. What therefore is now described as African literature in English and French is a clear contradiction, and a false proposition, just as 'Italian literature in Hausa' would be.[16]

In response to this, Achebe defended his position and that of other Anglophone writers such as Soyinka and Mphahlele in "The African Writer and the English Language" in 1964, which was included in *Morning Yet on Creation Day*. Achebe responds:

> There are not many countries in Africa today where you could abolish the language of the erstwhile colonial powers and still retain the facility for mutual communication. Therefore those African writers who have chosen to write in English or French are not unpatriotic smart alecks with an eye on the main chance—outside their own countries. They are by-products of the same process that made the new nation-states of Africa.[17]

Obi Wali and Ngugi, however, insist that the African experiences of Africans can be conveyed only in their mother tongues. Unlike Achebe, Ngugi was stirred by Obi Wali's article in *Transition* about writing in English. In his "Return to the Roots," however, Ngugi later criticized Wali's article for not sufficiently emphasizing the fact of European imperialism in Africa.[18] Eventually Ngugi made two decisions. The first, made while in detention, was to write creatively only in Gikuyu; the second, announced in 1986, was to say a complete "farewell to English."[19] The gesture of Ngugi's farewell to English was his publication of *Decolonising the Mind* (1986). He says in a statement of the book: "This book, *Decolonising the Mind*, is my farewell to English as a vehicle for any of my writings. From now on it is Gikuyu and Kiswahili all the way." In the preface of the book, he makes clear his opinion on African writers' use of European languages as follows:

> If in these essays I criticise the Afro-European (or Euroafrican) choice of our linguistic praxis, it is not to take away from the talent and the genius of those who have written in English, French or Portuguese. On the contrary I am lamenting a neo-colonial situation which has meant the European bourgeoisie once again stealing our talents and geniuses as they have stolen our economies. In the eighteenth and nineteenth centuries Europe stole art treasures from Africa to decorate their houses and museums; in the twentieth century Europe is stealing the treasures of the mind to enrich their languages and cultures. Africa needs back its economy, its politics, its culture, its languages and all its patriotic writers.[20]

In contrast to Ngugi, Achebe maintains his position concerning African literature and, undeterred by criticism, justifies his use of English:

> As you know, there has been an impassioned controversy about African literature in non-African languages. But what is non-African language? English and French certainly. But what about Arabic? What about Swahili even? Is it then a question of

how long the language has been present on African soil? If so, how many years should constitute *effective occupation*? For me it is again a pragmatic matter. A language spoken by Africans on African soil, a language in which Africans write, justifies itself.[21]

In one of his earlier essays, "African Writer and the English Language (1964)," Achebe has had to defy colonialist critics' doubts on African writers' use of English. Actually there have been many studies on African-English in linguistics.

> I do not see any signs of sterility anywhere here. What I do see is a new voice coming out of Africa, speaking of African Experience in a world-wide language. So my answer to the question *Can an African ever learn English well enough to be able to use it effectively in creative writing?* is certainly yes. If on the other hand you ask: *Can he ever learn to use it like a native speaker?* I should say, I hope not. It is neither necessary nor desirable for him to be able to do so. The price a world language must be prepared to pay is submission to many different kinds of use. The African writer should aim to use English in a way that brings out his message best without altering the language to the extent that its value as a medium of international exchange will be lost. He should aim at fashioning out an English which is at once universal and able to carry his peculiar experience.[22]

Here Achebe asserts the validity of Afro-English. The presented questions connote typical colonialist's attitude toward Africa; infantilization, primitivization and decivilization of the Other by their use of pidgin. In the first chapter of *Black Skin, White Masks*, Frantz Fanon discusses language issues in the colony. According to him, using the colonizer's language affects both the colonizer and the colonized. The colonized suffering from an inferiority complex is "elevated above his jungle stats in proportion to his adoption of the mother country's cultural standards."[23] The more he renounces his blackness, his cultural heritage, the whiter he becomes. However, the colonizer infantilizes and patronizes the colonized by treating him as a child. When a white man with good intentions speaks pidgin to a "pidgin-nigger-talker," it also makes him angry, because according to Fanon, such action comes from "absence of wish, [this] lack of interest, [this] indifference, [this] automatic manner of classifying him [the colonized], primitivizing him, decivilizing him."[24]

The language issue in African literature cannot be solved easily. If one neglects one's mother tongue, as Wali argues, there can be no way to expect and develop literature in the language. Wali takes an example from English literature: "One wonders what would have happened to English literature, for instance, if writers like Spenser, Shakespeare, Donne, and Milton had neglected English, and written in Latin and Greek simply because these classical languages were the cosmopolitan languages of their times."[25]

There exists, however, another perspective. One can argue the language issue in national literature. In literature in English, for instance, one can mane a few; English literature, American literature, Canadian literature, Australian literature and New Zealand literature, etc. There are also multilingual national literatures in countries like Switzerland, Belgium, The Netherlands and India. In Swiss literature, literary works can be produced in at least three languages. In the case of India, there are more than twenty official languages.

The point is this: it seems that even in the discussion of African literature the colonial attitude of the past is still pervasive; the very designation of African literature in singular blurs the unique experiences of Africans' own, whatever they may be; they could be tradition, culture, tribal custom, and/or contemporary sociopolitical experiences, as if in African literature there is no distinction in geographical, cultural and historical entity, just as European imperial powers divided the African continent by their interest regardless of Africans' own cultural and sociopolitical distinctions. As one acknowledges the differences within European nations, one should acknowledge the differences in Africa and its people, culture and tradition, etc. Ironically, most critics and writers seem to have lost their vision and insight, inflamed in the heat of discussion to find "the path" for African literature.

Many voices should be allowed in African literature for the best of that continent's mind and vision to be expressed. The importance of cultural and historical contexts should be more emphasized in creating and studying African literature than certain criteria such as language. Thus, in other words, *national criteria* can be more important in determining critical standards than mere *linguistic criteria*.[26] In that sense, African literatures in the plural seems more proper than in the singular. As Achebe mentions, let African literatures speak themselves instead of herding them onto a single path. Still they are in an early stage compared to the western literatures, any precocious and restrictive judgment on artistic activities might harm their sound development rather then benefit it.

Colonialist Criticism
Achebe deplores colonialist critics and their influence on the African psyche

in his essay, "Colonialist Criticism:"

> If colonialist criticism were merely irritating, one might doubt the justification of devoting a whole essay to it. But strange though it may sound, some of its ideas and precepts do exert an influence on our writers, for it is a fact of our contemporary world that Europe's powers of persuasion can be far in excess of the merit and value of her case. Take for instance the black writer who seizes on the theme that "Africa's past is a sadly inglorious one" as though it were something new that had not already been "proved" adequately for him. Colonialist critics will, of course, fall all over him in ecstatic and salivating admiration—which is neither unexpected nor particularly interesting. What is fascinating, however, is the tortuous logic and sophistry they will sometimes weave around a perfectly straightforward and natural enthusiasm.[27]

Colonialist critics, according to Achebe, do not see African literature from the proper perspectives. Instead, they blur the uniqueness of African literature, for instance, by using a word such as *universal*. In his articles written in the 1960s, it seems he does not show much abhorrence for the word "universal." Without thinking much of the word and its connotation, he himself might have used it in his essays. Later, faced with and bothered by increasing colonialist criticism, he might have come to think about vocabularies used in the criticism of African literature. The following is, for instance, a paragraph taken from Eldred Jones's article. Though he means well, the narrative still seems imbued with a colonialist's attitude and rhetorical tone:

> Much more fundamental than the mere reproduction of syntax is the conveying in its totality of an experience in a way that reflects its environment without precluding it from general applicability. In looking at the African author's work we may be able to recognize its Africanness; we must be able to see its universality. Fortunately the two things often go together. A work which succeeds in realizing its environment to the full often achieves this universality. The happy paradox is that, to be truly universal, one must be truly local.[28]

Having mentioned this, Jones discusses poems by African poets to make his point of how well Africans use French and English to express their feelings. Yet, as he praises their works by the degree of "universal" appeal, the word "universal" seems to suggest how much it appeals to European aesthetics. Surely such a subtle tone bothers conscious African writers like Achebe. To Achebe, the word "universal" stands for Eurocentricism: "I should like to see the word *universal* banned altogether from discussions of African literature until such a time as people cease to use it as a synonym for the narrow, self-serving parochialism of Europe, until their horizon extends to include all the world."[29] Prior to this essay of Achebe's, an African critic, Ernest Emenyonu, also expressed a similar opinion regarding contemporary critics' approach to African literature.[30] He criticizes the critics' ignorance of African history, tradition and culture, and adds that such ignorance creates false voices on African literature and its authors.

This kind of attitude in literature has a parallel with the course of history: the rise of Imperialism. The imperialist rhetoric was crafted carefully under the brocade of sublime ideology. The careful meditations on European Imperialism and its practices in the African colonies are well captured in Joseph Conrad's *Heart of Darkness*. The Conradian voice against European Imperialism is very evident in the story. However, his use of language to create African images in the psyche of white men set the ultimate stereotypical African discourse in modern literature of the colonial era. The tone of colonialist criticism in the present has its origin in many European literary works on and about Africa and its people.

Achebe and Conrad

If Conradian discourse on Africa is an ultimate example of African discourse during the colonial era, Achebe's is its counterpart in the post-colonial era as a discourse of decolonization. The African continent in Conradian discourse merely stands for "darkness" and "void" in one's (European's) psyche rather than for its own geographic spatial specificity. Africa is an unknown and unfamiliar world to Conrad and his contemporaries, not only for its strange culture and people but also for its remoteness from the "familiar" and "progressed" world of western civilization.

As Marlow, the narrator of *Heart of Darkness*, explains in the story, the title of the story seems to have been taken from contemporary cartography:

> Now when I was a little chap I had a passion for maps. I would look for hours at South America, or Africa, or Australia and lose myself in all the glories of exploration. . . . But there was one yet—the biggest—the most *blank*, so to speak—that I had a hankering after.
>
> True, by this time it was not a *blank space* any more. It had got filled since my boyhood with rivers and lakes and names. It had ceased to be a blank space of delightful mystery—a white patch for a boy to dream gloriously over. It had become a place of *darkness*.[31]

In a map, blank space actually means actually means unknown and unexplored areas to Europeans. As the story proceeds, the blank space with a big river "resembling an immense snake uncoiled," that is, the Congo, reveals its content. It is filled with people and the ugly reality of imperialism. Marlow's impressionistic mode of story-telling creates a contrast between darkness and light, which becomes a powerful sinister symbol for the moral corruption of white men, and the lack of civilization of black men. Conrad's creation of African discourse resembles going *backward* against the flow of time. The following can be the most typical paradigm of African narrative by the west:

> Going up that river was like *travelling back* to the earliest beginnings of the world, when vegetation rioted on the earth and the big trees were kings. An empty stream, a great silence, an *impenetrable* forest. The air was warm, thick, heavy, sluggish. There was no joy in the brilliance of sunshine. The long stretches of the waterway ran on, deserted, into the gloom of overshadowed distances. On silvery sandbanks hippos and alligators sunned themselves side by side. The broadening waters flowed through a mob of wooded islands. You lost your way on that river as you would in a desert and butted all day long against shoals trying to find the channel till you thought yourself bewitched and cut off for ever from everything you had known once—somewhere—far away—in another existence perhaps. There were moments when one's past came back to one, as it will sometimes when you have not a moment to spare to yourself; but it came in the shape of an unrestful and noisy dream remembered with wonder amongst the overwhelming realities of this strange world of plants and water and silence. And this stillness of life did not in the least resemble a peace. *It was the stillness of an implacable force brooding over an inscrutable intention.* It looked at you with a vengeful aspect.[32]

Conrad's description of surroundings is so subjective and impressionistic that it creates a mood as if one were to travel to a place resembling the surrealistic paintings of Salvador Dali. The world seen through Marlow's eyes is incomprehensible and inscrutable, and constantly remains an enigma. The unknown and unfamiliar world even appears to bear a malicious intention. It seems to have a "vengeful aspect" with its "stillness of an implacable force brooding over an inscrutable intention." The fear of the unknown is projected into the description of the surroundings.[33] This feeling reaches its climax when Marlow sees a group of black men in motion in contrast with the "motionless foliage."

> But suddenly as we struggled round a bend there would be a glimpse of rush walls, of peaked grass-roofs, a burst of yells, a whirl of black limbs, a mass of hands clapping, of feet stamping, of bodies swaying, of eyes rolling under the droop of heavy and motionless foliage.
> The steamer toiled along slowly on the edge of a black and incomprehensible

> frenzy. The prehistoric man was cursing us, praying to us, welcoming us—who could tell? *We were cut off from the comprehension of our surroundings*; we glided past like phantoms, wondering and secretly appalled, as sane men would be before an enthusiastic outbreak in a madhouse. We could not understand because we were too far and could not remember *because we were traveling in the night of first ages, of those ages that are gone*, leaving hardly a sign—and no memories.[34]

Marlow's reasoning of the mysterious, "incomprehensible frenzy" is based on the idea of progress, that is, Social Darwinism. Since the white men, "us," are far advanced in terms of civilization and culture, they cannot recall the faintest memory of their "prehistoric" existence which might have been like those of the black men on the river bank.

Conrad's choice of words referring to the black man in *Heart of Darkness* is an excellent measure of the contemporary view of black man and Africa in general. It is "us" and "we" versus "they"; the civilized versus the primitive. The "they" is not even completely human. Conrad's terminology reveals an unconscious fixation on "myth of the Other" through dehumanization: "the savage"(38), "an improved specimen"(38), "a whirl of black limbs"(37), "black shapes," "black shadows of disease and starvation," "these moribund shapes," "the black bones"(20), "bundles of acute angles," "these creatures," "strings of dusty niggers with splay feet"(21), etc.[35] Conradian discourse on Africa does not convey an attempt to bridge the gap between "Us" and "the Other." The Other exists in a complete shadow of darkness, rendering only its "inscrutable intention." No matter how hard Marlow tries to distance himself from black men's "incomprehensible frenzy," however, in a brief moment he cannot help but doubt his belief in the myth of the Other:

> No they [the black men on the river bank] were not inhuman. Well, you know that was the worst of it—this suspicion of their not being inhuman. It would come slowly to one. They howled and leaped and spun and made horrid faces, but what thrilled you was just the thought of their humanity—like yours—the thought of your remote kinship with this wild and passionate uproar. Ugly.[36]

The black men are not the same human beings as the white men, simply because to Marlow they live in the first ages of human progress. To him, they are rather closer to animals than to human beings like himself. Yet Marlow shudders at the thought of sameness in "Us" and "the Other." Later when he meets the ultimate figure symbolizing white man's civilization and idea, Kurtz, he also shudders at the realization of the horrible moral degradation in the continent of darkness. The sinister darkness in the black Africa becomes an ultimate symbol for the moral deterioration of European ideology, Imperialism. "White" outside means "black" inside. However, Conrad has not gone far enough to create a symbolic meaning of vice versa.

In an essay titled "An Image of Africa," Achebe strongly reacts against such a dehumanized image of black man. He accuses Conrad of choosing "the role of purveyor of comforting myths."[37] Though he is aware that Conrad's main focus in *Heart of Darkness* is not on Africa itself but on Europeans and their morality, Achebe accuses him of being "a bloody racist" for the following reason:

> Africa as setting and backdrop which eliminates the African as human factor. Africa as a metaphysical battlefield devoid of all recognizable humanity, into which the wandering European enters at his peril. Of course, there is a preposterous and perverse kind of arrogance in thus reducing Africa to the role of props for the breakup of one petty European mind. But that is not even the point. The real question is the dehumanization of Africa and Africans which this age-long attitude has fostered and continues to foster in the world. And the question is whether a novel which celebrates this dehumanization, which depersonalizes a portion of the human race, can be called a great work of art. My answer is: No, it cannot. I would not call that man an artist, for example, who composes an eloquent instigation to one people to fall upon another and destroy them. No matter how striking his imagery or how beautiful his cadences fall, such a man is no more a great artist than another may be called a priest who reads the mass backwards or a physician who poisons his patients.[38]

Achebe acknowledges that Conrad is not the originator of such negative images of Africa and its people, but the man bringing "the peculiar gifts of his own mind to bear on it."[39] Achebe asks to avoid perpetuation of such a negative portrayal of Africa as a dumping ground for sickness in Western civilization:

> For reasons which can certainly use close psychological inquiry, the West seems to suffer deep anxieties about the precariousness of its civilization and to have a need for constant reassurance by comparison with Africa. If Europe, advancing in civilization, could cast a backward glance periodically at Africa trapped in primordial barbarity it could say with faith and feeling: There go I but for the grace of God. Africa is to Europe as the picture is to Dorian Gray—a carrier onto whom the master unloads his physical and moral deformities so that he may go forward, erect and immaculate.[40]

Achebe's criticism of Conrad is powerful and moving because he speaks emotionally yet frankly about how he reads Conrad. His essay eloquently shows how an African reader's perspective differs from that of a westerner's.

At the same time, his reaction illustrates how far and how much dehumanization of the Other pervaded the public mind at the time of Imperialism.

This essay of Achebe's defense and argument against Conrad's negative description of Africa has brought forth a response by Wilson Harris years later. His article begins as follows:

> I read Chinua Achebe's article on Joseph Conrad with much interest and some sympathy. My sympathy rests on an appreciation of his uneasiness in the face of biases that continues to reinforce themselves in post-imperial western establishments. Perhaps the west does have the bad conscience Achebe attributes to it and is seeking, therefore, some assuagement of its guilt.[41]

Yet Harris does not agree with Achebe's view, because Achebe's charge on Conrad and his work is a "mistaken one." According to Harris, Achebe does not understand the nature of "the novel form as a medium of consciousness." Since Achebe comes from Africa where "tradition tends towards homogeneous imperatives," he might have not been able to comprehend the "interaction between sovereign ego and intuitive self" in art, especially in the novel form. Harris says:

> It is in this respect that I find it possible to view *Heart of Darkness* as a frontier novel. By that I mean that it stands upon a threshold of capacity to which Conrad pointed through he never attained that capacity himself. Nevertheless, it was a stroke of genius on his part to visualize an original necessity for distortions in the stases of appearance that seem sacred and that cultures take for granted as models of timeless dignity....
> The novel form Conrad inherited—if I may restate my theme in a more complex way—was conditioned by a homogeneous cultural logic to promote a governing principle that would sustain all parties, all characterizations, in endeavoring to identify natural justice, natural conscience behind the activity of a culture.[42]

Harris praises Conrad for revealing the "hideous biases within a context of heterogeneous bodies and pigmentations" in imaginary art. He gives examples of how well Conrad creates parodies to criticize European ideas through Kurtz and through an exquisite employment of words, especially of the adjective.

In the article, however, the focus of Harris's argument differs from Achebe's. It seems both Achebe's and Harris's arguments are powerful and logical in each perspective. Harris does not touch the subject of racism as Achebe does in his article. Instead, he accuses Achebe of not acknowledging the greatness of Conrad's work as a novel. If Harris can defend Conrad's position by saying that he inherited the novel form as a cultural logic and transcended its intrinsic limitation, the same argument can be applied to Achebe's position. In the age of decolonization ("post-Imperial" in Harris's word), Achebe is surely justified in being upset after reading a literary work so marked by the Imperial era. Achebe's resentful voice is the product of the present postcolonial era and its ideology.

As discussed earlier, Conrad's writing is a paradigm of Africa's image in the western mind. As a strong African voice in the postcolonial era, or neo-colonial era, and by writing true African stories, Achebe has begun a counter revolution of shattering the myth of Africa and blacks which has been perpetuated in the western mind through various media.

Achebe's works are answers to the Conradian discourse on Africa which is mainly an expression of the west's fear of the "impenetrable," "implacable" world "brooding over an inscrutable intention." Achebe's Africa is a world of familiarity and cultural dignity in realistic circumstances, whereas Conrad's Africa exists in an impressionistic and surreal place of "darkness: which hardly can be detached from the west's psychological dimension.

Nancy Schmidt notes that "critics frequently point out weakness in plot and character development in Nigerian fiction, without indicating that plot and characterizations in Nigerian fiction are very similar to those in West African oral literature."[43] She mentions evidence of the influence of forms of oral literature in Nigerian fiction. They are: first, the emphasis on action and narrative and the relatively infrequent use of description; second, the use of proverbs. These aspects typically characterize the mode of Achebe's fictional narrative.

Achebe uses Igbo proverbs to illustrate situations more clearly. In *Things Fall Apart*, the narration goes: "Among the Ibo the art of conversation is regarded very highly, and proverbs are the palm-oil with which words are eaten."[44]

Achebe also uses African words in the narrative without providing their meanings such as *chi*, *obi*, *osu*, etc. Readers at first bewildered by unfamiliar words, can soon grasp their meanings from the context or are indirectly given their closest counterpart in English. Such a technique of using African words and native proverbs in English text creates unique African narratives. This can be a secret and successful ingredient in Achebe's African narrative in English.

The following analysis of Achebe's works, *Things Fall Apart*, *Arrow of God* and *No Longer at Ease*, will contrast with the Conradian discourse on Africa in such a way as to illuminate "heart of darkness" about Africa and its people. "The savages" and "the dark shadow" in *Heart of Darkness* do not exist in Achebe's world: instead, the whites are lepers and subhuman to "we" the blacks before their direct contact with the Other, "the whites."

The fear of the unknown and the in-between barrier seem a part of human nature. Yet Achebe's confident voice from Africa becomes a paradigm of postcolonial African discourse. He presents an inside look at intricate African life with its own dignity and flaws. Through his writings, Achebe captures a true African soul. He also synthesizes the historical legacy of colonialism with African culture and tradition.

Things Fall Apart: Disintegration of Tradition

Things Fall Apart (1958)[45] is Achebe's first novel and it remains his best-known novel. It is more than the tragedy of a traditional hero's downfall. It is a story about African tradition and African dignity depicted through the life of the Igbo people. It is a story about the consequence of Africa's contact with whites and Christianity. It is also partly a story about colonialists. Achebe has successfully interwoven all these issues concerning history, tradition, religion, and races, and has created a powerful story. For this reason, it has acquired a reputation of being both fictionalized history and an anthro-pological documentation of traditional Igbo society.

The novel consists of three parts. Part One is centered in Umuofia and shows its culture through the main character, Okonkwo. The thirteen chapters of this part focus on Okonkwo and his relationship with others, including his immediate family and the cultural tradition itself. Part Two, from chapter fourteen to nineteen, describes Okonkwo's life during his exile in Mbanta. And the final six chapters are Part Three, which deal with Okonkwo's return to Umuofia and his tragic death.

The story's hero, Okonkwo, is an embodiment of Igbo tradition. His tragic downfall in the end symbolizes the imminent disintegration of Igbo tradition and values. He is a very impressive masculine character. In the beginning of the novel he is introduced as a man of wealth and great success, having three wives. When he was still young, he had won the fame as the greatest wrestler around the nine villages, ultimate proof of his masculinity and manliness.

In contrast with Okonkwo, his father, Unoka, is an unsuccessful man. Even when Unoka was young, he was lazy and improvident and was quite incapable of thinking about the future. Unoka has more feminine traits than masculine ones. Unlike his well-built wrester and warrior son, Unoka is thin and slightly stooped (8–9). He loves music and is very good on his flute. When he plays his instrument, his face is "beaming with blessedness and peace" (9). However, Unoka is a "failure." He has no title and no money. He is a loafer and a debtor. Above all, he never likes wars because he cannot bear the sight of blood. These characteristics make him a "coward." He ends his life without any title and with heavy debts.

Okonkwo is deeply ashamed of his father. Having such a "failure" and "coward" as a father, Okonkwo had learned the word *agbala*. The word indicates another name for woman, indicating men who have no title (17). The shame of having such a father makes Okonkwo suffer from the deepest fear, the fear of failure and of weakness. The fear is not external but lies deep within himself. Actually it is "the fear of himself, lest he should be found to resemble his father" (16–17). "The fear of his father's contemptible life and shameful death" (21) haunts Okonkwo throughout his life. Thus he rules his household with authority and power. He does not even show his love to his children, because he thinks that "to show affection was [is] a sign of weakness: the only thing worth demonstrating was [is] strength" (30). Therefore he seldom speaks and expresses his emotions unlike his own father. When he tells stories, they are only "stories of the land—masculine stories of violence and bloodshed" (52).

Okonkwo's extreme masculinity is a reaction to his father's feminine characteristics and failure in life as a man. The author extends the contrast between both men's personalities to every aspect of Igbo society and its traditions, exploring in this way the delicate balance of masculinity and femininity. Even crops in Igbo are divided by such norms: women's crops are coco-yams, beans and cassava; the king of crops is yam, which stands for manliness (25, 34, 35).

The symbol of power, however, is often embodied in feminine essence. The Feast of the New Yam, for instance, is held to give thanks to Ani, the earth goddess and the source of all fertility. The goddess, Ani, is probably the most important deity in Igbo: "She was [is] the ultimate judge of morality and conduct. And what was [is] more, she was [is] in close communion with the departed fathers of the clan whose bodies had been committed to earth"

(37). Umuofia, feared by neighboring villages for its power in war and magic, has an old war-medicine named *agadinwayi*, old woman. The village of Umuike is famous for its markets, because its people make a powerful market-medicine in the shape of an old woman with a fan (107). The Oracle of Hills and Caves who governs people's spirituality in Umuofia is a woman, too. Thus, even though Igbo men despise women for their weakness and insignificance, the power in Igbo tradition is kept and manifested symbolically through feminine embodiments. The delicate balance of two principles of masculinity and femininity in Igbo society is in a way similar to the philosophy of *yin* and *yang* in Taoism.

Due to his rigidity in perspective, Okonkwo occasionally violates traditional norms and disrupts their structural balance. Okonkwo breaks the sacred peace by beating his youngest wife heavily during the Week of Peace for her negligence in her duty. Another time, he beats his second wife on the joyous day of the New Yam Festival, blaming her for a withered banana tree. Annoyed by the beaten wife's murmuring, he almost kills her with his gun. Disgraced by such minor violations of traditional norms, resulting from his hot temper, Okonkwo, however, always obeys the traditional norms by showing his willingness to accept whatever punishment is decided as suitable for his mistakes. Yet the most significant episode illustrating Okonkwo's rigid characteristics is his killing of a boy who was like an adopted son to him.

The unfortunate boy is one of two hostages taken from other villages as a means of appeasement for a murder committed against an Umuofian. The poor boy, Ikemefuna, lives in Okonkwo's house for three years. He gets along very well with Okonkwo's eldest son, Nwoye. When the people of Umuofia decide to kill the boy, following the order of the Oracle of Hills and Caves, Okonkwo does not heed his friend's advice not to participate in the killing of Ikemefuna. On the night of his death, Ikemefuna walks along with his adopted father, Okonkwo, and other men in the village. To get rid of his ominous fear, he walks to the beat of song which he sings in his mind. He senses something wrong when one of the men clears his throat:

> The way he said it sent cold fear down Ikemefuna's back. His hands trembled vaguely on the black pot he carried. Why had Okonkwo withdrawn to the rear? Ikemefuna felt his legs melting under him. And he was afraid to look back.
> As the man who had cleared his throat drew up and raised his machete, Okonkwo looked away. He heard the blow. The pot fell and broke in the sand. He heard Ikemefuna cry, "My father, they have killed me!" as he ran towards him. Dazed with

fear, Okonkwo drew his machete and cut him down. He was afraid of being thought weak. (59)

Okonkwo does not have to participate in killing the boy in order to obey the Oracle. Because of his fear of failure and weakness, Okonkwo kills the boy he loves as much as his own son. His wise friend, Obierika, blames him for his action saying that "What you have done will not please the Earth. It is the kind of action for which the goddess wipes out whole families"(64). Okonkwo defends his action by claiming that he only fulfilled his duty in obedience to the Oracle, who is a messenger of the Earth goddess, Ani. Yet the death of Ikemefuna makes Okonkwo uneasy. He cannot sleep or eat for several days.

Calamities keep plaguing Okonkwo's life, yet the way he deals with them makes his a great masculine hero. Okonkwo inadvertently commits a "female *ochu*," the murder of a clansman. As Okonkwo fires his gun as a part of the funeral ceremony for the death of the old and venerable man, Ezeudu, a piece of iron from the explosion pierces a boy's heart and kills him. As a penalty for his "crime against the earth goddess" (117), he has to flee from his land to his mother's land. Okonkwo and his family are in exile for seven years in Mbanta.

> His [Okonkwo's] life had been ruled by a great passion—to become one of the lords of the clan. That had been his life-spring. And he had all but achieved it. Then everything had been broken. He had been cast out of his clan like a fish onto a dry, sandy beach, panting. Clearly his personal god or *chi* was not made for great things. A man could not rise beyond the destiny of his *chi*. The saying of the elders was not true—that if a man said yes his *chi* also affirmed. Here was a man whose *chi* said nay despite his own affirmation. (121)

Despite this ill-fated incident, Okonkwo survives the ordeal of exile. While his best friend, Obierika, takes good care of his home in Umuofia during his absence, in Mbanta his maternal uncle provides a shelter for him and his family. The nature of Okonkwo's crime and its subsequent punishment again illustrate the wisdom in Igbo custom of balancing the masculine and the feminine. The uncle explains the philosophy with simple language:

> A man belongs to his fatherland when things are good and life is sweet. But when there is sorrow and bitterness he finds refuge in his motherland. Your mother is there to protect you. She is buried there. And that is why we say that mother is supreme. . . . Your duty is to comfort your wives and children and take them back to your fatherland after seven years. But if you allow sorrow to weigh you down and kill you,

they will all die in exile. (124)

Okonkwo does not learn the lesson which he could have gotten from his exile—the need for balancing feminine and masculine traits in himself. His violent crime (masculinity) is punished by the seven-year exile, a feminine solution. However, he is not changed. Okonkwo still has no patience with unsuccessful and unmanly men. He is till a masculine hero. After his return from the exile, he deplores the changes in Umuofia. He thinks the people of Umuofia have all become "women," mainly because they have accepted the church and allowed their own people to convert to Christianity, and they also have allowed the white men to rule them. The white men have brought to Umuofia their own government along with the religion. Umuofia is no longer the same old place, and Okonkwo's return is far from the glorious one he dreamed of during his exile:

> Okonkwo was deeply grieved. And it was not just a personal grief. He mourned for the clan, which he saw breaking up and falling apart, and he mourned for the warlike men of Umuofia, who had so unaccountably become soft like women. (168)

Okonkwo tries to encourage people to resist the white man's power. One of the converts, Enock, desecrates one of the *egwugwus*[46] by lifting its mask, which is considered one of the greatest crimes a man can commit. Upon that incident, the Mother of the Spirits weeps "as if the very soul of the tribe wept [weeps] for a great evil that was [is] coming—its own death" (171–72). And subsequently people destroy the church to pacify the spirit of the clan (175). For such action, Okonkwo is mainly responsible: he speaks violently about the matter, and his clansmen listen to him. Though people do not agree to kill the missionary or drive away the Christians, at least they agree to destroy the church. The consequence of their action is, however, very serious. In a way, it brings their proud cultural heritage closer to its "falling-apart." The wail of the Mother of the Spirits is a prefiguration for such a symbolic death of tradition.

Two days after the destruction of the church, the six leaders of Umuofia, including Okonkwo, are humiliated under the power of the District Commissioner. The bitterness and anger over that experience later drive Okonkwo to kill one of the white men's messengers at the community gathering. Later the Commissioner and his men come to arrest Okonkwo; they find only his body hanging in the tree. Okonkwo's suicide is again "an offense against the Earth" (190). His body cannot be buried by his clansmen because of the abomination for suicide according to the custom, which, however, echoes somewhat his father's shameful death. Besides, his father seemed to have predicted what might happen to Okonkwo, as he said: "A proud heart can survive a general failure because such a failure does not prick its pride. It is more difficult and more bitter when a man fails alone" (27). Unoka's remark foreshadows Okonkwo's whole life. Though Okonkwo survived all the calamities which struck him, his pride could not stand the humiliation from the Other. His vengeful act of killing the messenger is his final reenactment of his warrior spirit, and yet his unbending pride ironically destroys him. Obierika says to the District Commissioner: "That man was one of the greatest men in Umuofia. You drove him to kill himself; and now he will be buried like a dog" (191).

With the tragic down fall of the great man of Umuofia, the process of "falling apart" in Igbo society must accelerate. When he kills the messenger, Okonkwo himself seems to sense that the course of history cannot be turned back and the process of "falling apart" is inevitable. The only alternative left to him is death:

> He [Okonkwo] knew that Umuofia would not go to war. He knew because they had let the other messengers escape. They had broken into tumult instead of action. He discerned fright in that tumult. He heard voices asking: "Why did he do it?" (188)

The two most foreshadowing incidents in the novel are the death of Ikemefuna and the annihilation of Abame: the former is caused by the rigidity of Igbo values and the vulnerability of Igbo culture to Christianity; the latter is caused by the violent nature of white colonial power disguised by the gentle doctrines of Christianity and the ideology of Imperialism. The conflict in the religious doctrine of "all men are equal before the God" and the use of militant power under the rhetoric of "civilizing the primitive" is the intrinsic ambivalence in white's approach to the native.

The rigidity of Igbo tradition is apparent in many episodes in the story. As in the case of Unoka's despicable death, when a man is afflicted with swelling in the stomach and the limbs, he is not allowed to die in his home but is abandoned to the Evil Forest (21). Also there are the *osu*, the outcast and the untouchable in Igbo. The *osu* is taboo and is not allowed to mix with the freeborn in anyway. If twins are born, they have to be thrown away in the Evil Forest. When Nwoye hears for the first time the cry of abandoned twins, he shudders:

> Nwoye had heard that twins were put in earthenware pots and thrown away in the forest, but he had never yet come across them. A vague chill had descended on him and his head had seemed to swell, like a solitary walker at night who passes an evil spirit on the way. Then something had given way inside him. It descended on him again, this feeling, when his father walked in, that night after killing Ikemefuna. (60)

Ikemefuna's death also leads to Nwoye's estrangement from his father. Nwoye tries to be an ideal son to his powerful and strict father. In order to please him, he intentionally shuns the feminine side of him. There is a great deal of influence form Ikemefuna, too. Nwoye has always considered Ikemefuna his own elder brother. His death and its cause make Nwoye question the value of the society and the authority and the strength of his father. With the coming of the church in the town, he finds an alternative in the new religion. The fact that Nwoye's conversion is voluntary is very significant. It signifies the intrinsic vulnerability in Igbo tradition and its value system. Largely, the rigidity in Igbo tradition makes Nwoye question the existing values and turn himself to the newly arrived alternative, Christianity.

Nwoye never forgets the chilly moment of his first realization about the fate of Ikemefuna and twins, and continues to doubt his society's values. When he first hears the missionaries talking about the Holy Trinity and singing hymns, he feels a kind of relief like having an answer for his doubt and question:

> It was the poetry of the new religion, something felt in the marrow. The hymn about brothers who sat in darkness and in fear seemed to answer a vague and persistent question that haunted his young soul—the question of the twins crying in the bush and the question of Ikemefuna who was killed. He felt a relief within as the hymn poured into his parched soul. The words of the hymn were like the drops of frozen rain melting on the dry palate of the panting earth. Nwoye's callow mind was greatly puzzled. (137)

Despite the fact that his father wants him to be a great farmer and a great man (34) in the traditional context, Nwoye converts to Christianity. Besides embracing a fine young man like Nwoye, the new religion welcomes *osu*, outcast, twins, and anybody who cannot fit into the main stream of Igbo society. Thus, Chielo, the Oracle of Hills and Caves, calls the converts "the excrement of the clan," and Christianity "a mad dog that had [has] come to eat it up" (133). Compared to Igbo tradition, Christianity seems very flexible in its treatment of Igbo people, especially outcasts. Such religious embraces create puzzlement among the native: one like Chielo and Okonkwo, for instance, shows complete rejection and hate; the other is attracted to Christianity for its religious doctrines, as in the case of Nwoye. For the advent of Christianity in Igbo, the death of Ikemefuna is like a propitious sacrifice. Particularly it affects Nwoye's life and his decision to convert. In this respect, Donald J. Weinstock sees Ikemefuna as a Christ-figure.[47]

Implications of the advent of Christianity in Igbo are to signify the encroachment of Imperialism in the region and to contrast two different value systems through their clashes. Thus such processes make the intrinsic vulnerability of Igbo tradition surface to Igbo people's consciousness, especially by re-enforcing their rigidity through characters like Okonkwo.

Yet Okonkwo himself ponders his son's conversion with much abomination. He considers converts to be "effeminate men." He shudders at the thought of his other sons following Nwoye's step and praying to the white man's god. It is like the prospect of annihilation (142). Okonkwo comes to terms with the fact in Igbo cultural context. Considering his nickname, "Roaring Flame," he believes it is natural that he has a woman for a son: "Living fire begets cold, impotent ash" (143). Okonkwo's abomination of Christianity is similar to that of the grandfather in Yŏm Sang-sŏp's *Samdae*. Even though the cultural settings are different from each other, the conflicts between the old and the new, tradition and western values, render the same kind of implication to people's lives along with the generation gap.

Okonkwo's masculine pride and rigidity are also responsible for Nwoye's conversion, even though Okonkwo himself does not realize it. Okonkwo blames his father for having such a son, because Nwoye takes after his grandfather in many ways. In fact, what Okonkwo lacks in himself is shown through the characteristics of Obierika, his best friend.

Obierika is not a man of action like Okonkwo, but a man of thought. He is a wise and respectable man, who has the ability to predict and prepare for the future. Above all, unlike Okonkwo who has an absolutely rigid view of "the Law of the Land" and obeys it in masculine ways, Obierika is more flexible in his obeisance to the law. And sometimes he doubts and questions the nature of the law (67). When Okonkwo has to be exiled for his murder of a kinsman, Obierika mourns his friend's calamity: "Why should a man suffer so grievously for an offense he had committed inadvertently?" (118). He also advises Okonkwo not to participate in the killing of Ikemefuna. He is always loyal to his friend. Unlike Okonkwo who suffers from the fear of weakness, Obierika does not think that compassion is a sign of weakness. Yet he remains as loyal as Okonkwo to "the law of the land."

One of the most important answers for people's passive reaction indicated in the episode where Okonkwo kills the messenger as his act of resistance is the shadow of the Abame incident. The Abame incident brings history into fiction; Achebe historicizes the story by putting it into historical context.

Obierika brings the news about the town of Abame to Okonkwo in the second year of his exile. Obierika says "Abame has been wiped out" (127). When a white man enters the town riding his bicycle, the people of Abame kill him and tie the bicycle to a tree, following the order of their Oracle. Out of revenge, other white men later kill the villagers on a market day. Obierika says:

> But I am greatly afraid. We have heard stories about white men who made the powerful guns and the strong drinks and took salves away across the seas, but no one thought the stories were true. (130)

Okonkwo's reaction to the news is typical of a warrior: "They should have armed themselves with their guns and their machetes even when they went to market" (130). Two years after the new of Abame, Obierika also brings news about the arrival of missionaries to Umuofia. The encroachment of the white men and their imperial power to this part of Africa is done very fast, faster than the African people can prepare to react or accept such changes in life.

According to Wren, Obierika's story of the murdered white man corresponds to the case of Dr. J. F. Stewart:

> The one case is that of Dr. J. F. Stewart, who at 1:00 p.m. on 16 November 1905, set off on his bicycle from Owerri (today the capital of Imo State) intending to ride to Calabar via Bende. At a branch in the 'road' (really a track), he turned toward Obizi—a serious error, according to a letter to the Colonial Office from H. M. Douglas. 'Native,' he said, who reported the matter to Owerri, reported that Stewart was stripped, bound, and beaten, and afterwards 'his body was cut up and shared. His bicycle also was broken up and shared' (Colonial Office file 520/35 and 32). A. E. Afigbo investigated local tradition about the death of Stewart and found that the Ahiara people 'took him to their neighbours . . . to show them *what* they had caught'; 'they did not know he was a human being,' though he might have been a ghost' (*The Warrant Chiefs*, 1972, p.67).[48]

On 13 December, a captain and other black soldiers "punished" the Abame people. About the death of Stewart, there seem to have been several versions of the account. Still Stewart's death became a major justification for the "Bende-Onitsha Hinterland Expedition, "which destroyed the Oracle at Awka, subdued the Ahiaras and other resistant groups, and opened the way for motor-road construction."[49] It opened the land to the colonials and missionaries.

The horror of the Abame incident lay deep inside the Igbo people. The annihilation of their neighboring town is felt very closely: it becomes an ultimate reference of what might happen to them if they behave "unwisely" in dealing with whites. In their closed society, Igbo people cannot acquire accurate knowledge about the Other. Their ignorance about white men is obvious, as depicted in the conversation between Obierika and his in-laws. They think white men are lepers. In Igbo, the polite name for leprosy is "the white skin." Thus white men are considered to 'have no toes" (71). Igbo people also call white men albino, whereas they call themselves "we," "ordinary men." And a bicycle is an "iron horse" to them.

With the Abame incident, Achebe brings history to the fictional world. He historicizes the world of *Things Fall Apart* and gives the background its temporal and spatial specificity in the historical context of West Africa. Suddenly the epic world of tradition depicted in Part One is shifted to that of the novel in a Bakhtinian sense.

Before the contact with whites, the traditional Igbo society is completely walled off from the outside world. It lacks any relativity and in no way is it similar to the present Nigeria. It is the world of "epic past," "monochromic and valorized (hierarchical)."[50]

Until readers are told by Obierika about Abame, they hardly can locate the time setting, whether the novel is about the world of five hundred years ago or of one hundred years ago. The traditional world is the absolute past to which neither the present readers nor the author himself can return in experience. With the news about the Abame incident, the story enters the world of the novel; it is connected to the temporal procession of history and to the present world.

Upon their contact with the whites, Umuofians are confused and divided among themselves by the differences. Above all, the ways the whites approach them bewilder and perplex the Umuofians:

"Does the white man understand our custom about land?"
"How can he when he does not even speak our tongue? But he says that our customs are bad; and our own brothers who have taken up his religion also say that

our customs are bad. How do you think we can fight when our own brothers have turned against us? The white man is very clever. He came quietly and peaceable with his religion. We were amused at his foolishness and allowed him to stay. Now he had won our brothers, and our clan can no longer act like one. *He has put a knife on the things that held us together and we have fallen apart.*" (162; emphasis mine)

Obierika's accurate observations of how white men have gained power in Igbo society illustrate well the double-faced policy of Imperialism; the gentleness of Christianity by embracing almost everybody and the merciless use of military power to kill anybody in the name of "pacification" or "punishment." Such ambivalence accelerates the division among the Igbos and confuses them. Among white characters in the story, the differences in dealing with the natives are well portrayed through Mr. Brown and Mr. Smith. Mr. Brown as a missionary shows his eagerness to understand Igbo culture and tradition, whereas Mr. Smith opposes such attempts openly. Mr. Smith sees things "as black and white" (169). Anyhow, the existence of the whites make the Igbo people fall apart by encouraging them to "put a knife on the things that held [them] together."

The novel, of course presents an inside look at many details of Igbo customs which show their virtues and dignity: the ceremonial greetings using kola nuts and chalk between the elders on a visit, the settling with the suitor for the bride-price (67–71), the celebration of the New Yam Festival, the traditional trial by *egwugwu* and the Evil Forest (83–89), etc. The rich details of Igbo customs in the novel make it a document of anthropological value. Igbo tradition and society as a whole become a character, which play very important roles to illuminate the theme of the novel. Politically, Igbo society is democratic rather than dictatorial. When the missionaries ask who the king of the village is, they answer that they do not have a king, instead "we have men of high title and the chief priests and the elders" (138).

The Igbo society and its tradition presented in the novel in detail, ultimately help readers to understand Okonkwo as a tragic hero in an Igbo cultural context. In the eyes of the Commissioner, Okonkwo's death is merely an interesting anecdote. He thinks the story of Okonkwo's suicide would be worth putting into his upcoming book, *The Pacification of the Primitive Tribes of the Lower Niger*, but it would only deserve "a reasonable paragraph" not even a chapter. The colonialist cannot understand the depth of Okonkwo's tragedy, and above all, he refuses to do so, because it would "give the natives a poor opinion of him" (191). This is a typical colonialist attitude to rule over the native. In order to create an aura of superiority over the native, colonialists like the Commissioner emphasize the importance of bureaucracy. Even the title of the Commissioner's book carries the implication of the myth of the Other. By claiming to be an expert on Africa and its culture, he perpetuates the myth of African primitives. The impenetrability of "the Other" is obvious. In the episode of Okonkwo's suicide, Achebe handles well the two different perspectives, African and European. He creates a well-calculated irony: Africans still dwell in the crumbling and "falling apart" norms of tradition; Europeans lack the capacity to understand the tragic human dimension of the Other.

By presenting a close and inside look at Igbo society through the tragic hero, Okonkwo, Achebe shows the weakness as well as the strength of Igbo society. He also presents the dignity of Igbo culture and tradition. All these elements in one culture are well captured along with its contrast with other value systems, Christianity and the white dominance in politics.

One can sense such a theme from the title of the novel. Lloyd W. Brown elaborates on the implication of the title taken from Yeats's poem, "The Second Coming" (1921):

> In Yeats's work the vision of human history projects a succession of gyres, of epochal cycles in which the pre-Christian era gives way to the age ushered in by Christ's first coming, and the Christian phase must be followed in turn by a new and terrifyingly unknown cycle—by the new "cradle" and the new "Bethlehem" of another era or "coming." Achebe's nineteenth century Africa witnesses the end of an era and the beginning of twentieth century Europeanization, with all its implied consequences to another stage—the future history of post colonial Africa. . . . Namely, in evoking Yeats's themes, Achebe implies that the sense of history and tradition, the burdens of cultural continuity, decay, and rebirth, have all been the African's loss as well as the Westerner's. And in the process the novelist has exploited the European's cultural criteria—his literature and historiography—in order to reverse the white man's exclusivist definitions of history and culture.[51]

With the evocation of African tragedy through Western literary metaphor and form, Achebe shows his ingenuity as an artist. His allusion about the course of African history of Yeats's (western) philosophical rendering transcends cultural and historical differences. Yet Achebe's use of Igbo words and Igbo expressions makes this work an anti-Conradian African discourse: his debts to his African oral tradition and proverbs are immense.

Achebe's third novel, *Arrow of God*, further illustrates the process of falling apart. Achebe continues the fictionalization of history and anthropological documentation without losing his aesthetic sensibility.

Arrow of God: Is It Ulu's?

Arrow of God is Achebe's third novel, published in 1964. Robert M. Wren considers it to be "the most complex, richly-textured novel to come out of Africa."[52] Its temporal background fills the time gap between the two previous novels, *Things Fall Apart* (1958) and *No Longer at Ease* (1960). It is set mainly in the early 1920s about a decade after Okonkwo's tragic death in *Things Fall Apart*. The action takes place in Umuaro, which consists of six villages or clans. Umuaro is a neighboring town of Umuofia in *Things Fall Apart*. Situations and incidents in the first novel (and even in *No Longer at Ease*) are echoed throughout *Arrow of God*. Achebe finally succeeds in this novel to present a full picture of the complicated Igbo culture and its dynamic relations with the people and outsiders of the tradition.

Umuaro as a community plays a very significant role in the novel; it is more than a background. The important characteristics of Umuaro are brought forth through the spiritual leader, Ezeulu. He is the Chief Priest of Ulu, and the whole story unfolds, focusing on and around him. One of the important white characters, Winterbottom, explains the meaning of the title, Ezeulu, to one of his subordinates: "The prefix *eze* in Ibo means king. So the man is a kind of priest-king" (121). As the main protagonist, Ezeulu's personality reflects the complex nature of social changes under the white men's colonial rule and the meaning of Igbo tradition in this context. Ezeulu's tragic transformation from the imposing spiritual leader to a lonely deranged man reveals the deeper meaning of Igbo culture falling apart than the tragic death of Okonkwo in *Things Fall Apart* does: it touches the spirituality in Igbo culture. After the reading the novel, however, readers can finally realize that Umuaro itself remains the real hero of the novel. Due to the Igbo people's tenacity to life, the survival of its culture is ensured even under the drastic social change.

In chapter Two, the narrator provides the origin of Umuaro's formation:

> In the very distant past, when lizards were still few and far between, the six villages—Umuachala, Umunneora, Umuagu, Umuezeani, Umuogwugwu and Umuisiuzo—lived as different people, and each worshipped its own deity. Then the hired soldiers of Abam used to strike in the dead of night, set fire to houses and carry men,

> women and children into slavery. Things were so bad for the six villages that their leaders came together to save themselves. They hired a strong team of medicine-men to install a common deity for them. This deity which the fathers of the six villages made was called Ulu. Half of the medicine was buried at a place which became the Nkwo market and the other half thrown into the stream which became Mili Ulu. The six villages then took the name of Umuaro, and the priest of Ulu became their Chief Priest. From that day they were never again beaten by an enemy. (16)[53]

Umuaro as a community has been formed out of the fear of slavery-attack. Uniting six villages together was necessary to ensure their survival, and yet it became a source of bitterness for the ambitious leaders of every other clan. For instance, Nwaka from Umunneora and its priest, Ezidemili, are the chief political rivals of Ezeulu. When Umuaro wages war against Okperi claiming the possession of some part of the land, the political rivalry between Nwaka and Ezeulu becomes so obvious that their different opinions divide the people of Umuaro. Eventually Nwaka's opinion dominates the public mind and war breaks out. The African war, stemming out of tribal enmity, is abruptly ended by the intervention of the white rulers. The colonial use of military force is no match for the natives, and their ruling over the Igbo people meets no more a violent resistance than Okonkwo's killing of a messenger shown in *Things Fall Apart*. The Abame incident which appeared in the first novel is also echoed throughout *Arrow of God* as a powerful metaphor for the horror of white men's expedition:

> The next day, Afro, saw the war brought to a sudden close. The white man, Wintabota, brought soldiers to Umuaro and stopped it. The story of what these soldiers did in Abame was still told with fear, and so Umuaro made no effort to resist but laid down their arms. (31)

The white man, Winterbottom, also solves the problem which ignites the war; he gives the disputed land to Okperi. He also orders soldiers to break all the guns in Umuaro. People keep the memory of their humiliation by naming the babies born that year after the gun-breaking incident. Captain Winterbottom is described as a representative of white colonialism in Nigeria.

As a counterpart character to Ezeulu, the story of Winterbottom's life discloses the inner conflicts among the whites hidden behind the façade of a pompous bureaucracy. To the people of Umuaro and Okperi, Winterbottom has ultimate power. Yet it becomes clear that he is also a victim of colonial policy and a failure in the system. He is often angry and frustrated by high-handed orders from his superiors. He is not promoted, whereas one of his junior officers becomes his superior. Winterbottom says: "Any fool can be promoted, provided he does nothing but try. Those of us who have a job to do have no time to try" (61). He also complains about the colonial administration:

> The great tragedy of British colonial administration was that the man on the spot who knew his African and knew what he was talking about found himself being constantly overruled by starry-eyed fellows at headquarters. (63)

However, the conflicts and tensions among the white characters can be categorized as situational. Achebe uses the white characters to mirror the Igbo people in order to expose an irony. The irony is this: description about Winterbottom's unsuccessful marriage and his illness prove him to a vulnerable mortal, yet, to the natives' eyes he is seen as an embodiment of the western colonial power. Despite the fact that tensions among the whites are presented well, they do not arouse the same degree of pathos as the tensions in Umuaro politics. Yet, the internal political turmoil and enmity among the Igbo leaders continue only within the boundary of their power.

To present the complex relationships among Igbo people and their relations with their new white rulers, the perspective in the narration alternates between the whites' point of view and the natives' point of view; it allows a certain degree of objectivity in story-telling, and at the same time, its deconstructive presentation allows readers to connect the stories about the past of Umuaro and its people with Achebe's other two novels. The language coordinates along with the switching of narrative perspectives. For instance, the white man's name, Winterbottom, is called Wintabota, when the story is told from Ezeulu's perspective. The narrative tone is also changed according to the point of view. Mr. Wright observes the nature of blacks while building the road between Umuaro and Okperi. The narration accords with this white colonial's sentiment:

> In fact he had got very much attached to this gang and knew their leaders by name. Many of them were, of course, bone lazy and could only respond to severe handling. But once you got used to them they could be quite amusing. They were as loyal as pet dogs and their ability to improvise songs was incredible. (86)

The white man's view on blacks is amicable and yet unmistakably dehumanizing; it echoes Conrad's suspicion on black's humanity in *Heart of Darkness*. Above all, the tone is so similar to that of Joyce Cary's *Mister*

Johnson that the quotation seems to have been taken from the book. Achebe skillfully provides two different perspectives in the story whose contrast effectively illuminates the paradox of being the Other.

Ezeulu's speculation of his power in the beginning of the story is a very important epiphany in the development of the plot. Ezeulu, as the Chief Priest of Ulu, speculates on the nature and the significance of his power:

> Whenever Ezeulu considered the immensity of his power over the year and the crops and, therefore, over the people he wondered if it was real. It was true he named the day for the feast of the Pumpkin Leaves and for the New Yam feast; but he did not choose the day. He was merely a watchman. His power was no more than the power of a child over a goat that was said to be his. As long as the goat was alive it was his; he would find it food and take care of it. But the day it was slaughtered he would know who the real owner was. No! The Chief Priest of Ulu was more than that, must be more than that. If he should refuse to name the day there would be no festival—no planting and no reaping. But could he refuse? No Chief Priest had ever refused. So it could not be done. He would not dare. (3)

Ezeulu questions how much power he has over the people. The story is developing toward the answer to Ezeulu's questions. As mentioned, his duties are to observe the moon and season and to name the date for the most important festivals in Igbo. Ezeulu is well aware of the implications of such duties and the importance of his role as the Chief Priest of Ulu in Umuaro. He imagines his immense power could change the fate of whole villages; if he should refuse to name the day for the New Yam Feast, then there would be no planting and reaping. Later he is tempted to execute his power. When he actually does, he only realizes that it brings his own destruction. His elated feeling at the pensive moment when he considers the greatness of his power is later proven to be illusory. Unable to face such a reality, Ezeulu becomes deranged.

His speculation on the "immensity of his power" signals more complicated issues in internal politics as well as in relations with the white men in Igbo. Facing the political threat from other leaders, Ezeulu's "friendship" with Captain Winterbottom secures his power more firmly until the python incident breaks out in his own household. Oduche's zeal for the new religion changes his perspectives in life. In order to testify his faith, Oduche almost kills a python by confining it in the box. Such action enflames again the dormant political power game and brings outrageous reactions from Umunneora, where a python is a sacred beast owned by their deity, Idemili.

The difference in the treatment of the python antagonizes the Igbo people and even some Christian converts. Yet the changes in social values gradually encroach upon the Igbo mind, and the increase in Christian activity is partially responsible for such changes. Ezeulu himself realizes the power of the new religion and shows his willingness to know about the religion. When Ezeulu decides to send one of his sons, Oduche, to church, he justifies this decision by asserting that people should learn the white man's deity to have such "great power and conquest" (47). As time passes, Ezeulu becomes afraid that "the new religion was [is] like a leper" (47).

Nwaka and Ezidemili try to use this unfortunate incident to attack Ezeulu. The fact that Ezeulu offered his son as a sacrificial lamb to Christianity is caught in the political web and is distorted. Ezeulu wants his son to be his "eyes" to the new religion. He wants to respond to the changes in the world. That was Ezeulu's original intention to send Oduche to church. Instead of opening his eyes to the new world, his decision to send his son brings him more problems than solutions. Along with Ezeulu's alleged friendship with Winterbottom, Ezeulu's political enemies use Oduche's conversion as an excuse to attack him. They claim that Ezeulu betrayed Umuaro to the white man and Christianity.

Besides the white men's colonial rule, the nature of Umuaro's federacy is also an important factor in Ezeulu's political conflicts with other leaders. Emmanuel Obiechina Explains about the inner conflicts:

> Ulu's dominance in the structure of a traditional power is itself a result of social change. It represents a certain centralizing trend somewhat at odds with the federalizing, segmentary political relationships of earlier times. The centralization has not been consolidated or it would have led to a priest-kingship such as that of Ununri in Igboland and probably like the obaship among the Yoruba. This lack of consolidation is exploited by Ezidemili. He is always harking back to the golden age of the people's history "in the days before Ulu" when "the true leaders of each village had been men of high title like Nwaka." This near-enactment of the Cassius-Brutus-Caesar syndrome is interesting because it supports the point that a feeling of greater security is behind the attack on Ulu's authority; the "security" role of Ulu is completely left out of Ezidemili's tirade. His conspiracy could only work at a time of increased security. The presence of the colonial administration and the end of the trans-Atlantic slave trade explain this feeling. But it should not be forgotten that the colonial presence generated its own insecurities, since the "pacification" involved the use of force.[54]

Ezidemili and Nwaka's political attack on Ezeulu gains its force when Winterbottom summons Ezeulu to Okperi to appoint Ezeulu to Paramount

Chief of Umuaro. Captain Winterbottom and Tony Clark expect that this decision will bring Ezeulu's total transformation to a more imposing leader, who commands authority over his own people. The two white men relish their power to create another African king, rendering ironical and paradoxical effects; the criticism of British colonial policy and of African corruption through abuse of the parasitic nature of their power. Captain Winterbottom says, "I have never found the Ibo man backward in acquiring the airs of authority" (121). He also criticizes the Chief of Okperi, who is appointed by the colonial government:

> "The man was a complete nonentity until we crowned him, and now he carries on as though he had been nothing else all his life. It's the same with Court Clerks and even messengers. They all manage to turn themselves into little tyrants over their own people. It seems to be a trait in the character of the negro." (121)

The narration, however, attributes the main reason for Africans' desire of power to the British colonial policy over the Igbo people who never had kings before: "This was what British administration was doing among the Ibos, making a dozen mushroom kings grew where there was none before" (65). Without acknowledging it as the outcome of their policy, the two white men conclude that the tyranny of leadership is an innate characteristic of the blacks. It is a typical colonial attitude. Achebe's depiction of traditional Igbo life defies such a conclusion. The African experiences of abuse and violence under the presence of colonial power create the inversion of such abuse and they inflict it on their own people; violence begets violence. In *The Wretched of the Earth* with similar perspectives, Frantz Fanon explains the nature of violence in Africa as a colonial legacy.

Ezeulu rejects the white government's offer to be a Paramount Chief. After ordering Ezeulu's arrest, Winterbottom breaks down due to his deteriorated health. The people of Umuaro consider it Ulu's punishment for incarcerating their priest. During the long and humiliating imprisonment, Ezeulu's reputation keeps changing between heroism and powerless defeat. The Umuaro people's passivity toward such humiliation from the white colonial government indicates Umuaro's political impotence. The direct and indirect experiences with the whites make the Igbo people passive, or sometimes, apathetic, and helpless.

Obika, the most masculine character in the story, is beaten by Wright. People, including Ezeulu, react to the news, demonstrating their concern through mere talk and speculation. No action is taken to compensate for the humiliation. Though deeply disturbed by his son's being whipped by the white man, Ezeulu only wishes that Wright would have punished Obika's delinquency by different means, such as fines or a warning, rather than humiliating corporal punishment. The incident shows how white colonialism treats the natives; it indicates the dehumanization and/or infantilization of them. The fact that the most masculine black character in the story is beaten symbolizes the emasculation of the Igbo spirit.[55]

Through Ezeulu, readers see not only the internal politics and the spirituality of Igbo culture, but also the intricate relationships among wives and sons and daughters in the polygamous household. This inside look at life—quotidian matters, the marriage ceremony, wife abuse, and Ezeulu's friendship with Akuebue, who is less impressive than Obierika in *Things Fall Apart*—has little to do with the colonial incursion.

As shown through elaborate ceremonies, the Pumpkin Festival and the New Yam Feast are the two most important communal events which represent the spirituality and the dignity of Igbo culture. The Pumpkin Festival is a feminine festival, whereas the New Yam Feast is rather a masculine one. As A. M. Kemoli observes in the discussion of violence and peace in Igbo society, "an equilibrium between peace and violence can only be maintained when a society agrees to stick together and to do constant ritual purifications."[56] Through these festivals, people seek to purify their sinful souls and to reunite themselves in symbolic ways. The enmity between clans disappears amid the festival atmosphere (76). The balance in male-female principles shown in *Things Fall Apart* is also important in *Arrow of God*. During the celebration of Akwu Nro, a minor ritual before the New Yam Feast, Edogo is concerned about the look of his mask, whether it has too much of a Maiden Spirit (229).

Ezeulu appears as an imposing Chief Priest of Ulu in the Pumpkin Festival:

> He struck the metal staff into the earth and left it quivering while he danced a few more steps to the *Ikolo* which had not paused for breath since the priest emerged. All the women waved their pumpkin leaves in front of them.
>
> Ezeulu looked round again at all the men and women of Umuaro, but saw no one in particular. Then he pulled the staff out of the ground, and with it in his left hand and *the Mother of Ofo* in his right he jumped forward and began to run round the market place.... As the fleeting Chief Priest reached any section of the crowd the women there waved their leaves round their heads and flung them at him. It was as though thousands and thousands of giant, flying insects swarmed upon him. (82)

Ezeulu's power as a spiritual leader seems to be at its height. As the Chief Priest of Ulu, he also has to name the day for the New Yam Feast. It is considered to be the most important ceremony in Umuaro. The significance of the New Yam Feast in Umuaro is to unite all people in a sense of spiritual communion with ancestral spirits:

> The festival thus brought gods and men together in one crowd. It was the only assembly in Umuaro in which a man might look to his right and find his neighbour and look to his left and see a god standing there—perhaps Agwu whose mother also gave birth to madness of Ngene, owner of a stream. (232)

However, the significance of this festival is more than its spirituality and symbolism; the feast is also practical. On that day, each person in Umuaro offers a good-sized seed yam to their deity, Ulu. Fro the heap of these offered yams, Ezeulu as the Chief Pries selects thirteen yams to reckon the new year as seen in the first chapter. And also the people know the population of six villages from the size of the heap of offered yams.

This year Ezeulu refuses t name the day for the festival. Struck by several calamities, Ezeulu decides to hit the people of Umuaro in that way. He thinks he carries the will of Ulu. Oduche's python incident provides Ezeulu with a new perspective to look at the conflicts between Ulu and Idemili, in other words, between him and Ezidemili:

> Who was Ezeulu to tell his deity how to fight the jealous cult of the sacred python? *It was a fight of the gods. He was no more than an arrow in the bow of his god.* This thought intoxicated Ezeulu like palm wine. New thoughts tumbled over themselves and past events took on new, exciting significance. Why had Oduche imprisoned a python in his box? It had been blamed on the white man's religion; but was that the true cause? What if the boy was also an arrow in the land of Ulu? (219; emphasis mine)

Ezeulu wonders who carries the true will of Ulu. Oduche's misbehavior in imprisoning a python might have been an act of Ulu with an unknowable purpose. Yet he is certain that he is an arrow of his god, Ulu. His decision is Ulu's and vice versa. When Ezeulu is asked whether he will accept the position of Paramount Chief, he answers that "tell the white man [Clark] that Ezeulu will not be anybody's chief, except Ulu"(196). His certainty of being an arrow of Ulu, however, turns out to be questionable in the end. It is uncertain whether he has been an arrow of Ulu or of Christian God. This question is raised by Ezeulu's refusal to declare the day of the New Yam

Feast and its consequence.

People become desperate to find a solution to soothe their god's rage against them, otherwise they might miss the sowing season of the year. The catechist of the Umuaro church, Goodcountry, takes advantage of the crisis. He thinks the Chief Priest's action is "a blessing and an opportunity sent by God" (243). Goodcountry issues a message that "whoever made [makes] his thank-offering to God could [can] harvest his crops without fear of Ulu" (246). Thus, the church flourishes and Umuofians are able to overcome the crisis. Yet, the harvest is done under the name of their son.

Ezeulu, being isolated from everybody, does not expect such an outcome. Besides his illusion of holding "immense power," his loneliness prevents him from detecting any of the people's responsive movements. Even his Christian son, Oduche, fails to be his "eyes" to the new religion. The news brought by his best friend, Akuebue, about the church's offer awakens Ezeulu's conscience, yet the whole situation is beyond his control:

> Perhaps if the silence in which Ezeulu was trapped had been complete he would have got used to it in time. But it had cracks through which now and again an incomplete driblet of news managed to reach him: this had the effect of deepening the silence, like a pebble thrown in a cave.
> Today Akuebue threw such a pebble. He was the only man among Ezeulu's friends and kinsmen who still came now and again to see him. . . .
> "It troubles me," he said, "because it looks like the saying of our ancestors that when brothers fight to death a stranger inherits their father's estate." (250)

Ezeulu's rage against his own kinsmen leads to his own destruction and hurts them all. The foreign religion takes over the power of Ulu and averts the crisis. Ezeulu himself senses the paradox of his action and its consequence through his nightmarish and ominous dream of being deserted by his own family and hearing a Christian's delirious laughter (253).

Ezeulu's fear of being deserted by his own god, Ulu, and his kinsmen comes true with Obika's sudden death. Obika's death shakes all of Umuaro as well as Ezeulu. Ezeulu questions, "Ulu, were you there when this happened to me?" (259). Ezeulu seems to take his favorite son's death as a sign and manifestation of Ulu's desertion of him. Unable to face the possibility fact that he may not have been an arrow of his god, Ezeulu goes mad. His madness is treated by the people of Umuaro as the most feasible and natural outcome of his recent conflicts, based on the history of his mother's madness. The fear of desertion by his god is combined with the fear of insanity in Ezeulu's mind. For instance, even after Ezeulu wakes up from his sinister dream, "a vague fear remained [remains] because the voice of the python had [has] ended as the voice of Ezeulu's mother when she was [is] seized with madness" (253).

The Umuaro people become confused about how to interpret their Chief Priest's action and its consequence; whether "a priest like Ezeulu leads a god to ruin himself" or "a god like Ulu leads a priest to ruin himself" (243). As Ezeulu wonders whether or not Oduche might be an arrow of Ulu not of the Christian god, readers also wonder the same thing about Ezeulu. As he talks of himself, he is "Known" and at the same time he is "Unknowable" (149). Ezeulu's decision to make the people suffer is to let people know his humiliation from the white colonials. He inflicts his anger on his own people instead of directing it toward the white men. Ezeulu's arrogance, however, blocks him from having a clear insight into the nature of his power.

As an arrow of god, Ezeulu's execution of his power or Ulu's power brings his own destruction:

> In destroying his priest he had also brought disaster on himself, like the lizard in the fable who ruined his mother's funeral by his own hand. For a deity who chose a time such as this to destroy his priest or abandon him to his enemies was inciting people to take liberties; and Umuaro was just ripe to do so. (261)

Ultimately, the Umuaro people emerge victorious as the final winner in the trial and so they justify themselves. They consider the crisis as a fight between Ezeulu and themselves, not as "a fight of the gods." The people's final judgment is simple:

> Their god had taken sides with them against his headstrong and ambitious priest and thus upheld the wisdom of their ancestors—that no man however great was greater than his people; that no man ever won judgment against his clan. (261)

The real hero is not Ezeulu but Umuaro as a community. M. M. Mahood sees this point clearly:

> The community of Umuaro has continuity as well as cohesion. It is, like all Ibo communities, an acephalic society in which custom and tradition—'rules rather than rulers'—perform the functions elsewhere vested in overlords. Through the involvement of members of Ezeulu's household in various rites of passage such as marriage and second burial, Achebe gives us a feeling of the continuity of custom; the continuity of tradition is ensured by the principle that a man is always to tell the truth to his son. The white men at Okperi pride themselves on their clocks and calendars; 'they've no idea of time,' says Winterbottom, though half an hour later he is

remembering with pride that whole age group has been named from his destruction of Umuaro's firearms. Yet their lives are without the continuity seen in the lives of their Ibo neighbours; they are at the mercy of every change of policy emanating from Enugu and Lagos.[57]

The juxtaposition of Igbo life and white colonial life creates contrasts and similarities. In the novel, however, their unity found in cultural traditions, divisions aroused from political enmity and family feud, are all a part of a mechanism to ensure the continuity of Umuaro. Ezeulu's charismatic personality is destroyed; Winterbottom as a symbol of colonial power dwindles to that of a mere victim of the colonial system.

The traditional heroes, such as Okonkwo in *Things Fall Apart* and Ezeulu in *Arrow of God*, become a sort of mythical figures, as the next generation takes over. The gap in Igbo people's way of life created by the incursion of white civilization has widened more than ever. Such an issue, along with the coming of new generation, is dealt in Achebe's second novel, *No Longer at Ease* (1960).

No Longer at Ease: African Corruption as the Second Coming

Achebe's second novel is set in the modern city of Lagos, during the 1950s. It is the time when the British accelerated the Africanization of the Administration prior to Nigeria's independence in 1960. It seems the author dealt with his immediate reality facing problems created by colonial legacy. As Wren says, "Achebe, writing in the later 1950s, wished apparently to deal with the alienation such educated young men as himself felt in the new nation moving swiftly toward independence."[58] The novel focuses on corruption as a social problem rather than on Nigeria's anticipation of its independence.

The novel's protagonist is Obi Okonkwo, the grandson of Okonkwo and the son of Nwoye in *Things Fall Apart*. Like his grandfather's tragic ending, Obi's prospects of a successful life abruptly disappear. Okonkwo's downfall is like a classic tragedy, whereas Obi's is a modern tragedy which continues into the present Nigerian society. Achebe makes clear that along with the presence of the British, the African mind and society are plagued by the social disease of corruption. In order to deal with such African corruption as a theme, Achebe presents Obi's personal tragedy as closely related to the history of Nigeria.

The story starts with the trial of Obi Okonkwo who is charged with bribery, immediately raising the most important question through the judge: "I cannot comprehend how a young man of your *education* and brilliant *promise* could have done this" (10; emphasis mine).[59] In a way, Obi's moral confusion is predictable, considering the end of *Things Fall Apart*. With the traditional hero's death and the conversion of the next generation as represented by Nwoye, the coming chaos is inevitable. Corruption becomes an African condition.

In *Things Fall Apart*, the Commissioner fines all of Umuofians as a punishment for their destruction of the church. The native court messengers arbitrarily increase the fine from two hundred to two hundred fifty bags of cowries. The fifty bags, of course, are for themselves. Such a corruptive behavior by the native under colonial government becomes rampant by the time set in *No Longer at Ease*, almost a half century later. Corruption comes from the abuse of power. It has been institutionalized. Instead of heading for "progress," the African society becomes a state of anarchy, lost somewhere between the traditional values and the authoritative administration policies by the colonial government. Such drifting African minds are well portrayed in the image of Lagos.

Obi inherits two different worlds and is caught between them; his grandfather's tradition and his father's Christianity, collectivism based on kinship relations and individualism nurtured by his western education. He constantly sways between the two worlds. The dichotomy inside himself eventually destroys him since he is unable to identify himself entirely with either of them. In addition there is always the lure of moral corruption which is one manifestation of the colonial legacy.

Obi Okonkwo is the first person in the village of Umuofia to receive a university education and a post in the senior service. His future seems assured as Nigeria's independence approaches. His university education is financed by the Umuofia Progressive Union (U.P.U.). The people of Umuofia raise money for scholarships as a means of putting their sons in senior positions or "European positions" in the government. Obi is the first person to be selected and goes to England to study for his B.A. degree. The U.P.U. has so far spent eight hundred pounds for Obi's education. After Obi's arrest on corruption charges, they remain faithful to him because he is a kinsman. The U.P.U. has also hired a lawyer to defend their only "palm-fruit." An often-quoted proverb explains their sentiment: "The fox must be chased away first; after that the hen might be warned against wandering into the bush" (13).

Obi as a beneficiary of the Umuofia Scholarship Scheme is expected to repay his debt over four years, thus he is considered an investment "which must yield heavy dividends" (37). Therefore, Obi's return from England is a felicitous event not only for his family but also for all Umuofians. Since Umuofians have paid for Obi's education, Obi is, in a way, obligated to the people. Yet Obi's experiences in England have changed him. He no longer behaves in the way he is expected to. For the welcome reception in honor of him, for instance, he neither dresses up in a formal suit nor makes a great speech. Obi fails to satisfy his kinsmen's expectations by not showing signs of being a successful man. He should have made ostentatious gestures to create a certain aura of importance in order to impress the crowd.

Obi's individualism prevents him for being one of them, even if Umuofians call him "one of us." He has an identity problem which is revealed in his language. When he comes home from England, he embarrasses himself and his family because he could not read verses in the Bible well enough. His Igbo is not fluent any more. He excuses himself by telling a lie that it is because he has read the English Bible. Also in the U.P.U. meeting, he gives a speech which starts off in Igbo and finishes in half English and half Igbo (81). Though Obi likes poetry, like his father Nwoye and great-grandfather Unoka, his poetic sensibility is expressed in English not in his native language. He reads and writes English poetry. He finds solace in English literature rather than in his own culture and kinsmen.

Obi's alienation from the tradition seems to have begun when he was young. He grew up in a Christian household. His father and mother were very pious. In fact, his father is now retired from church after serving for twenty-five years as a catechist. As a child, Obi was alienated from the Umuofia tradition, most of which his parents avoided as superstition. Obi remembers how difficult it was for him to tell good folk tales in school. Obi's upbringing as a Christian and his western education have made him different from others, as one of Obi's school friends, Joseph, indicates in his question:

> "You know book, but this is no matter for book. Do you know what an *osu* is? But how can you know?" In that short question he said in effect that Obi's mission-house upbringing and European education had made him a stranger in his country—the most painful thing one could say to Obi. (72)

Here Joseph refers the fact that Obi's girlfriend, Clara, is an *osu*, an outcast and untouchable, who is not allowed to marry a free born in any way according to the traditional norm. Torn between personal love and traditional obligation to his kinsmen, Obi chooses to marry Clara even though he expects strong opposition from his parents. Obi's individualism, mixed with a sense of naïve idealism, makes him determined. Obi thinks, "Family ties were [are] all very well as long as they did [do] not interfere with Clara" (76). He almost believes that if he could convince his mother about the matter, all would go well. Obi's love affair with Clara bring out his characteristics, and shows how they cause inner and outer conflicts for him. Internal conflicts affect his relationship with his parents, especially with his mother; external conflicts indicate how he sees Igbo tradition and even Christianity.

When Obi finally faces his parents with his impending marriage, he fails to convince them with his appeal to Christianity and idealism. He argues with his father, Isaac Okonkwo (Nwoye):

> "What is *this thing*? Our fathers in their darkness and ignorance called an innocent man osu, a thing given to idols, and thereafter he became an outcast, and his children, and his children's children forever. But have we not seen the light of the Gospel?" (126)

Unlike Obi's idealistic view on the issue, Isaac Okonkwo has respect for Igbo tradition even though it contains bad customs such as the treatment of *osu*. The fact that Clara's father is a good Christian like himself does not alter his opinion. Isaac Okonkwo (Nwoye) tells his son, Obi:

> "*Osu* is like leprosy in the minds of our people. I beg of you, my son, not to bring the mark of shame and of leprosy into your family. If you do, your children and your children's children unto the third and fourth generations will curse your memory. It is not for myself I speak; my days are few. You will bring sorrow on your head and on the heads of your children. Who will marry your daughters? Whose daughters will you sons marry? Think of that, my son. We are Christians, but we cannot marry our won daughters." (127)

Obi's mother's opposition is stronger than his father's. She says to Obi: "But if you do the thing while I am alive, you will have my blood on your head, because I shall kill myself" (129). Considering Obi's strong bond to his mother, such a reaction from her convinces Obi that he cannot marry Clara by any means. Of all her children, Obi is the closest to his mother's heart and neighbors call her "Obi's mother." One day when his mother washed his clothes, her hand was badly cut by Obi's razorblade which he had mistakenly left in his pocket. After seeing his mother bleeding due to his mistake, Obi was touched by her love for him. Since that incident, he always thinks of his mother very affectionately and the feeling of a special bond between them becomes mutual. To Obi, his mother is the source of his identity and strength. That is why he has thought that all would go well if he could convince his mother about his intention to marry an *osu*.

After his return from England, Obi as an educated man struggles to hold himself to high moral standards. But corruption is ubiquitous. He encounters it even on his return ship. On his first visit home, he observes how the lorry driver and the policemen exchange money. From the beginning of his work in the civil service, there are constant temptations to give and take bribes. He passes such ordeals successfully. Yet his idealism alienates him further from his Umuofian kinsmen and the majority of Nigerians, by differing his opinion and attitude on every issue. He thinks that "the public service of Nigeria would remain corrupt until the old Africans at the top were replaced by young men from the universities" (42). He has no respect for job experience. As a man of experience, the president of the U.P.U. warns Obi that "Book stands by itself and experience stands by itself" (82). Obi's economist friend, Christopher, has a more realistic and broad view on the corruption issue and he seems well adjusted to social reality. He turns his educational background into an asset, whereas Obi's education seems continually to alienate him to the margins of society. Christopher's language reflects his flexibility and skills in social mobility:

> Whether Christopher spoke good or "broken" English depended on what he was saying, where he was saying it, to whom and how he wanted to say it. Of course that was to some extent true of most educated people, especially on Saturday night. But Christopher was rather outstanding in thus coming to terms with a double heritage. (106)

The two men's differences in dealing with the western and traditional elements inside of them are similar to the contrast between Okonkwo and Obierika in *Things Fall Apart*. In a way, Obi resembles his tragic grandfather in his stubbornness. Eventually Obi is destroyed by his lack of identity. He fails both to live up to his idealism and to fulfill his obligation toward his kinsmen. However, his failure exists on a personal level; the author limits the scope of his tragedy in *No Longer at Ease*, unlike the historical failure embodied in his grandfather's death in *Things Fall Apart*.

Obi's new start in life after taking a "European post," is rather smooth until he faces the *osu* issue and the squeeze of financial shortage. His job pays very well, about sixty pounds a month, considering the fact that his father receives an annual pension of twenty-five. He has a car and a chauffer. The luxury and prestige in life gnaw at his conscience until he no longer can see moral issues in things clearly. His idealism tarnishes gradually, as he tries to impress fellow Umuofians with his ostentatious ness. Yet he neglects the importance of his spiritual ties to his roots. He alienates himself by accusing the U.P.U. of meddling with his private life.

The Umuofia Progressive Union in Lagos is his home away from home. By being together once a month Umuofians in the city assure themselves a sense of identity infused with a pride for their ancient town. Obi begins to drift away from the U.P.U. and does not share such spiritual union and ties to the land and people. He does not realize the importance of such spiritual ties, even though his father advises him: "In a strange land one should always move near one's kinsmen" (125).

Lagos is a big city with many divisions, a microcosm of Nigeria. One can see language divisions; English for colonialists and educated Africans, pidgin English and native language such as Yoruba and Igbo, etc. Only by the language can people be united with each other in the big, diverse and divided city like Lagos. For instance, at the time when Clara and Obi are confronted by a policeman, his rude bureaucratic attitude changes completely when he finds out they are Igbo. Speaking same language makes the policeman acknowledge them as kinsmen. When Clara and Obi first met in a party in England, Clara spoke Igbo to Obi. Because of her language, Obi felt close to her. Unlike Obi, Christopher uses his language to deal with people of different educational and cultural backgrounds. Clara also uses her varied linguistic skills to deal with different groups of people. The language differences in the city (or Nigeria) are well manifested in the song sung by a group of traders. The song goes:

> "An in-law went to see his in-law
> Oyiemu—o
> His in-law seized him and killed him
> Oyiemu—o
> Bring a canoe, bring a paddle
> Oyiemu—o
> The paddle speaks English
> Oyiemu—o" (49)

Obi thinks about the meaning of the song and concludes that "the burden of the song was 'the world turned upside down'" (50), in which a paddle suddenly speaks a foreign language and no one understands it. In a way, Lagos, or the whole of Nigeria, is "the world upside down," in anarchy.

The city is also divided by wealth. To Obi, it is no longer a city of "lights and motorcars." Both the glory and the ugliness of the city are well captured in the following:

> His [Obi's] car was parked close to a wide-open storm drain from which came a very strong smell of rotting flesh. It was the remains of a dog which had no doubt been run over by a taxi. (22)

In Lagos, dogs are often run over because they are thought to bring good luck for a new car. The rotten smell of dead dog symbolizes the smell of corruption and of poverty, in large, some degree of social sickness. In contrast with the bright side of the city, the scenes from the slum area where Obi stands reveal "the real Lagos" to him. The image of "the real Lagos" is far from the one he used to imagine when he was in England. His nostalgic poem about Nigeria and Lagos depicts the feeling of sweetness when one embraces the beauty of nature such as "a tree," "the ecstasy of jocund birds and flimsy butterflies," and "the tender glow of the fading sun" (23). The life in Lagos is far removed from the idyllic and peaceful world Obi used to imagine during his youth. The present Lagos is teeming with all kinds of people from all over Nigeria for money and jobs.

Lagos is also divided between native and European, the colonials. Obi feels the division sharply in the differences between Lagos mainland, crowded with natives, and Ikoyi, once a European reserve. Since Obi has a senior "European post," he lives in Ikoyi. On his way back to Ikoyi from Lagos mainland, his mood changes drastically:

> Going from the Lagos mainland to Ikoyi on a Saturday night was like going from a bazaar to a funeral. And the vast Lagos cemetery which separated the two places helped to deepen this feeling. For all its luxurious bungalows and flats and its extensive greenery, Ikoyi was like a graveyard. It had no corporate life—at any rate for those Africans who lived there. They had not always lived there, of course. It was once a European reserve. But things had changed, and some Africans in "European posts" had been given houses in Ikoyi. Obi Okonkwo, for example lived there, and as he drove from Lagos to his flat he was struck again by these two cities in one. It always reminded him of twin kernels separated by a thin wall in a palm-nut shell. Sometimes one kernel was *shiny black* and *alive*, the other *powdery white* and *dead*. (24; emphasis mine)

Interestingly enough, Obi prefers the world of Africans to the world of Europeans. He is comfortable and identifies with the life in Lagos mainland. Thus, he considers the life in Ikoyi dead. His ambivalent attitude toward the two heritages makes him marginalized in both worlds.

The divided world of Obi Okonkwo inherits is his colonial legacy. The sharp division felt in the descriptions of Lagos mainland and Ikoyi makes the society and its people alienated from the colonial government consisting of Europeans. Thus in Nigeria, people call the government "they." It has nothing to do with the natives. It is "an alien institution" and the Nigerian people's only concern is "to get as much from it as they [can] without getting into trouble" (38). This kind of attitude toward their government produces a mentality that enables an educated Nigerian to ask not only for his fees, a generous allowance and a nice job, but also money for his fiancée (112). This mentality is the source of the corruption, which Mr. Green deplores. Yet Mr. Green fails to see the problem of the colonial legacy in African society.

Mr. Green is an idealistic colonial officer, who claims to know Africans very well. He says that "the African is corrupted through and through" (11). According to Mr. Green, by having "been sapped mentally and physically," Africans' corruption cannot be corrected even by western education and the achievement of equality (11). Mr. Green especially hates the mentality of so-called educated young Africans. He and his European secretary also are critical of the fact that there are too many holidays and there is too much prestige in being a civil servant. For instance, there are four months' leave for Moslem holidays and local leave. Mr. Green says that "The idea of local leave was [is] to give Europeans a break to go to a cool place like Jos or Buea. But today it is completely obsolete" (144). In response to this, Obi defends that it is not the fault of Nigerians:

> "You devised these soft conditions for yourselves when every European was automatically in the senior service and every African automatically in the junior service. Now that a few of us have been admitted into the senior service, you turn around and blame us." (44)

Obi's pride as a young idealist before his downfall makes Obi even feel sorry for Mr. Green. In Obi's eyes, it seems Mr. Green is lost due to the presence of educated young men like him in Africa. It is ironic. As a colonized person, Obi cynically pities the fact that Mr. Green lost the opportunity to "bring civilization to the dark continent" as his predecessors did decades ago:

> It was clear he loved Africa, but only Africa of a kind: the Africa of Charles, the messenger, the Africa of his garden boy and steward boy. He must have come originally with an ideal—to bring light to the heart of darkness, to tribal headhunters performing weird ceremonies and unspeakable rites. But when he arrived, Africa played him false. Where was his beloved bush full of human sacrifice? In 1900 Mr. Green might have ranked among the great missionaries; in 1935 he would have made do with slapping headmasters in the presence of their pupils; but 1957 he could only curse and swear. (103)

Here Obi summarizes the course of colonialism in the land and suggests colonialism is no longer effective in the present day Nigeria. He, however, fails to recognize what they have lost in the name of colonialism, because his perspective has been altered to a western one due to his Christian upbringing and western education. Also, his personal plights are too severe to give him any insight on the matter.

Obi's mother's death and his financial crisis become immediate causes of his moral corruption. Besides the fact that Obi suffers from financial shortage due to his excessive expenditure, he has to take care of Clara's abortion before they separate from each other. Obi arranges an illegal abortion for Clara, which causes him more financial pressure. In the middle of emotional and financial trials, he reveals his selfishness. Instead of comforting Clara, he thinks of his own feelings though he tries to consider her position. His mother's death comes at the worst time, in the midst of such emotional and financial turmoil. He does not even attend her funeral. Confining himself in his flat, he only reminisces about her memory:

> These thoughts [a town, Aninta's surrender to the white government] gave Obi a queer kind of pleasure. They seemed to release his spirit. He no longer felt guilt. He, too, had died. Beyond death there are no ideals and no humbug, only reality. (156)

With his mother's death, Obi frees himself from their special bond. Thus Obi's fragile and struggling idealism finally dies with her death. Clara and his mother, not his education and Christian upbringing, symbolize Obi's love and spirituality. And the two women disappeared from his life forever: "The two events following closely on each other had dulled his sensibility and left him a different man" (10). Without the two beloved women in his life, he no longer possesses the moral strength to resist corruption. Instead, he acquires a warped vision. His idealism gives way to "the beat of the high life" (157). Despite the fact that the president of the U.P.U. advises him, Obi follows "the sweetness" of Lagos (82) and perishes.

As Lloyd Brown states, Obi Okonkwo is "a twentieth century magus."[60] The philosophical link between the novel and T. S. Eliot's "The Journey of the Magi" are undeniable. The title, *No Longer at Ease*, is taken from the poem:

> We returned to our places, these Kingdoms,
> But no longer at ease here, in the old dispensation,
> With an alien people clutching their gods.
> I should be glad of another death.

Through characters like Obi Okonkwo, Achebe tried to extend T. S. Eliot's invocation of the meaning of Christ's birth and crucifixion in western civilization to include African experiences. As an African magus, Obi has been to England and returned to his homeland. Consequently, his perspectives have been changed. However, he fails to come to terms with all the changes in society and even in himself.

The united communal spirit shown through the Umuofia Progressive Union has two conflicting sides: its goodness is manifested, for instance, in loyal support for Obi even after his arrest; its bad affect is to give pressure for fulfilling obligations to kinsmen. There are many recurring sayings in Igbo about kinsmen. One is that "anger against a brother was [is] felt in the flesh, not in the bone" (13). The other is "a kinsman cannot be bought in the market, neither is a brother bought with money" (123). Ironically, Obi's self-pride and individualism nurtured by the support from his kinsmen blind his sense of belonging. As Umuofians think, Obi is "a very foolish and self-willed young man" (13). Obi, with an individualistic spirit takes the best offer, the scholarship and emotional support, and fails to recognize his obligation to repay them. Thus, his failure is tragic and yet remains a personal one.

The first and final image of Obi is his appearance in the court, which is very disturbing. There seem to be no absolute answers for Obi's downfall and nor clues about his future. But, without a doubt, the second coming for Africans, after colonialism, is the coming of corruption, a moral anarchy with political independence.

The world described in Achebe's three novels discussed here, *Things Fall Apart*, *Arrow of God* and *No Longer at Ease*, is the world of "becoming" from traditional to modern. Bakhtin defines the epic world as the world about the past and its glory. Achebe, singer of tales and creator of novels, brings the epic world into present with familiarity of time. The remote world of the past in its pastness suddenly comes close to us with its irrevocable contact with the white and its civilization. There is no going-back to epic world of Okonkwo's glory. Achebe shows us the epic world's disintegration by the consequence of contact with the whites. The two worlds collide with each other, each with different strength. The dialectic world is the present Africa. The epic narrative in part one of *Things Fall Apart* instantly changes to the novelistic narrative by attaining its temporal location in history with the news brought by Obierika; "Abame is no more." This temporal familiarity to readers is the world of novel, according to Bakhtin.

In general, allusions to historical events appear in the three novels with consistency. *Arrow of God* has the most historical allusions. In this respect, more or less, the three stories are connected to each other. They are the trilogy about Igbo people's saga. By providing an in-depth look at the complicated political and cultural issues in his novel, Achebe creates the ultimate postcolonial narrative in the African novel.

Chapter Four

"Pickling" History in Rushdie's Works

Rushdie's Literary World

Salman Rushdie, an Indian-born English writer, achieved literary fame in 1981 with the Booker Prize Award for his second novel, *Midnight's Children*. Then he acquired further fame and recognition two years later when he published a sibling of *Midnight's Children*, *Shame*. Recently he has emerged as a symbol of a writer who finds himself at risk in life for what he has written. In 1989 Rushdie's *The Satanic Verses* raised the controversial question of an individual's free speech versus religious authority and sanctity; the novel so inflamed the late Imam Ayatolah Khomeini that he ordered the author killed and the book banned in Moslem countries. The ensuing turmoil enveloped every aspect of Islamic society, crossing all the delicate boundaries of politics, diplomacy, economy and human rights as well as of religion. The sensationalism of this unfortunate incident has made Rushdie's name familiar to the general public, and yet the literary approaches to his works seem still to be at the beginning stage.

Rushdie's works are part of the legacy of the historical and inter-cultural relationships between Britain and India. In both countries, through their past colonial relations, there have been many mutual cultural influences. Indian aesthetics and culture has inspired English literature for centuries. The very epitome of Indian spirituality and aesthetic sensibility, Rabindranath Tagore, gained universal recognition by being awarded the Nobel Prize in 1913 and by being knighted by the British after that. In the 1930s, younger generations of Indian writers began what has developed into a great contribution to Indian literature in English, especially in the genre or the novel. Among these Indian writhers are R. K. Narayan, Raja Rao and Mulk Raj Anand. Salman Rushdie continues in this tradition. Critics find traces of these early modern writers in his works and consider them to be successful blends of Indian and western literary sensibilities imbued with a creative originality.

For example, William Walsh's article, "India and the Novel," discusses

Rushdie in this context:

> The novel [*Midnight's Children*], dramatizing the history of independent India in the person of the beak-nosed wildly extravagant Muslim, Saleem Aziz, . . . , combines the rush and fluency of Mulk Raj Anand, the speculative and metaphysical habit of Raja Rao, the shrewd psychological acumen of R. K. Narayan with the linguistic wildness, inventiveness and fantasy of G. V. Desani.[1]

Rushdie's main literary theme is history and its interplay with the individual. He has a deep understanding of history, and he is academically trained in the subject. He fictionalizes the most critical and realistic elements of contemporary life. Moreover, Rushdie himself embodies the paradoxes caused from exposure to different civilizations as happened to modern India herself before and after her independence.

Rushdie effectively expresses his profound sense of historic consciousness by linking historical events to his own life, even if the bond seems arbitrary to readers. He admitted as much in his travelogue, *The Jaguar Smile: A Nicaraguan Journey*.[2] This forged bond reminds readers of the historicity of human experience which echoes throughout Rushdie's works. Thus an individual's life has a deep historical meaning and significance for Rushdie. Though coincidental, it is important that Salman Rushdie was born in 1947, the year India achieved Independence. When one reads *Midnight's Children*, one cannot help relating the author's voice to that of the protagonist, Saleem Sinai, whose birthday coincides exactly with the moment of India's birth as a new nation. The fact that Saleem is a highly self-conscious protagonist-narrator, together with biographical similarities with the author, makes this work a pseudo-autobiography.

An important inspiration responsible for the birth of *Shame* comes from a real incident which happened in London, where a Muslim father killed his own daughter for disgracing the family. Each character of the novel represents either an allegorical personification of a quality or a fictionalized real character within a range scaled from 'shamelessness' to 'shame.' The voice of the author-narrator clarifies his ambiguous bond between the real and the fictional for his reader: "The country in this story is not Pakistan, or not quite. There are two countries, real and fictional, occupying the same space, or almost the same space."[3] The world of *Shame* reflects Pakistan, and yet it is not the story of Pakistan only. Both the historicity and fictionality of literary works are constantly fluctuating in Salman Rushdie's world. If one can call history or actuality a referent, Rushdie's works can be considered various shadows of history.

The second aspect of Rushdie's significance can be drawn from a more general speculation. Rushdie's India or Pakistan is different from that of Rudyard Kipling or E. M. Forster. It is a view from *inside* not from *outside*. It is a passage *from* India not *to* India. Despite the fact that he lived in London as a British citizen at the time of publication, he seemed to claim his past as his own and identify himself with it: "it [the photograph of the house in India] reminds me that it's my present that is foreign, and that the past is home, albeit a lost home in a lost city in the mists of lost time."[4] *Midnight's Children* and *Shame* are the manifestations of his dreams of "a lost home."

It seems Rushdie's national history is vivid and his sense of identity is found from Indian culture. This fact distinguishes him from another celebrated author, V. S. Naipaul. Naipaul's voice in his books is hollow and devoid of center. In his *India: A Wounded Civilization*, for instance, one senses nihilism as well as a deconstructive mode of searching for identity. He does not seem to belong anywhere, which turns him toward cynicism and heartlessness, whereas Rushdie is not ready to put down the Indian past. Even further he maybe exploits the "exotic" past. And yet concerning religion (Islam and Hinduism), he is confused; if not, at least he dislikes the exclusivity of each. With the metaphor of a hold in one's heart, he expresses his ambivalence toward religion. Like Aadam Aziz in *Midnight's Children*, Rushdie seems to have a hole in his heart for having abandoned his faith in Islam, which in turn, makes him aware of an individual's vulnerability to totalitarian history. The image of a hole as a metaphor has become his escape route to skepticism or agnostic vision against fanaticism.

The threats of the immensity and significance of ancient Indian grandeur, modern India and Pakistan's disease-like dream and corruption, are all mixed together in the two novels. Maybe the author himself is overwhelmed and disillusioned by the course of History in both countries, which can mirror other recently formed independent countries, liberated from colonization, since readers are struck by his immense demand to consume all symbols, metaphors, historical events, Hindu mythology, Islamic visions, quotidian matters such as conflicts and love, etc. Heavy metaphors enrich the stories, and yet they also may raise the question of whether or not Rushdie himself has successfully internalized all of them. He throws metaphors to readers, as if desperately creating meanings. He can write and fictionalize the past, and yet he rejects the role of prophet. However, it produces an interesting ambiguity whether his works leave room for either optimism or pessimism for the future through his unique narrative voice and fantastic realism.

Rushdie and English

The use of English in India is obviously a major heritage from her colonial past. English as the official language in India dates from Thomas B. Macaulay's "Minute of Education" in 1835. Since then Western values have permeated educated Indians. Ironically the language of the ruler triggered the unity of Indians and their fight for national freedom. After centuries of English presence in India, there are likely common experiences shared by both British and Indians. Rushdie's literary charm and success can be found in the fact that he recaptures Indian elements and realities within a Western literary frame. Like Saleem Sinai, the protagonist of *Midnight's Children* who inherits the dichotomous world within himself, Salman Rushdie is testimony to that synthesizing process of Indian and British heritage.

Besides the historical viewpoint on the use of English by Indians, there is another important aspect of it in present times; namely a political aspect. Rushdie's choice of English also defines his relation to his medium. Although his choice of the language could have a historical meaning, it also could have an extremely personal and private one. English is literally the international language of contemporary society, as if the structure of power lies in the hand of English speaking countries. When one reads a blanket statement like the following, he or she hardly can disagree to what it implies: "No writer from the third world can avoid being political in a fairly narrow sense of the term, especially he is writing in English. His subject matter, however 'domestically' or 'privately' focused, will almost certainly involve direct reference to far-reaching political, social and economic changes."[5] Since the author's intended audience is likely to be primarily the English and American reader, his very choice of English as medium has political implications. Here Rushdie is no exception. He addresses the powerful using their medium, accusing them of imperialistic attitude or of neocolonialism toward Third World countries, most of which are the ex-colonized. Sometimes he tends to appeal to humanity. He knows what it is like to be weak, as he mentions in the introduction of *The Jaguar Smile*. Nevertheless, it is ironic that his choice of "political" identity with British citizenship and of the English language could be a testimony of his personal affinity to the west or at least of "westness" in his own being, while he finds his cultural identity through his "Indian" past.

Midnight's Children: Children of History

The "Perforated Sheet" as a Prefiguration for the Whole Structure

The opening chapter, "The Perforated Sheet" offers a reader a frame of the whole novel with most the important aspects of Salman Rushdie's literary concerns and narrative style. It is a rather sudden revelation or epiphany for the whole panorama, and yet very effectively presented. The narrator begins the story "guided only by the memory of a large white bed sheet with a roughly circular hole," "which is my [his] talisman, my [his] open-sesame."[6] furthermore, the metaphoric image of "a hole" is one of many good examples which make the text somewhat symbolic rather than realistic. The author's serious use of metaphors as literary devices to capture the complex meaning of life creates a fictional world similar to that of Gabriel Garcia Marquez's magical realism, but with a stronger egocentric and solipsistic narrative tone. The first chapter is in many ways the prelude of the novel, since it introduces the main messages and tone of the novel. Many secrets and clues for the plot development are lurking among the powerful metaphors.

The novel begins with the narrator-protagonist's birth and its significance. The opening sentence, "I was born in the city of Bombay...," seems rather plain for a start. Yet the mentioning of birth has metaphorical significance; a beginning of a new life, new nation and above all the novel itself. More importantly the time of the narrator's birth forges a strong bond between his personal life and the modern history of India. He was born at the exact moment of India's arrival at independence, on the stroke of midnight on August 15, 1947. From this coincidence of timing the author reaffirms that Saleem's own existence is closely tied to history; the historicity of Saleem's life. The protagonist-narrator, Saleem Sinai, is certainly aware of this forged bond: "thanks to the occult tyrannies of those blandly saluting clocks I had been mysteriously handcuffed to history, my destinies indissolubly chained to those of my country" (3).

For the rest of Sinai's life there seems no way to escape from the parallelism. His life, "handcuffed to history" and heavily tainted by the shadow of Fate, leaves no room for an individual's control. He was "left entirely without a say in the matter" (3). The feeling of helplessness is overwhelming through the author's choice of words and frequent use of passive voice. Sinai is "tumbled forth into the world," only to be "handcuffed to history" by the "occult tyrannies" of the time. His fated life is interplay of centrality in history and sense of helplessness and powerlessness. The issues like centrality versus periphery, reality versus fantasy, history versus fiction, all these are constantly flickering throughout the novel.

The moment of Saleem's birth is celebrated and shared with the public. The sinister darkness of midnight at clocks' strike, however, forebodes bad omen for Saleem's future as well as for Independent India. Furthermore, the narrator mentions that it is a "crime-stained" birth, an image captured in a blood-stained sheet with a hole. The narrator sets up a sinister mood in his narrative in a very effective and powerful way, in contrast with the actual celebrating mood for the nation's independence and his birth to the family. Rushdie's ingenious use of metaphors makes possible the expansion of textual meaning by its plurality. For example, the metaphor of blood is associated with birth, death, violence and shame. Its image also signifies the same messages in *Midnight's Children*'s sibling, *Shame* (1983). More importantly, blood is closely linked with one's identity, as shown in the "Alpha and Omega" chapter leading to the revelation of Mary Pereira's crime and Saleem's true identity.

In the first chapter, the image of a hole as the narrator's "open-sesame" functions like a movie camera zooming from the world of the past into the present like a time-machine. Rushdie uses the image of a hole in a stained sheet as a kind of interchangeable zone of thin blue line between reality and fantasy, history and fiction. As the hole leads us to another world, different in time and space like magic, Saleem starts "remaking" his own life guided by memory. The "holey, mutilated square of linen" is his "talisman" and "open-sesame" for him to devote himself to the creative activity of "writing" as an artist.

The saga of Saleem Sinai begins when his grandfather, Aadam Aziz, comes back from Europe. Saleem calls it "the point at which it [his life] really began" (4). The narrator-protagonist relates his grandfather to "a creator" of his life in a sense with an association of blood image, as he cites the Quran: "Recite, in the name of the Lord thy Creator, who created Man from clots of Blood" (4). His grandfather's new beginning in India is stained with three drops of blood and also he is the creator of the stain on sheet. Besides he has a symbolic name conjuring up all metaphors together. His first name, Aadam evokes a powerful association with the first Man, Adam. Saleem makes his grandfather Aadam the "Adam" of his family myth.

Aadam's return to his old place after medical training in the West does not lead to an easy and smooth start. He finds himself in conflict with his old self. Experiences in Germany have altered his perspective on life. Now he sees things in India through traveled eyes: "Instead of the beauty of the tiny valley circled by giant teeth, he noticed the narrowness, the proximity of the horizon; and felt sad, to be at home and feel so utterly enclosed" (5). Western education makes him doubt and ultimately it deprives him of a sense of identity, making him feel detached and unsuited to his own homeland. An inexplicable feeling of alienation makes him further feel "as though the old place resented this educated, stethoscoped return" (5).

With an uneasy feeling, and yet with a sincere and desperate hope, he tries to reunite himself with the past by turning to Islam. His attempt to achieve oneness through religious communion is only received with hostility and resentment of Indian soil. The rejection of westernized Aadam Aziz by the old India leads to his resolution to abandon religion, which leaves a hole in him. According to the narrator, this vacancy in an inner chamber makes him "vulnerable to women and history" (4). This episode of Aadam abandoning Islam and thus inflicting a symbolic hole in himself seems like the creation of an original sin in Saleem's personal mythology, as Adam and Eve committed the original sin of disobeying the God by eating a forbidden fruit. Its results are passed on to the next generation, as we see in Saleem's life. In a way, it legitimizes Saleem's celebrated public birth which is the tangible source of his claim for centrality in history.

Along with the image of the hole, there is Aadam Aziz's nose; it plays a significant role in indicating the gravity of history. Aadam Aziz's exceptional "patriarchal" nose (8) can sense the future and warn him in advance if something is wrong. Tai explains: "It's the place where the outside world meets the inside you" (13). The hole in the heart stirs the history of Aziz and India in motion. Because of the hole and his vulnerability to women and history, Aadam is led to meet his prospective wife through a hole in the sheet. The perforated sheet stands between "doctor and patient" (21). Dr. Aziz's heart falls through a hole for the patient, Naseem. He gets to know her body bit by bit as a doctor. After about three years, he can finally put her body together in his mind. He still has not seen her face. In the same way, he only can grasp fragments of Indian reality and randomly bump against its collective history.

Through the anecdote of the perforated sheet, Salman Rushdie introduces us to the idea of fragmentation of the whole. Its concept plays an important role in Rushdie's literary works and is helpful to an understanding of his narrative art. The literary ingenuity of Rushdie makes the image of the holes poise the agony of fragmentation and the struggle for unity, as readers see Aadam's personal ordeal faced the old Indian tradition. The metaphoric fragmentation of a whole significantly characterizes a Rushdian approach to history: the sporadic presentation of events in modern India helps to give a sense of historicity in an individual's life.

The agony of fragmentation brings with it the desire for unity. The connection can be easily found in the inner struggles of female characters, in Naseem and her daughters' relationships with their men and to life in general. The "whole" could mean a person, History or truth. The metaphor of the fragmentation of the whole might stand for our struggle to understand what is going on around us, particularly when we have access only to pieces of truth. In Rushdie's works, its concepts also can be applicable to the structure of the novel. Here and there ambushes of heavy messages are scattered and yet all are eventually linked to the whole unified message.

The first chapter is the beginning: the beginning of the story, the creation of personal myth, the prelude for its mood and setting, the sources of the conflicts and the introduction of the main theme. Later chapters mainly show more details of the close relationship between an individual's life and the course of history. In this sense, "The Perforated Sheet" is the epiphany of the book.

Search for Identity
"To understand just one life, you have to swallow the world" (126).

The children of midnight inherit the colonial past and mirror the society of independent India. People hail their births as seeds of hope for India's future. Saleem is searching for the validity of this legacy in contemporary India where every aspect of life is swept by a greater vortex of politics. As India suffers from political turmoil and chaos after Independence, Saleem is also hurt and affected by them in one way or another.

Being "handcuffed to history" by the odd timing of his birth, Saleem has been aware of the feeling of being watched and being the center of events regardless of his own will. Throughout all of the political and historical events of modern India, desperately but vainly does he fight for his own individual independence. Yet often, especially in Books I and II, his self-conscious narrative deceptively succeeds in convincing readers that he is in control of contemporary events and in the center of history. In terms of individualism, however, a sense of futility and pessimism gradually color the general tone of the story.

Besides Saleem, there are a thousand more children of midnight. According to him, each of them possesses his or her own unique power as a mark of their fate to become mirrors of the nation. Saleem writes "in plain unveiled fashion, about the midnight children":

> ". . . during the first hour of August 15th, 1947—between midnight and one a.m.—no less than one thousand one children were born within the frontiers of the infant sovereign state of India. . . . What made the event noteworthy (noteworthy! There's a dispassionate word, if you like!) was the nature of these children, everyone of whom was, through some freak of biology, or perhaps owing to some preternatural power of the moment, or just conceivably by sheer coincidence (although synchronicity on such a scale would stagger even C. G. Jung), endowed with features, talents or faculties which can only be described as miraculous. (234)

Saleem suggests that this extraordinary characteristic of the midnight's children including himself is due to history having arrived "at a point of the highest significance and promise" (235). Their lives are linked directly to the modern history of India and also to the ancient past.

Among them, Saleem is the one who gets the attention of the media and receives a letter from Prime Minister Nehru, which sums up Saleem's central place in the history. His birth is received as the transformation of new India's hopes, desires and expectations. After the *Times of India* hails Saleem as Midnight's Child, Jawaharlal Nerhu writes him: "You are the newest bearer of that ancient face of India which is also eternally young. We shall be watching over your life with the closest attention; it will be, in a sense, the mirror of our own" (143). Saleem's family also has great expectations and hopes for him. Mary Pereira's little cradle songs for baby Saleem reflects that anticipation: "Anything you want to be, you can be; You can be just what-all you want: (148).

Saleem's being the chosen baby of midnight owes a great deal to Mary Pereira's own "private revolutionary act" of changing two infants' name tags. The poor baby of an ex-colonialist is put in the hands of a rich privileged Moslem family; a baby born to wealth is condemned to a life of deprivation. Grown-up Saleem lives with the fear of being discovered and of being chased by the changeling, Shiva.

Saleem is an ugly baby whose features suggest symbolic qualities. He inherits his grandfather's prominent nose—"which was also the nose of grandmother from France"—and eyes "as blue as Kashmiri sky," "which were also eyes as blue as Methwold's" (135).

I was not a beautiful baby. Baby-snaps reveal that my large moon face was too large; too perfectly round. Something lacked in the region of the chin. Fair skin curved across my features—but birthmarks disfigured it; dark stains spread down my western hairline, a dark patch coloured my eastern ear. And my temples: too prominent: bulbous Byzantine domes. (144–45)

Besides the eccentricity of his features, the baby is unusual in his behavior: He grows so fast that his appetite drains his mother's breast milk; he never cries; he never blinks because his eyes are too blue to do so. After worried Amina and Mary takes turns opening and closing his eyelids, he learns his first lesson of life: "Nobody can face the world with his eyes open all the time" (146). This symbolism echoes his notion that "most of what matters in our lives takes place in our absence" (14). Furthermore, Saleem, as the narrator, defends and justifies his multiple inheritance and grotesqueness in his life. He responds to an assumed doubt from readers: "If I seem a little bizarre, remember the wild profusion of my inheritance . . . perhaps, if one wishes to remain an individual in the midst of the teeming multitudes, one must make oneself grotesque" (126). Above all, according to Saleem, one's life is transmuted into grotesqueness by "the eruption of history" (61) into it. Since he is the child of "the time: fathered by history" (137), his grotesqueness is the essence of his being along with its historicity.

When Ramran prophesies Saleem's life, it appears rather like uninterpretable riddle to readers as well as to Amina Sinai. But Saleem's sudden revelation of Mary Pereira's crime, changing the babies, finally provides readers the main clue to understanding their meanings of these riddles and derived metaphors about "Blue Jesus." When Padma is first told the secrecy of Saleem's birth, she protests to him: "All the time, you tricked me." The angry and surprised reaction from Padma, who has been a loyal and intensive listener and spoken for suspicious readers as their mouthpiece, seems to reflect Saleem's success as a story-teller in creating metaphoric meanings in his life such as centrality and historicity. Padma's anger may also be directed toward herself because of her credulity and faithfulness as a listener without raising her eyebrows as well toward his perfect building-up of symbolism in his life. Saleem explains to her:

No: I'm no monster. Nor have I been guilty of trickery. I provided clues . . . but there's something more important than that. It's this: when we eventually discovered the crime of Mary Pereira, we all found that it *made no difference*! I was still their son: they remained my parents. (136)

After the painful disclosure of his identity, the cynical narrator tells us that nothing much is changed except that his position as the center of attention is taken by his sister, Brass Monkey. But the change of his position means a lot in reality. Mary Pereira starts to sing to the Monkey "the little ditty which had been my [his] theme-song all my [his] days: 'Anything you want to be, you can be . . ." (304). His position is literally "usurped" and his sister is given the burden of their father's dream about the future. It is a visible indication of Saleem's significant shift from the historic center to its periphery.

Despite the fact that his early disintegration leaves cracks all over his body, he is still used to thinking of himself as the midnight child of India. His attempt to hold all midnight's children together and to form a council is the true beginning of a self-realization process and yet the path toward confirming his identity is doomed to be difficult. In his safely cocooned life filled with egocentricity, self-importance and self-pride, he anticipates the moments of triumph, which will reassure him. Instead, when they actually meet, the other children revolt and challenge his self-claimed leadership among the midnight's children.

Furthermore, Saleem's gifted ability to hear them all as the "all India radio" gnaws at his dreams and confidence rather than confirming them. Things slip out of his control, and the power of the multitudes pushes him to the margin of events as happened in the contemporary politics of India. The heat of politics reaches his private domain and affects his life. He is gradually drained of power and hope in the Midnight Children's Conference as well as in contemporary history, while India suffers from the grip of the Dictator, Indira Ghandi. Saleem hates her so much that he calls her the Widow, the epitome of negativity and despair in Indian politics.

Among the challenges from the other children of the Midnight Children's Conference (MCC, Shiva's is the most poignant. It is because Saleem is Shiva's alter ego, and vice versa. Shiva is the dark side of reality and is also an avatar of anger and destruction. In Hinduism, "Shiva" is the god of destruction and the greatest dancer, whom people regard as the most powerful of deities. Having a symbolic name after the god, the changeling Shiva inherits his extraordinary power over the knees. Superstitious and symbol-loving Saleem explains: "Shiva and I were born under Capricorn rising; the constellation left me alone, but it gave Shiva its gift" (265). The gift of power saves Shiva from his father's brutal attack to maim his leg in order to make him a crawling beggar. When Saleem asks him to join the

MCC, Shiva challenges Saleem's supposed leadership in the Conference: "So! Lissen, my father said I got born at exactly midnight also—so don't you see, that makes us joint bosses of this gang of yours!" (263). Unlike Saleem, he has a daring and rebellious personality. Saleem wants the MCC to be a kind of loose federation of equals, whereas Shiva sees it as a grand organization with a strong boss, run like the one he has been running in a back alley of Matunga. Saleem believes that things can be managed for *a reason* or *a purpose*. Shiva strongly opposes this by accusing him having the naïve sentimentality of the rich:

> "Rich kid," Shiva yelled, "you don't know one damn thing! What purpose, man? What thing in the whole sister-sleeping world got reason, yara? For what reason you're rich and I'm poor? Where's the reason in starving, man? God knows how many millions of damn fools living in this country, man, and you think there's a purpose! Man, I'll tell you—you got to get what you can, do what you can with it, and then you got to die. That's reason, rich boy. Everything else is only mother-sleeping *wind*! (263-64)

Saleem dwells upon his idealistic world of insulation; Shiva lives in the midst of stark reality and experiences the world. To Shiva, the world is divided into the haves and the have-nots, the powerful and the powerless. The conflicts and differences between them flare up again and again until the MCC falls apart on the day of the Chinese invasion and Saleem's exile to Pakistan. The disintegration process of the MCC reflects Indian society in a quandary of dispute. Since these children as a group are a mirror of the nation, they are not immune to prejudices and world-views of the adults in that nation. Children from Maharashtra loathes Gujaratis, and fair-skinned northerners revile Dravidian 'blackies'; there are religious rivalries; and division by social class; conflicts between the rich and the poor, between the castes; the increased pressures of poverty and Communism among the low-born. Saleem pleads to the members of the MCC against the trend:

> Do not let this happen! Do not permit the endless duality of masses-and-classes, capital and labour, them-and-us to come between us! We ... must be a third principle, we must be the force which drives between the horns of the dilemma; for only by being other, by being new, can we fulfill the promise of our birth! (306)

Here Saleem shows his optimism and hope for the better society. And still he believes in the midnight children's extraordinary power and legacy.

Soon this turns out to be a mirage of hope and idealism. Childhood as the third principle is eventually "murdered," as the political situation and social problems are aggravated. As the poison of grown-ups is poured into children, the midnight children are sickened. On a symbolic level, Saleem's reference to gradual poisoning reflects the sickness in Indian society which would allow a dictatorship to emerge. The midnight's children finally take the ultimate poison, "a Widow with a knife." The Widow is Indira Ghandi whom Saleem considers a dictator. The Widow drains power out of every individual, and such power affects Saleem's adult life. As Saleem gradually loses his central role, he becomes impotent. His impotency is not only sexual but also metaphorical. Saleem had a sperectomy which denies future hope. It precludes the regeneration of midnight's children. Saleem's impotency suggests the ultimate exercise of the Widow's power.

Compared to Saleem's idealism, Shiva's perspectives on the world are materialistic and realistic. Unlike passive Saleem, he emphasizes active participation rather than sitting and contemplating things. The following is the response from Shiva, illustrating the extreme polarities of the two children's characteristics:

> No, little rich boy; there is no third principle; there is only money-and-poverty, and have-and-lack, and right-and-left; there is only me-against-world! The world is not ideas, rich boy; the world is no place for dreamers or their dreams; the world, little Snotnose, is things. Things and their makers rule the world; . . . For things, the country is run. Not for the people. For things America and Russia send aid; but five hundred million stay hungry. When you have things, then there is time to dream; when you don't you fight. (307)

To Shiva, to have things is to acquire power. Saleem's points of view are fundamentally bourgeois, whereas Shiva's way of looking and solving matters is like a Marxist. It reflects the rebellious and revolutionary spirit, with which the lower classes always try to gain power and upward mobility in society.

Interestingly, all these conflicts of ideas and views between Saleem and Shiva are actually conflicts in Saleem's own mind. Another irony is that it doesn't sound at all like a ten year old boy's confusion in his search for values. As the narrator Saleem acknowledges, he puts it all down in an adult's language. Anyhow, Saleem is struggling to hold his crumbling self together. His chaotic states of mind reflect social disillusion filled with ugly reality. As a kind of self-doubt, Shiva's voice is constantly ringing in his head due to his ability to "broadcast" and communicate with others through telepathy. Again, it suggests that his conscience is polarized by the extreme ideologies in conflict. Extremism in ideas represents existing factions and differences in Indian society and also in one's own self. Saleem's awkward efforts to unite the midnight children and to resolve all conflicts and differences among them reflect the failure to bring the whole of India together in harmony.

Saleem's odyssey to grow up ultimately leads him to his identity. He tries to settle down as is. Yet telepathic communication with Shiva all the time increases the chances of revealing the secret of their birth. He is afraid of being a split self, of having his "prestigious" bourgeois living usurped, and, most of all, of losing his centrality in history. After Mary's public disclosure of her secret crime, Saleem's fear increases. Shiva is the most ferocious and powerful of the children. Saleem eventually gets rid of Shiva's voice from his head by exiling him, since he is determined to guard his position:

> I was obliged to come to the conclusion that Shiva, my rival, my changeling brother, could no longer be admitted into the forum of my mind; for reasons which were, I admit, ignoble. I was afraid he would discover what I was sure I could not conceal from him—the secrets of our birth.... I resolve that my destructive, violent alter ego should never again enter the increasingly fractious councils of the Midnight Children's Conference; that I would guard my secret—which had once been Mary's—with my very life. (339)

Despite Saleem's firm determination to "exile" Shiva, Saleem himself with the twist of Rushdian irony is exiled to Pakistan in 1958. There he discovers that "somehow the existence of a frontier 'jammed' my [his] thought-transmissions to the more-than-five-hundred; so that, exiled once more from my home, I [he] was also exiled from the gift which was my [his] truest birthright: the gift of the midnight children" (341). Even during adulthood, however, Saleem cannot shut Shiva completely out of his life. Impotent Saleem is to have Shiva's son as his own. With an ironical twist of fate Saleem fulfills Ramran's prophesy: "He will have sons without having sons!" (99). Saleem and Shiva's life cannot be separated. Both of them experience the contemporary events in history and yet their reactions to them are totally opposite to each other.

Nevertheless, Saleem keeps running away from Shiva till he flees or is pushed to the edge. He never intends to tell Shiva the truth of his birth. He even tells readers Shiva is dead, which he confesses is a lie (529). His attempt to keep the self-claimed legitimacy of being the center seems desperate and even despicable. He has a false identity and he wants to keep it. He prefers to remain the son of a rich bourgeois rather than to be identified as a poor Indian entertainer's son. Maybe he desperately wants to hold onto dear life rather than be crushed between Shiva's superhuman and possibly revengeful knees. Saleem's identity is a world of paradox in which he chooses to dwell.

What's the use of hiding from Shiva? Saleem is the one who claims centrality in history and to be responsible for what happened. However, Shiva is the one born with all the symbolic characteristics; possibly the true symbol of Indianness. As Shiva is elusive in Saleem's private record of Indian life, maybe the True India is hiding from us or from the record of history. Also Rushdie seems to indicate that the British colonial heritage in India which Saleem inherits cannot be undermined or ignored. The British colonial heritage and its Western influence in post-independent India also have as much validity and legitimacy as the ancient Indian heritage of Tai. Neither Saleem nor Shiva can represent the whole of India alone. Each of them complements the other; together they represent the Whole India.

Centrality and Marginality
After about thirty years, Saleem finally realizes that he is no longer the center of historical events. His celebrated birth is just an emblem of a symbol for the birth of a new nation. His individuality serves nothing more than to witness all the events in modern India. He does not play a central role in the making of history but is merely a spectator and victim of the circumstance.

Saleem's leadership in the Midnight Children's Conference fails to unite all the members. His frustration brings him to a gradual realization of his identity and his role in the drama of history. He becomes aware the he is like anybody else, a victim of the terror inflicted in the name of history. He is not at the center, as he used to believe, but at the periphery of events. While Saleem struggles with his gradual realization of his role and position in modern India, his body shows signs of the seriousness of his agony: his skin begins to crack all over "like an old jug" (37). He thinks he shall "eventually crumble into (approximately) six hundred and thirty million particles of anonymous, and necessarily oblivious dust" (37). And yet he still possesses his solipsistic centrality in a paradoxical sense, even if he loses the sense of controlling events.

> Who what am I? My answer: I am the sum total of everything that went before me, of all I have been seen done, of everything done-to-me. I am everyone everything whose being-in-the-world affected was affected by mine. I am anything that happens after I've gone which would not have happened if I had not come. Nor am I particularly exceptional in this matter; each "I," everyone of the now—six-hundred-million-plus of us, contains a similar multitude. (457)

Here he spreads himself to each one of the over six hundred million in the Indian population and becomes a universal and ubiquitous self. He is everyone and at the same time a unique being who has a sense of history. He is "everyone everything whose being-in-the-world affected was affected by" his. This paradox of centrality is innate in every individual's life. When he says "I am anything that happens after I've gone which would not have happened if I had not come," there is very little room for contingency. Saleem is aware of this immanent fact of life, so he wants to claim his own share of the role in historic events through his activity of writing about them. He is afraid of being in the periphery. Before he slips into the anonymity of six hundred and thirty million particles after the celebrated publicity of his birth, he decides to rescue himself or history from doomed oblivion through the act of writing. He also is very conscious of his literary gift. He feels obliged to write his past and history, as one of the Midnight's Children and possessor of "such mastery of the multiple gifts of cookery and language" (38). In other words, he consciously historicizes his past.

Out of the split life of Saleem's day and night, Rushdie creates a unified vision of life, in which no element is meaningless in the making of history. Rushdie's metaphorical allusions to Saleem's job of producing pickles during the day and writing during the night are juxtaposed with the question of defining what history is. Pickling is metaphorically transcended to the preservation of history, as shown in the following:

> And my chutneys and kasaundies are, after all, connected to my nocturnal scribblings—by day amongst the pickle-vats, by night within these sheets, I spend my time at the great work of preserving. Memory, as well as fruit, is being saved from the corruption of the clock. (38)

His nightly engagement in writing "preserves" memory in order to save it from oblivion. However, we as readers can ask: if his own pickles are "the pickles," then how can his writing on his life be the mirror of India's history? A proper response should include the point where we can draw the line between fiction and history. Saleem only emphasizes the importance of writing (records), in other words the documentation of his own life. Besides his own claim of centrality, how much objectivity and validity does his writing have in terms of history? Can his personal involvement in re-writing history be considered as an antithetic challenge to the impersonal discourse of history books? Maybe, yes. Saleem answers the question in the following way:

> I supervise the production of Mary's legendary recipes; but there are also my special blends, in which, thanks to the powers of my drained nasal passages, I am able to include memories, dreams, ideas, so that once they enter mass-production all who consume them will know what pepperpots achieved in Pakistan, or how it felt to be in the Sundarbans . . . believe don't believe but it's true. Thirty jars stand upon a shelf, waiting to be unleashed upon the amnesiac nation. (549)

In his ego centric and solipsistic manner of story-telling, we hardly can distinguish between private episodes and historical events. His writing is a privatization of Indian history and an act of self-redemption out of the fear of oblivion. Perhaps this is the irony of Rushdie's world; the narrator tells Indian history from a confident omniscient point of view as if it was his personal property, and yet he admits that he does not experience all. In order to understand him, he claims, people may have to swallow the whole world. According to him, most important things in life always happen during one's absence (14–15). One has no control over them, but one represents them. The Rushdian irony or paradox is so pervasive that the self-confident, solipsistic narrative tone is gradually transformed into a sort of soliloquy of despair and helplessness, as in the final paragraph of the novel.

> Yes, they will trample me underfoot, the numbers marching one two three, four hundred million five hundred six, reducing me to speaks of voiceless dust, just as, in all good time, they will trample my son who is not my son, and his son who will not be is, and his who will not be his, until the thousand and first generation, until a thousand and one midnights have bestowed their terrible gifts and a thousand and one children to be both masters and victims of their times, to forsake privacy and be sucked into the annihilating whirlpool of the multitudes, and to be unable to live or die in peace. (552)

It is clear at this point that the whole struggle is between an individual and the mass concerning the issue of establishing an identity of one's own in history. Since for Saleem optimism is like a disease in life, pessimism gradually prevails in the struggle for an individual's identity. Thus his sense of centrality is also gradually replaced by a sense of marginality, still chained to the course of history.

Saleem's humble acknowledgment of anonymity and defeat comes suddenly in a reflection of his son's life as an exact mirror of his own:

> Looking into the eyes of the child who was simultaneously no-my-son and also more my heir than any child of my flesh could have been, I found in his empty, limpid pupils a second mirror of humility, which showed me that, from now on, mine would be as peripheral a role as that of any redundant oldster: the traditional function, perhaps, of reminiscer, of teller-of-tales . . . (534)

Legacy of British Colonial Rule in India

Salman Rushdie's treatment of the legacy of colonial rule provides a new insight into Indian perspectives on the past. The nature of Saleem's being tied to history symbolizes the Indian attempt to synthesize the past and the present after the nation's Independence. Saleem's biological father is a departing English colonial, Methwold, and his mother a poor Indian entertainer's wife, Venita. But he is raised as the son of rich Moslem family from Kashmiri, and yet he claims to be in the center of history due to the coincidence of his birth with that of India's Independence. Metaphorically, Saleem inherits the British colonial legacy (Methwold) and the Indian heritage (both his Indian grandfather and father).

William Methwold is the only English colonial fully described by Saleem. He has a symbolic and historical name, identical to that of an officer of the East India Company who, in 1633, saw a vision—"a dream of British Bombay, fortified, defending India's West against all comers" (106). The Methwold who has been carrying out 17th century Methwold's dream is a six-foot Titan with a center part in his hair. Metaphor-loving Saleem describes him in details which have sinister similarities to his Indian grandfather, Aadam Aziz:

> Methwold's hair, parted in the middle, has a lot to do with my beginnings. It was one of those hairlines along which history and sexuality moved, like tightrope-walkers. (But despite everything, not even I, who never saw him, never laid eyes on languid gleaming teeth or devastatingly combed hair, an incapable of bearing him any grudge.)
> And his nose? What did that look like? Prominent? Yes, it must have been the legacy of a patrician French grandmother—from Bergerac!—whose blood ran aquamarinely in his veins and darkened his courtly charm with something crueler, some sweet murderous shade of absinthe. (109)

This description of Methwold echoes his grandfather's appearance. The significance of his hairline "along which history and sexuality moved" is paralleled to the hole in Aadam Aziz's heart symbolizing his vulnerability to women and history. Also, each man has a very prominent nose, suggesting extraordinariness. Their singularity suggested by such a nose is nothing but the "vulnerability to women and history."

Methwold is a typical colonialist who can be identified with characters in Kipling's Indian stories. Setting aside stories like "The Strange Ride of Morrowbie Jukes," "At the End of the Passage," "The Phantom Rickshaw" and "Thrown Away" which deal with English Sahib's fear of unknown culture and of losing self-control, tales like "Beyond the Pale" and "To Be Filed for Reference" warn of the latent danger of immersion into the native culture in which native women are represented by destructive sensuality. Through the episodic adventures of English colonial officers' illicit love affairs with Indian women, Kipling allegorically expresses the danger of the split life and the immersion in an exotic cultural fantasy. He makes such colonials pay the high price for their dark nighttime love excursions. Kipling's framed stories are highly controlled: the final messages are about how to become an ideal colonialist; surface plot structure fulfills readers' fantasies about the exotic culture and fear of the unknown especially in a displaced situation. Like Trejago and McKintosh, Methwold has a weakness for women, and yet he has to hide this tendency within an English frame of mind. He seems well aware of that, when he says "beneath this still English exterior lurks a mind with a very Indian lust for allegory" (110).

Yet Methwold's center-parted hairstyle suggests his irresistibility to women, according to the narrator, and is his responsibility for Saleem's birth. To our readers' surprise, the precise hairline is that of his toupee. Methwold is bald. He deliberately seduces Wee Willie Winkie's wife and impregnates her. The dark spot in his conscience rises to the surface; the secret drips down to stain his face from forehead to eyebrow. The stain embodies his guilt. Saleem inherits his English father's guilt, for which people nickname him Stainface.

Often someone's sense of guilt and shame is manifested in this symbolic way in fiction. Methwold's stained face, for instance, reminds one of James Flory in *Burmese Days* by George Orwell. This novel is more or less Orwell's personal indictment of British Imperial rule, through which he distilled his Burmese experiences as an Imperial Policeman. Flory has a sinister and repugnant birthmark which brings about his downfall and represents the ultimate failure of his life. Flory is ashamed of his birthmark and tries to hide it:

> The first thing that one noticed in Flory was a hideous birthmark stretching in a ragged crescent down his left cheek, from the eye to the corner of the mouth. Seen from the left side his face had a battered, woe-begone look, as thought the birthmark had been a bruise—for it was a dark blue in colour. He was quite aware of its hideousness. And at all times, when he was not alone, there was sidelongness about his movements, as he maneuvered constantly to keep the birthmark out of sight.[7]

This birthmark disappears only when he dies. Through this powerful symbol Orwell suggests that some men are "branded by a stigma—whether of poverty, cowardice, guilt or failure—which clung [clings] to them all their days and could [can] not be eradicated."[8] For Flory, who can see the futility of British rule but lacks the power to do anything against the orthodoxy and its corruption, the birthmark stands for his own weakness, shame, guilt and failure.

Events which lead to the arrival of Independence are juxtaposed with events of the Sinai family. When Earl Mountbatten announces the Partition of India on June 4th, 1947, Saleem's parents leave for Bombay. When they arrive in Bombay, they are involved in the game "the transfer of power" (104) —a game to purchase Methwold's palaces. The departing colonial is "transferring power" by selling his English mansion to an Indian couple, as British Government is transferring power to the hands of Indians. William Methwold sentimentally justifies British rule in India: "Never seen the like. Hundreds of years of decent government, then suddenly, up and off. You'll admit we weren't all bad; built your roads, schools, railway trains, parliamentary system, and all worthwhile things. Taj Mahal was falling down until an Englishman bothered to see it. And now, suddenly independence. Seventy days to get out" (109–10). This echoes exactly the nineteenth-century (Kipling's) notion of "white man's burden," which supposedly brings decent civilization to pagan and ignorant natives. Methwold sets two conditions in his transactions: the new owners should retain every item in the house and the actual transfer should be effective at midnight on August 15th, since he has "a sort of itch to do it at the same time the Raj does" (110).

Rushdie does not appear to be openly critical about this Englishman's game. Yet he clearly shows its effect on the Sinais for better or worse. Methwold's Estate gradually changes them under Methwold's personal supervision.

> Every evening at six they are out in their gardens, celebrating the cocktail hour, and when William Methwold comes to call they slip effortlessly into their imitation Oxford drawls; and they are learning, about ceiling fans and gas cookers and the correct diet for budgerigars, and Methwold, supervising their transformation, is mumbling under his breath. Listen carefully: what's he saying? Yes, that's it. "Sabkuch tichtock hai," mumbles William Methwold. All is well. (113)

The significance of the Sinais' transformation goes beyond the mere acquisition of a British life style; their Indian soul is also changed. Indians living in British mansions symbolically inherit the British legacy in India. In politics, India's yearning for Independence and Democracy under British rule breeds a Western form of government in a different cultural setting. India, which used to be the whole Other under the British rule, faces fragmentation upon the arrival of Independence; Hindu against Moslem, the rich against the poor. British departure does not mean a total eradication of their political and cultural baggage. There are Christians like Mary and Joseph D'Costa among the Indians. Ironically, Joseph considers Christianity to be a white man's religion. To his wife, says he, "You can't get it into your head that that's the white people's religion? Leave white gods for white men. Just now our own people are dying. We got to fight back" (120). He also hates the rich. He foresees that "the air comes from the north now, and it's full of dying. This independence is for the rich only; the poor are being made to kill each other like flies. In Punjab, in Bengal. Riots riots, poor against poor. It's in the wind" (120).

What makes the Sinais' situation more complicated is the inner conflict between the new and the old. With the little time that remained before the final transfer, Methwold did his best to teach the Sinais what the British had long been trying to inculcate to its colony: the necessity of exclusivity, secluding interaction with Indians through the formation of British "Clubs."

What the Sinais are going through is the internalization of the colonial experience. It corresponds exactly to the hegemonic phases of colonialism in Abdul R. JanMohamed's categorization. In his article, "The Economy of Manichean Allegory: The Function of Racial Difference in Colonialist Literature," he distinguishes between "the dominant" and "the hegemonic" phases of colonialism and also between its "material" and "discursive ideological" practices. According to him, the natives who formerly refused to be subjugated in the early stage of colonial practice gradually internalize the colonialists' value imposed upon them:

By contrast, in the hegemonic phase (or neocolonialism) the natives accept a version of the colonizers' entire system of values, attitudes, morality, institutions, and, more important, mode of production. This stage of imperialism does rely on the active and direct "consent" of the dominated, though, of course, the threat of military coercion is always in the background. The natives' internalization of Western cultures begins before the end of the dominant phase. The nature and the speed of this internalization depend on two factors: the many local circumstances and the emphasis placed on interpellation by various European colonial policies. But in all cases, the moment of "independence"—with the natives' obligatory, ritualized acceptance of western forms of parliamentary government—marks the formal transition to hegemonic colonialism.[9]

This passage sums up what happens to the Sinai family through its objective and impersonalized sociopolitical language. Saleem gives us a realistic glimpse into what happened to Indians right before Independence through the process of the Sinais' immersion into Britishness and the transference of power by playing along with Methwold's "game." Sinai is the transformed and inherited Colonial Legacy, which he impregnates to produce the next generation, Saleem.

In supervising Sinai's transformation, Methwold is pleased that "all is well" (113). The impact of his rule (Britishness) upon Sinai and other Indians, for example, is later manifested in "a pigmentation disorder" (212). What Saleem or the author himself is suggesting by the pigmentation disorder is that India's economic situation during the first nine years after Independence thrives by becoming "white." Indian businessmen become pale by engaging in "the gargantuan (even heroic) efforts" of taking over from the British and becoming masters of their business, handling black money. Ahmed Sinai becomes British in effect, turning entirely white due to affliction of wide-spread Anglophilism. He is secretly pleased with his transformation into a white man because he has long envied Europeans' white skin. He remarks that "all the best people are white under the skin; I have merely given up pretending"; he makes darker neighbors feel "ashamed" (212). Ahmed Sinai becomes emblematic of the slavish mentality affected by the Anglophiles during the neocolonial phase in India.

Narrative Device: Frgmentation and "Angle-Poised" Perspective
The study of the subject is focused on the narrative mode in the novel through close analysis of reader and narrator relations, use of language in the text (both Indian and English), imagery and symbolism, etc. for capturing a synthetic vision of Indo-British sensibility.

Midnight's Children as a vision is created in "the pool of angle-poised light" (14), which suggests the narrator's objective and distanced views representing Western intellectualism in capturing reality. In order to grasp the meaning of life and personal identity, Saleem Sinai illuminates and recaptures the past within the limits of language, the sole medium of repository for past memory. Since the author deals with "a broken mirror" to the past, the structure of the story accords with Saleem's fragmentary visions.[10] Yet Rushdie's narrative mode is constructed with the very conscious and experimental strategy to create a sense of unity within a series of fragmented visions and episodes. He invites the reader's active participation in gluing the fragments together to achieve an artistic unity. Through visible tensions and dynamics between the narrator and his loyal listener, Padma, Rushdie plays with his own consciousness of authorial suspicion and artistic doubt on his ability to aesthetically reify history and fiction.

Saleem begins his story with a sense of urgency and fear: "I must work fast, faster than Scheherazade, if I am to end up meaning—yes, meaning—something. I admit it: above all things, I fear absurdity" (4). He consciously compares himself as a narrator to the legendary story-teller, Scheherazade in *Arabian Nights*, whose art of story-telling is responsible for her survival and that of other women in the kingdom under the misogynist prince Shahryar. The narrator's necessity and desire to capture the reader's attention resemble the plight and dilemma of Scheherazade. As Scheherazade's wit and charm in story-telling methods mesmerize the prince, who is eager to quench his curiosity each night, Saleem is also anxious to get the reader's attention and keep it with him. Besides telling the story of his personal life "handcuffed to the history of nation," Saleem or the author himself often engages in a series of arguments on the activity of creation and checks his own narratives in order to reveal his ultimate intentions or doubts on creating the perfect story as an art form.

In the beginning of the novel, Rushdie establishes an awareness and acceptance of the limitations and problems facing an artist—partiality, subjectivity and imperfection in formulating his message or the truth, as he mentions in his essay, "Imaginary Homeland." We can feel the agony and doubts of the author from the image of the narrator scribbling words after his personal memory and imaginary visions with a sense of fear and urgency. He is haunted by the fear of being unable to reclaim the past because of his "physical alienation from India." Rushdie faces this problem in the narratives with deliberate attempts to exploit the handicap rather than to succumb to the weakness. He mentions in the essay:

> This is why I made my narrator, Saleem, suspect in his narration: his mistakes are the mistakes of a fallible memory compounded by quirks of character and of circumstance, and his vision is fragmentary. It may be that when the Indian writer who writes from outside India tries to reflect that world, he is obliged to deal in broken mirrors, some of whose fragments have been irretrievably lost.[1F]

Rushdie conveys the difficulty each artist faces in order to create an artwork. It is a question of medium and form to capture all of reality. Since Saleem claims that one should swallow the whole world to understand him, he also tries to encapsulate all reality in his story-telling. But he has to consider the nature of language as a medium and the narrative form of fiction in order to achieve his artistic goal.

In the story we meet other premonitory characters suffering from the burden of creativity besides Saleem, who have to deal with artistic ambition and limitations of his medium and art form. Saleem's uncle Hanif is "the high priest of reality" in the Bombay film industry, which is dominated by unrealistic and fantastic movies (292). He loves details and linearity. He even plays cards differently in order to stick to his own principles. His "quest for this unattainable perfection" (295) is ultimately doomed to failure. He commits suicide like one of the characters of his own creation. Lifafa Das also tries to show "the whole world" through his peepshow box.

> The hyperbolic formula began, after a time, to prey upon his mind; more and more picture postcards went into his peepshows he tried desperately, to deliver what he promised, to put everything into his box. (I'm suddenly reminded of Nadir Khan's friend the painter; is this an Indian disease, this urge to encapsulate the whole of reality? Worse; am I infected, too?) (83)

We know he cannot possibly put the whole world into his little box, no matter how many postcards are carried inside. Both Uncle Hanif and Lifafa Das seem more ambitious than Saleem. They are doomed to be the victims of their own desire to "encapsulate the whole of reality." Saleem determines himself whether or not he is also infected by "the Indian disease." Yet Saleem as an artist grows and learns through witnessing the failures of these characters. They are reminders to Saleem. As Saleem tries to include everything that happened to him and India at the same time, he can sense the smell of failure. Since he is already aware of the dilemma of recreating reality in the form of fiction, he tries to transcend the mere mimetic aspect of employing language. He uses metaphors, patterns and intertextual dialogues between himself and readers. Yet he wants more positive feedbacks to reassure his self-confidence as a story-teller. As Saleem is constantly in doubt and suspect of failure, his narrative tone fluctuates between fear and pride.

In order to check the extremity in narrative devices, he also creates a surrogate reader among the characters, Padma, who helps readers to construct the whole structure of the story or to build a unity from the reflected images in broken mirrors. Padma has a simple and naïve taste for narratives traditional in their linearity and logic. She is a loyal and patient listener to Saleem, just as the prince listens to Sheherazade. Padma's role in the structural construction of the novel is far more important than that of being a passive character in the narration. Rushdie's creation of her is closely related to his view on solving the artistic limitation of writing the whole and the perfect out of "the broken mirror."

Padma often complains about Saleem's way of story-telling and yet tries to understand him as a person. Padma's reaction to his story becomes a barometer to test its readability. After sensing her bewilderment, Saleem explains, for example, what he means by "passive-metaphorical," "passive-literal" and "active-metaphorical" about his Midnight Children's Conference (286). She is also a critic of his story. Sometimes she awakens Saleem to his fallibility as a narrator by questioning the credibility of his linear chronology of historical events (265). At first, Saleem defends these kinds of mistakes by saying, "Padma: if you're a little uncertain of m reliability, well, a little uncertainty is no bad thing. Cocksure men do terrible deeds. Women, too" (254). The accumulation of these kinds of mistakes, however, casts doubt on Saleem's own confidence as well as in reader's mind. Saleem asks himself: "but if small things go, will large things be close behind?" He justifies his refusal to alter the sequence of historical events in his story: "What actually happened is less important than what the author can manage to persuade his audience to believe" (325). Still, we are told again that he lies, for instance, about Shiva's death. We as readers can notice Saleem's certain moments of frustration in connecting memories and of embarrassment in insisting on his unreliable information concerning "facts" and historical events. All these mistakes and suspicion on credibility in narration are intended by Rushdie as he mentions in his essay, "Imaginary Homeland."

The narrator often intentionally interrupts the stream of the story to invite the reader's active participation in practicing intertextuality. He tries to communicate to an imaginary reader, since he undermines Padma's ability to follow his narratives. He answers the imaginary reader's protesting questions about his use of language in young Saleem's speech. He defends his use of heavy, philosophical terms in order to explain what is actually going on. It is purely speculative language to him. There seems no way of expressing himself as a child and recapturing the reality of the world with children's language, according to him. He does not coordinate the style (use) of language and the mimetic nature of novel form. At other times, he attempts to convince Padma or the imaginary reader of the effectiveness of his way of telling a story, which is not linear. Though he is conscious of Padma's bent for "what-happened-nextism" (39), he does not seem to take heed of her need. Instead he counsels patience and demands aesthetic sensibility.

> While I, at my desk, feel the sting of Padma's impatience. (I wish, at times, for a more discerning audience, someone who would understand the need for rhythm, pacing, the subtle introduction of minor chords which will later rise, swell, seize the melody; who would know, for instance, that although baby-weight and monsoons have silenced the clock on the Estate clock tower, the steady beat of Mountbatten's ticktock is still there, soft but inexorable, and that it's only a matter of time before it fills our ears with its metronomic drumming music.) (116)

In order to achieve a balance in the experimental narrative, the author needs both Padma's "What-happened-nextism" linearity and "a more discerning audience's" taste for symbolism and subjectivity in the text. Ultimately Rushdie demands more sophisticated and complex intertextual readings from actual readers. The relationship among Saleem (the narrator), Padma (the listener) and the actual reader is triangular. The dramatic relationship between Saleem and Padma is a reenactment of the reader/text relationship. What separates Padma from the ordinary reader is her empathy for Saleem's fated life; she is a character before she is a surrogate reader.

Rushdie's mixture of Indian and English words in the novel enhances textual flavors like the mixed aromas of Indian spices enhance a tasty English dish. Often readers can understand out of a weird looking combination of English and Indian phrases even without comprehending their meanings. Rushdie's handling of Indian and English seems to be so revolutionary and exceptionally well-done that a critic, Rustom Bharucha, hails him as a liberator of Indian English of both the literature and the language from "its false Puritanism, its fake gentility."[12]

> It should be stressed that Rushdie does not indulge in Indianisms for their own sake.

> What he does instead is something so daring that only a writer of his gifts could pull it off. He deliberately makes English-English words and Indian-English words collide. Latinisms and the foulest Indian abuses are intimately linked. . . . Salman Rushdie is, perhaps, the only writer in the world today who could use the words "rutputty" and "lassitudinous" within three lines, and make you accept the validity of both these words (from different cultures) in his own fictional context.[13]

Rushdie also puts Indian accents and rhythms in his language, deriving from his knowledge and experience of Indian vernacular tongues. Thakur Guruprasad expounds on this subject in detail with examples from both *Midnight's Children* and *Shame* in his essay, "The Secret of Rushdie's Charm."[14] Unlike Guruprasad's linguistic approach, Mario Cuoto sees Rushdie's confidence in handling both English and Indian as "a testimony to the enduring legacy of Indo-British sensibility."[15] In comparison to G. V. Desani's "more Anglicised" style of English, the critic's following statements are illustrative of his views on Rushdie's effective handling of two languages to capture Indian essence in English.

> Rushdie uses phonemes and word patterns to suggest the vigour and liveliness of folk culture, the pace and variety of urban life, the mythology of Bombay films, the brash exuberance of affluence, the violence simmering and on the boil. He introduces the Western reader to a vocabulary expressing the Indian experience that goes well beyond the *koi hai*, *tamasha*, and *funtoosh* of colonial times. Rushdie, apart from straight borrowings from Hindi—*Jooloos*, *arre baap*, *ai o ai o*, *surahi*, and the ubiquitous nasbandi—delights with picturesque colloquialisms: hotch-potch-town, hankying and pankying, every which way, everywhichthing, Rani of Cooch Naheen, real ruputty point, went phutt. His prose, liberally sprinkled with Urdu, Hindi and Sanskrit names, the deliberately uncontrolled flow of sentence with repetition and sonorous content, suggests the chant of Indian traditional texts.[16]

According to Maria Cuoto, Rushdie's English bears witness to the vital infusion of Indo-British culture in his use of the accents and rhythms of Indian language.

As he does with everything else, Rushdie historicizes historical events about language and its politics in his fictional world by juxtaposing them with the life of Saleem Sinai. In 1956, India had been divided anew into fourteen states and six centrally-administered territories according to language. However, nothing was done with the state of Bombay. Thus the protest marches for pro-Marathi language versus for pro-Gujarati eventually evolved into political parties: the Samyukta Maharashtra Samiti (United Maharashtra Party) and the Maha Gujarat Parishad (Great Gujarat Party).

As a child in the midst of this political turmoil over languages, bicycling Saleem, pushed by Evie Burns, cashes into the pro-Maharashtra demonstrators. With this incident, he not only encounters history but also creates its course. He tells them a rhyme designed to make fun of the speech rhythms of the Gujarati language. The tune of little Saleem's rhyme starts the first of the language riots which killed fifteen and wounded over three hundred, according to narrator.

As Saleem acknowledges, he becomes "directly responsible for triggering off the violence which ended with the partition of the state of Bombay, as a result of which the city became the capital of Maharashtra" (229). In this episode, Rushdie also suggests an India after the Independence which was divided over issues of language and power. Ironically, fragmented India is briefly united and becomes a whole through wars for a short period of time under the spell of false optimism, which Saleem calls "the Indian disease."

Rushdie's use of the experimental narrative devices mentioned above makes this novel a uniquely pluralistic text. This novel is not only about India and an individual's struggle to grasp the meaning of history and his identity, but also about the act of reading by emphasizing the reader/text relationship. In his essay, "*Midnight's Children* and Reader Responsibility," Keith Wilson writes:

> *Midnight's Children* is, then, a novel centrally concerned with the imperfection of any narrative act, the compromises which govern the relationship of a writer with a reader who is hungry for linearity, and the impossibility of rendering a reality—however much concerned with public history—that is not petrified into false and subjective form at the point at which an artist attempt to render it. It is a novel that deliberately invites a question of the credentials of the novelist and of the illusory surface objectivity of the novel form.[17]

Rushdie's experimental use of narrative strategy to capture a sense of unity within a series of fragmented visions is very effective as he plays consciously with his own doubts and fears of aesthetic failure. It is a question of medium and form, in other words, the use of language for the form of fiction. Keith Wilson says: "the pickle jar is the ultimate vindication of Saleem's faith that "Everything has shape, if you look for it. There is no escape from form."[18]

Rushdie's use of metaphor makes every incident and person meaningful, and interconnected. He also broadens his vocabulary by his own unique way of employing Indian words to give cultural flavors and uniqueness. *Midnight's Children* can be considers not only an encyclopedia of modern Indian history and culture, but also a plural text about the question of medium and form in an artwork, about the deconstructive act of reading.

Shame: The Origin of Violence

Rushdie's third novel, *Shame* (1983) echoes *Midnight's Children*, in its concept and theme. Yet this other sibling of *Midnight's Children* had a bolder contour in plot development and appeals less to realism. As *Midnight's Children* is a novel about post-Independent Indian society, *Shame* is mainly about Pakistan, a country built by partition.

This section focuses on what Rushdie means by the notion of "shame," and how it is related to Third World politics in the post imperial era. The main characters, Sufiya and Omar, symbolize "shame" and "shamelessness" respectively. They are rather abstract and allegorical compared to two political figures, Raza Hyder and Iskander Harappa, whose resemblance to real political figures in Pakistan can make this novel a political satire. The distinction of character portrayals leads us to the question of periphery versus centrality in history. Allegorical characters are pushed to the margin and deprived of their autonomy; realistic characters seem to keep the hegemony in the course of history because of their active pursuit of power in life. The idea of periphery versus centrality is applicable not only to characters and their lives but also to nations like Pakistan and India; these, in turn, can be expanded to include all of the Third World nations.

Political Language in Fantastic Realm
The beginning of the story sets major conflicts caused by rigid paths of history; the clashes between the archaic past and the recent intrusion of Imperialism, and existing conflicts between Muslims and Hindus. One beginning is for the Omar Khayyam Shakil story; the other is for the Sufiya Zinobia story appearing in Book II "The Duelists."

Shame begins with the death of two patriarchs from which dual strands of the plot, the Omar story and the Sufiya story, start to intertwine. First, Rushdie show the death of the maternal grandfather or Omar Khayyam. Old Mr. Shakil hates everything in town. The town Q (Quetta) is split into the ole and the new; the town of the native and the town of "the alien colonizers." This scene suggests conflicts between the countries or between the native and the alien. Sufiya Zinobia's story starts with the life and death of her grandfather, Mahmoud the Woman. He has the nickname, according to the narrator, because of his unmanliness. This patriarch is running "a fifth-rate Empire" movie theater.

The Empire movie theater is a microcosm of contemporary society, as its name may suggest. The situation in the Empire reflects antagonistic social moods between Hindus and Moslems just right before the Partition. It shows us the nature of inner conflicts in the pre-partition era, after the showing the existing split of the native versus the alien in society. The power game and hatred between Hindus and Moslems reach Mahmoud's movie business. And his effort not to take either side of the conflict eventually kills him. Instead of showing one kind of movie, he chooses to alternate between Hindu and Moslem movies, offering double features. Unlike Mahmoud's expectation of winning support from both religious groups, he becomes the target of hatred from both sides. Someone sets a bomb and it blows up the theater and its owner. His daughter, Bilquis, escapes the blast. But she suffers from her symbolic sensitivity to wind for the rest of her life.

The narrator's description of Angrez Imperialists at the beginning of the story contains the cynical tone making their seemingly colorful and self-contended life resemble the "doomed glory" of the imminent withdrawal of the British Empire from the colony:

> . . . at the dome of a large Palladian hotel, which rose out of the intolerable Cantonment streets like a mirage, and inside which were to be found golden cuspidors and tame spider-monkeys in brass-buttoned uniforms and bellhop hats and a full sized orchestra playing every evening in a stuccoed ballroom amidst an energetic riot of fantastic plants, . . . the Hotel Falshman, in short, whose great golden dome was cracked even then but shone nevertheless with the tedious pride of its brief doomed glory; that dome under which the suited-and-booted Angrez officers and white-tied civilians and ringleted ladies with hungry eyes would congregate nightly, assembling here from their bungalows to dance and to share the illusion of being colourful—whereas in fact they were merely white, or actually grey, owing to the deleterious effect of that stony heat upon their frail cloud-nurtured skins, and also to their habit of drinking dark burgundies in the noonday insanity of the sun, with a fine disregard for their livers. (4)[19]

The description of the imperialists and their symbol, the hotel, is paradoxical and shows the superficial glory and the inevitable sign of suppressed and hidden decay. Rushdie's words effectively reveal the contradiction of the imperialists' life. He is both sympathetic and critical of these imperialists' fate of "doomed glory."

The presence of the Angrez imperialists here is shadowy and suggestive. Yet they represent the symbolic nature of irreconcilable foreign elements and their conflicts with the native. When the Shakil sisters invite these colonialists to their queer party, it becomes a symbolic gesture of reenacting the foreign invasion of India with their (or India's) own half-willed invitation along with the irresistible force of history. After these sisters succeed in selecting a father for their child, they voluntarily withdraw from the world and become self-imposed hermits. As a mule owner mentions, it is an ironic gesture of self-retreat: "For what your begums want this lock-shock now? Invasion has already occurred" (10).

Even though the narrator is successful in implementing a politically critical tone in the description of a dichotomous world eroded by the Imperialists, he fails to develop the mass's participation in history especially in the political arena. Unlike *Midnight's Children*, *Shame* does not have a moment of celebrating Independence from the grip of Imperialists. Also it is a world devoid of the picture of the mass. Just as the Shakil sisters commit a "crime of omission" in inviting Indian residents to their party, so the narrator deliberately omits communal involvement in events. Instead, he gropes after abstract idea, such as values, philosophy, virtues, symbols, ideology, history, with language put into fictional form. *Shame*, a fictional fantasy with "a slight angle to reality" (23) is being made by a "fantasist" (92), whereas *Midnight's Children* is told by a "realist" with a haunting memory of other failed realists.

Overall, *Shame* is a story about Pakistan and yet the narrator avoids direct comments on it. He is "only telling a modern fairy-tale" (72):

> The country in this story is not Pakistan, or not quite. There are two countries, real and fictional, occupying the same space, or almost same space. My story, my fictional country exists, like myself, at a slight angle to reality. I have found this off-centering to be necessary; but its value is, of course, open to debate. My view is that I am not writing only about Pakistan. (23-24)

He later names his fantasy land: Peccavistan, a bilingual pun of *I have Sind*, originating from the Latin 'Peccavi' (I have sinned) and the Indian word "Sind" (92-93). The feeling of guilt or sin haunts the entire novel. *Shame* claims to be both a universal allegory and a political satire or apologue.[20]

Shame: The Origin of Violence

The complex meaning of the term "shame" becomes clearer through close study of the novel's characters, political messages, sense of history and narrative structure.

The original word for "shame," according to the narrator, is *Sharam*: "A short word, but one containing encyclopaedias of nuance. It was not only shame that his mothers forbade Omar Khayyam to feel, but also embarrassment, discomfiture, decency, modesty, shyness, the sense of having an ordained place in the world, and other dialects of emotion for which English has no counterparts" (35).

Rushdie considers "shame" as "the origin of violence." He provides his initial inspiration of the novel drawn from contemporary reality. He tries to analyze this human emotion underneath every action. Then he expands his idea of "shame" and tries to universalize it through the story set in "Peccavistan."

According to the narrator, the inspiration for *Shame* comes from a real incident in London, in which a Pakistani father kills his own loving daughter in order to restore the family honor the daughter has been "dishonored" by a white boy. The narrator understands the father, who is left only with blood-cleansed and restored (?) honor and the grief of loss, and he ponders upon the notion of shame and shamelessness. The author formulates these ideas from the cultural differences between the West and the East.

> The news did not seem alien to me. We who have grown up on a diet of honour and shame can still grasp what must seem unthinkable to peoples living in the aftermath of the death of God and of tragedy: those men will sacrifice their dearest love on the implacable altars of their pride. (And not only men, I have since heard of case in which a woman committed the identical crime for identical reasons.) Between shame and shamelessness lies the axis upon which we turn; meteorological conditions at both these poles are of the most extreme, ferocious type. Shamelessness, shame: the roots of violence. (123–24).

Rushdie sees both shame and shamelessness as the origins of violence. All the characters and their world cannot be immunized from the violence and bloody destruction caused by shame. The world of *Shame* consists of such elements as sex and death, which balance the cycle of life with the symbolic act of sexual reproduction and its destruction by death. What meteorological conditions refer to might be social and political situations or the fate of private lives. Each character according to the degree of his closeness to the apex acts out his portion of shame, as the narrator repeats like a refrain, "shame the beast has many faces." Its incarnations are many. Yet the opposite poles of the shame scale are personified as the main characters in the story; Sufia Zinobia Hyder as the shame, Omar Khayyam Shakil the shamelessness. Both of them are grotesque mediums linking the fantastic tales of two families and corrupted power game in Pakistan together.

Omar Khayyam is the "dizzy, peripheral, inverted, infatuated insomniac, stargazing, fat" hero of the novel (19). This unlikely here is shamelessness personified. His grotesque and self-effacing three mothers name his after the famous Persian poet, who is more popular in the West than in his own country. He is "a peripheral man." Omar Khayyam Shakil suffers from an improbable vertigo; he fells that he exists at the edge of the world. His childhood is also exceptional and has certain symbolic significances:

> Omar Khayyam passed twelve long years, the most crucial years of his development, trapped inside that reclusive mansion, that third world that was neither material nor spiritual, but a sort of concentrated decrepitude made up of the decomposing remnants of those two more familiar types of cosmos, a world in which he would constantly run into—as well as the mothballed, spider-webbed, dust-shrouded profusion of crumbling objects—the lingering, fading miasmas of discarded ideas and forgotten dreams. (25)

This third world consists of discarded ideas and forgotten dreams. It is "the thing-infested jungle," "Nihau," "his mother-country" (26) in "the town of shame" (53). While roaring in this world like a zoo animal, Omar Khayyam absorbs knowledge and becomes "a self-taught prodigy" (32). This confined lifestyle, under the supervision of three mothers in his childhood, makes him grow up without a definite sense of autonomy and without the ability to relate to others. Under the three mothers' watchful eyes, he can only develop into "a sidelined personality, a watcher from the wings of his own life" (31). Unable to mingle with others, he only watches the world outside through his telescope. The three mothers' strange resolve to seclude him from society also contributes to his "sense of exclusion, of being, in the midst of objects, out of things" (31).

He dreams of the outside world with an intensity paralleled only by his sexual desire. Later he confesses to Farah Zoroaster, whom he impregnates with the help of his power of hypnosis, that "the sight of you through my beloved telescope game me the strength to break my mothers' power" (24). At twelve he attends school "with the weapons of learning" (37), which ironically liberates him. From the moments of first tasting the outside world, however, he is marginalized. Yet he enjoys his invisible status with "the delights of the spectator" (42). The effect of his upbringing as a marginal man continues throughout his whole life, even after he becomes famous and successful. When Rodrigues, Omar Khayyam's father figure, says "one must be Of the Essence," and steers Omar Khayyam's future toward a medical career. According to the narrator's explanation, Rodrigues ironically sees the boy's "possibilities of his true, peripheral nature" as "Essential" qualities. The narrator connects the role of doctor in life with the idea of centrality and periphery:

> What's a doctor, after all?—A legitimized voyeur, a stranger whom we permit to poke fingers and to insert so much as a finger-tip, who gazes on what we take our most intimate moments (birthdeathetc.), anonymous, a minor character, yet also, paradoxically, central, especially at the crisis . . . yes, yes. Eduardo was a far-sighted teacher, and no mistake. (47)

Omar Khayyam is a marginal man suffering from vertigo and shamelessness. When compared with the protagonist of *Midnight's Children*, Saleem, immense differences are evident in each character's manner of existence: one is marginalized; the other is central. Yet the ultimate outcome is the same; each of them ends up victimized by his own life.

The fictional and fantastic world of *Shame* is connected closely or analogously to the shameful and corrupted reality of Pakistani politics. The narrator opens his criticism on the subject using the "Defense Society" as an example. The outlook on life in the "Defense Society" is deceiving. It seems filled with beautiful gardens, perfumes, and the elegance of civility, and yet the hidden and unspoken reality is that it is based upon corruption of the society. The narrator also criticizes severe political repression in Pakistan. The political repression exists hidden under a superficial friendliness, as in the case of the police spy the narrator encounters. The spy, according to the narrator, seems "a nice guy, pleasantly spoken, honest-faced, and no doubt happy that he was hearing nothing worth reporting" (22). The fragile equilibrium between oppression and freedom is juxtaposed with the deceptively elegant and peaceful life in "Defense." The narrator cynically says "I was struck by how many nice guys there were in Pakistan, by the civility growing in those gardens, perfuming the air" (22). Civility hides all sorts of ugly truths. With this carefully put analogy, the narrator reveals the meaning of "shame" and one form of its numerous metamorphic masks.

> Wherever I turn, there is something of which to be ashamed. But shame is like everything else; live with it for long enough and it becomes part of the furniture. In "Defense," you can find shame in every house, burning in an ashtray, hanging framed upon a wall, covering a bed. But nobody notices it any more. And everyone is civilized. (22–23)

This kind of unnoticed shame harbors violence beneath its calm surface. It can manifest itself from time to time in the form of incarceration or as physical torture, as happens to the narrator's poet friend. He is hung upside down and severely tortured, because of an absurd accusation that he knows someone whom the government wants to capture. Shame also motivates the Pakistani father to kill his own daughter. Ultimately the narrator blames "shame" as "the roots of violence itself."

This "shame" has many faces. Even though the narrator focuses on a fictional land of shame in the East, Peccavistan or Pakistan, he often reminds us that "shame, dear reader, is not the exclusive property of the East." It can also be found in the mind of a senior British diplomat and his wife, for example, who seem to possess perfect civility (23). London is also a world of shame and violence. Ectoplasmic images, ghosts and phantoms like the girl killed by her father "inhabit a country that is entirely unghostly: no spectral 'Peccavistan,' but Proper London" (125).

Often the concept of shame is closely tied to sex as well as to violence. When Bilquis Hyder finds out that her daughter, Sufiya Zinobia, has turned into an idiot, she accepts the fact. Because of her guilt and shame for her perfidious behavior; she acknowledges that "she [Sufiya Zinobia] is my shame" (107). Since then, she calls her daughter Shame. She accepts the idiot daughter as a kind of divine judgment. Interestingly, Bilquis Hyder's illicit love affair which results in the death of the lover by her husband, Raza Hyder, reminds us strongly of the infidelity of Saleem's mother and Commander Sarbarmati's wife in *Midnight's Children*.

It seems that a character's sex life can be a barometer of his or her shame or shamelessness. Most of the male characters are on the axis of shamelessness with Omar Khayyam on the apex; female characters are on the axis of shame with Sufiya Zinobia on the apex. Omar Khayyam's early sexual maturity and his debauchery in adulthood are given as major evidence of his shamelessness. Sufiya Zinobia, the symbol of other people's (including her own mother's) shame, remains a virgin even after her marriage. After she is raped by four boys, whom she more or less taunts into committing the rape, she completely turns into a Beast with supernatural powers of destruction. Her extreme abhorrence of sex and Omar Khayyam's lust are a most unlikely match, and yet they complement each other as a couple.

After all, as the narrator puts it, *Shame* is Omar Khayyam's love story. He releases his shamelessness or lust through his strange relationship with wife's ayah, Shahbanou. Sufiya Zinobia's vague awareness of the affair and the ayah's pregnancy infuses her with "fault and shame" (241). Her metamorphosis into a supernatural beast after having being raped seems to suggest vileness and violence behind sexual motives. Omar Khayyam's shamelessness in his debauchery is by extension the shame of Sufiya Zinobia. Rushdie suggests that sexual violence and immorality such as rape and adultery are part of the world of shame.

Even with the negative connotation of sex as a cause of violence, the world of *Shame* also maintains its balance through the cycle of life and death; sexual reproduction and death for destruction. Sexual innuendo and symbols in relation to the subject are prevalent throughout the novel. For example, unlike Sufiya Zinobia's asceticism, her sister Naveed the Good News has uncontrollable fertility enough to squash her old personality. She was beautiful and smart unlike her sister, Sufiya. Her beauty fades away as she copes with her army of children. Naveed the Good News's delivery of children cannot be a blessed and sacred moment in human life; it rather suggests a moment of humiliation and loss of human dignity. The narrator's voice seems to suggest that excessive fertility is also a source of shame.

> Begum Naveed Talvar, the former Good News Hyder, proved utterly incapable of coping with the endless stream of humanity flowing out between her thighs. . . . He came to her once a year and ordered her to get ready, because it was time to plant the seed, until she felt like a vegetable patch whose naturally fertile soil was being worn out by an over-zealous gardener, and understood that there was no hope for women in the world, because whether you were respectable or not the men got you anyway, no matter how hard you tried to be the most proper of ladies they would come and stuff you full of alien unwanted life. (228)

Naveed, struck by "the terror of the arithmetical progression of babies marching out of her womb" (251), commits suicide by hanging herself. Her pregnant body looks as if she'd "swallowed a whale" and is the visible evidence of her shame. Her nickname "Good News" and even further women's fertility are ridiculed thoroughly. The shame she feels toward her fertility ultimately kills her.

The nightlife in the women's quarter at Hyder's house illustrates people's hypocrisy in regard to sex. The narrator seems to ridicule the Hyder women's vain attempt to hide their shame:

> ... in that house in which it was believed that the mere fact of being married did not absolve a woman of the shame and dishonour that results from the knowledge that she sleeps regularly with a man; which was why Bariamma had devised, without once discussing it, the idea of the forty thieves. And of course all the women deny that anything of that nature ever took place, so that when pregnancies occurred they did so as if by magic, as if all conceptions were immaculate and all birth virgin. The idea of parthenogenesis had been accepted in this house in order to keep out certain other, unpleasantly physical notions. (76–77)

This kind of hypocrisy about sex is similar to the hypocrisy of life style in the "Defense," where people choose not to face the existence of shame. When the narrator talks about "shame," he also talks about hypocrisy, corruption, political repression, betrayal, violence and death.

The narrator's analogy of shame as "a liquid stored in a vending machine" leads to the question of "unfelt shame," since shameful things are done shamelessly by many people (131). He creates Sufiya Zinobia, the moron, as the sensor for those of unfelt shame. He somehow suggests that the nature of Sufiya Zinobia's physical suffering from the burden of shame committed by others can be transformed into the altruistic sufferings of a saint. He asks us: "What is a saint? A saint is a person who suffers in our stead" (153). Sufiya Zinobia's blush is altruistic; she blushes for the world.

This Sufiya Zinobia, the notion of shame itself, is the heroin and is introduced in the second part of the novel. However, her image or whole picture is very elusive when compared with that of other more realistic characters. This is not only because of her extraordinary and beastly behavior but also because of the narrator's presentation. The significance of her existence in the story is symbolic; as a character she interacts little with other characters.

> I did it to her, I think, to make her pure. Couldn't think of another way of creating purity in what is supposed to be the Land of the Pure ... and idiots are, by definition, innocent. Too romantic a use to make of mental disability? Perhaps; but it's too late for such doubts. Sufiya Zinobia has grown, her mind more slowly than her body, and owing to this slowness she remains, for me, somehow clean (*pak*) in the midst of a dirty world. (129)

If shame as an emotion is hard to describe, the reincarnation of shame is elusive, unreal and nefarious. Readers are kept from Sufiya's inner feelings and consciousness, which in turn effectively enhances her idiocy. Like Benjamin in *The Sound and the Fury* by William Faulkner, her idiocy mirrors the world in her "innocent" eyes. Yet she is much more unrealistic in many ways than Benjamin.

Sufiya Zinobia is a rubescent who blushes even at her birth. She is the wrong miracle for her parents who want to have a son. To the narrator, the metaphoric characterization of her is significant. He mentions that three "actual" incidents inspired him to create this kind of anti-heroine just like the unlikely hero of the novel, Omar Khayyam. The narrator also reminds us of the last sentence of *The Trial* by Franz Kafka and its relevance to the story of Sufiya Zinobia: *"Like a dog' he said; it was as if he meant the shame of it to outlive him"* (126). All people in his mind are related to the subject of shame and violence: Anna killed by her father; a girl molested and beaten by white boys; a boy burned himself to death. If the feeling of shame and fury are vented, as the narrator imagines, the intensity of emotion will turn into "energy, fire and light." After all, "blush is slow *burning*" (132). Sufiya Zinobia's blush and its heat manifest shame.

At the age of twelve out with a three-old mind, Sufiya Zinobia's horrible power of destruction is evidenced by her killing of two hundred and eighteen turkeys tearing off their heads and drawing out their guts. It is "the beast inside the beauty," combining the two opposing elements of a fairy-tale in a single character (151). Her violent behavior and insomnia result from the release of accumulated shame. Shameful deeds by others leave their marks on the sensor, Sufiya Zinobia. As the other characters' stories unfold, the narrator simply suggests that their shameful deeds cause Sufiya Zinobia's blush and its eventual violent eruption, when the pressure of unfelt shame reaches its limit. Sufiya Zinobia herself seems shocked by her potent destructive power.

> One can only speculate: Was Sufiya Zinobia trying, like a good daughter, to rid her mother of the gobbler plague? Or did the anger, the proud outrage which Raza Hyder ought to have felt, but refused to do so, preferring to make allowances for Pinkie, find its way into his daughter instead?—What seems certain is that Sufiya Zinobia, for so long burdened with being a miracle-gone-wrong, a family's shame made flesh, had discovered in the labyrinths of her unconscious self the hidden path that links *sharam* to violence; and that awakening, she was as surprised as anyone by the force of what had been unleashed. (150–51)

After the violent killing of the birds, she suffers from a fever which brings huge blotchy rashes, boils, vermilion lumps and appalling black buboes, etc. The dark violence of shame has turned inwards. Her physical suffering is more or less a self-sacrificing act:

> The plague of shame—in which I insist on including the unfelt shame of those around her, for instance what had not been felt by Raza Hyder when he gunned down Barbar Shakil—as well as the unceasing shame of her own existence, and of her hacked-off hair—the plague, I say, spread rapidly through that tragic being whose chief defining characteristic was her excessive sensitivity to the bacilli of humiliation. (152)

As if it were fated, the incident draws Omar Khayyam and Sufiya Zinobia together as doctor and patient at first, like Aadam Aziz and his fiancée are drawn together as doctor and patient in *Midnight's Children*. In each of their own stories, significant events occur from the moment of their meeting. Omar Khayyam as a practitioner of medicine is interested in psychosomatic behavior. Above all, he is a specialist in the field of immunology. It is not unrelated to his strong defense mechanism against shame. He is totally immune to it; Sufiya Zinobia's extreme sensitivity to "the bacilli of shame" is diagnosed as an immunological disorder: "Total breakdown of the immune system." Omar Khayyam's obsession with the disease, however, turns into a love for the girl. He shamelessly courts an idiot with the intent of being in the center of political power. It paves a way of climbing up the social ladder; Omar Khayyam approaches Sufiya Zinobia's father, even though he knows that Raza is the one who orders the killing of his own brother, Barbar Shakil. He claims that "his obsession with Sufiya Zinobia has cured his vertigo" (156). He shamelessly marries a girl who is thirty-one years his junior.

Omar Khayyam's existence in the periphery plays an important role in bridging the gap among the characters through his relationship to them, whether they are realistic characters like Hyders and Harappas or unrealistic like Sufiya Zinobia and the three mothers. He brings the fragmented structure of the story together. He is on the borderline of each character's life and yet he is the common denominator in their lives.

Finally the shame felt by Sufiya Zinobia turns her into a beast. Because the weight and pressure of shame are too much to bear, "it blows up in your face" (189). Like this symbolic remark, the book ends with an apocalyptic explosion. In the end, Shame, the origin of violence, destroys everyone.

Shame *as a Political Satire*
In addition to telling a story about the abstract concept of shame, the narrator

offers political satire and social criticism. The rivalry between Raza Hyder and Iskander Harappa is meant to ridicule the politics of Pakistan, and their characterizations are drawn from the real political figures, Zia Ulhaq and Ali Bhutto.

Raza Hyder and Iskander Harappa are cousins-in-law. Their duel begins over 'Pinkie' (Atiyah) Aurangzeb, the Marshal's wife, and it lasts until their death: "Its initial prize was the body of the Marshal's wife, but after that it moved on to higher things" (112). Iskander Harappa was, according to his wife, "world champion of shamelessness, international rogue and bastard number one" (115), and he indulged in debauchery along with Omar Khayyam. Eventually, he decides to give up the life of playboy and to reform himself, which has something to do with his daughter's influence on his life. His reformation also brings about the development of his wife, Rani's personality, transforming her into the confident and victorious wife of the political prominent. Iskander Harappa becomes popular and gains political power by killing his cousin, the former president Mir Harappa.

At first Raza Hyder is Iskander Harappa's protégé, but he manages to ruin Iskander Harappa's political career by accusing him of killing Mir Harappa. Raza Hyder eventually kills Iskander and becomes president himself. His scheme for political ascendancy relies on military power, and treachery and murder are common. Because of his shameful acts in political game, the initials CMLA, standing for Chief Martial Law Administrator, acquire new meaning, *Cancel My Last Announcement*.

Isky and Raza's political fight resulted in with Isky's defeat like the rivalry that existed between Danton and Robespierre during the French Revolution. Questioning the nature of the two men's political rivalry and its effect on the country, Rushdie attempts to transform their power game into an allegorical or a symbolic conflict innate in human nature, much as Georg Buchner did in his play, *Danton's Death* where the conflict becomes one of the epicures against the puritan. In his play, Buchner uses the character Danton to suggest, according to the narrator of *Shame*, that "the people are like Robespierre" (265). This narrator of *Shame* is able to find an inconsistency in this statement in the play by observing "the people's" cheering of Danton.

The defeated Danton and Isky also can be heroes to the same people who admire Robespierre. Thus the falls of Danton and Isky do not mean the defeat of Epicureanism in human nature, as Buchner suggests in his play. According to *Shame*'s narrator, Isky is not just Danton the epicurean; he also can be Robespierre. The shawls Rani creates as a means of preserving truth in history belie the fact that Isky commits and perpetuates Terror as much as Raza does. By the same token, Raza cannot simply be Robespierre, the puritan, acting in the name of God: "Isky and Raza. They, too, were Danpierre and Robeston. Which may be an explanation; but it cannot, of course, be an excuse" (267).

Since the differences in the personalities of Raza Hyder and Iskander Harappa are so similar to those of Robespierre and Danton created by Buchner, the narrator compares these two pairs of characters carefully. According to the narrator, Buchner believes that the true dialectic of history is the conflict between differing human natures, for example, the epicure versus the puritan, rather than the conflict between conflicting ideologies like left versus right, capitalism versus socialism and black versus white. However, Rushdie seems to disagree with this view. As he indicates in Raza's revival of Islam, Rushdie explains that Raza's devotion to Islam is a disguised form of tyranny, and the fall of Isky is a further defeat of Democracy in Pakistan.

The subversive nature of power is evident in Isky and Raza's rivalry. Raza was once the protégé of Isky. Now General Raza means Death itself to Iskander.

> *From darkness into light, from nothingness into somethingness. I made him, I was his father, he is my seed. And now I am less than he. They accuse Haroun of killing his father because that is what Hyder is doing to me.*
> Then another step, which takes him beyond such aching simplicities. The father should be superior and the son, inferior. *But now I am low and he, high.* An inversion: the parent becomes the child. *He is turning me into his son.* (254)

The narrator not only makes Isky a symbolic son but also turns him into an actual son, who has come into the world still-born with the umbilical cord around his neck. The image of the baby in the earlier chapter of the story, "The Wrong Miracle," is an epiphany of Iskander's death:

> An umbilical cord wound itself around a baby's neck and was transformed into a hangman's noose (in which other nooses are prefigured), into the breath-stopping silken rumal of a Thug; and an infant came into the world handicapped by the irreversible misfortune of being dead before he was born. (86)

Iskander is also hanged after he is dead. The killing of Iskander symbolizes Raza's revenge for this still-born child.

The narrator draws a parallel of between a hangman's noose and an umbilical cord around the baby's neck. At the same time the juxtaposed images of Isky in the cell and the baby in his mother's womb are so effectively matched that there seems to be no distinction between death and life. Birth means death. Isky thus understands the meaning of his death and the nature of his political rivalry:

> Because now he understands the cell, the throbbing walls, the smell of excrement, the drumbeat of a foul invisible heart: death's belly, an inverse womb, dark mirror of a birthplace, its purpose is to suck him in, to draw him back and down through time, until he hangs foetal in his own waters, with an umbilical cord hang fatally round his neck. He will leave this place only when its mechanisms have done their work, death's baby, traveling down the death canal, and the noose will tighten its grip. [. . .] The killing of Iskander Harappa avenges the still-born child. Yes: *I am being unmade.* (254)

After Isky's death, Pinky also commits suicide and Sufiya Zinobia disappears. The attic room where Sufiya Zinobia is confined is also an echo of Isky's prison cell. The disappearance of her from the room makes Raza worry that "Shame should come to me" (270). Raza hears Isky's monologue which is full of Machiavellian advice encouraging himself to commit cruelties in order to maintain power. At the same time he hears God's voice:

> Nor was Iskander's the only voice. We have already seen the first appearance of the spectre of Maulana Dawood; it returned to perch, invisibly, on the President's right shoulder, to whisper in his ear. God on the right shoulder, the Devil on his left; this was the unseen truth about the Presidency of Old Razor Guts, these tow conflicting soliloquies inside his skull, marching leftright leftright leftright down the years. (263)

These buzzing voices in his ears drive him to be a dictator acting in the name of God, and it characterizes the nature of Zia Ulhaq's rule of Pakistan.

In criticizing the politics of Pakistan, the narrator's voice seems detached from the political events. And yet with a satiric pun like CMLA and the narrative asides, he manages to deliver the feelings of horror and corruption in Pakistan's political game, and indeed that in Third World politics. These two characters' rivalry represents the stereotypical scenario of politics in the newly born nations.

The Myth of the Nation: Islam

Despite his corrupted dictatorship being actually maintained by military power and political murder, Raza Hyder can manipulate the public mind by building an image of himself as a pious man holding the Koran. Raza Hyder rules Pakistan under the catch phrase of "Stability, in the name of God" (276). In order to achieve "stability," he exerts military power and gets rid of his political enemies, including Iskander Harappa and even his own brother-in-law. From the way Raza Hyder rules the nation, especially his appeal to Islam, the narrator criticizes Pakistan's politics and the role of Islam in it.

Raza tries to escape from "the monologue of the hanged man [Iskander Harappa]," which buzzes constantly in his head. It is the sound of Raza's own conscience which he tries to ignore by all means. He clings desperately to Islam and uses people's religious faith to maintain his regime, by claiming "Iskander Harappa never believed in God." Raza distances himself from his predecessor drastically and disguises himself by wearing the garment of a pious man in public. However, it is ironic that Raza's way of using religion in politics is a very important and efficient method of killing democracy, too.

> What Raza did: he banned booze. He closed down the famous old beer brewery at Bagheeragali so that Panther Lager became a fond memory instead of a refreshing drink. He altered the television schedules so drastically that people began summoning repair men to fix their sets, because they could not understand why the TVs were suddenly refusing to show them anything except theological lectures, and they wondered how these mullahs had got stuck inside the screen. On the Prophet's birthday Raza arranged for every mosque in the country to sound a siren at nine a.m. and anybody who forgot to stop and pray when he heard the howling was instantly carted off to jail.... They [the beggars] had underestimated God, however; in the first year of his rule Raza Hyder incarcerated one hundred thousand beggars and, while he was at it, a further twenty-five members of the now-illegal Popular Front, who were not much better than mendicants, after all. He announced that God and socialism were incompatible, so that the very doctrine of Socialism on which the Popular Front had based its appeal was the worst kind of blasphemy imaginable.... The incompatibility doctrine made Raza very popular with the Americans, who were of the same opinion, even though the God concerned was different. (273–74)

Raza Hyder clearly uses Islam to maintain his dictatorship and to force people to follow him.

The narrator is critical of Raza's so-called Islamic fundamentalism in Pakistan. Obviously the creation myth of Pakistan is Islam. This "Land of Pure" was created by Partition and united its two separate bodies, the East and the West Wing, with faith in Al-lah. Knowing this creation myth of Pakistan, the narrator questions the nature of Raza Hyder's Islamic revival in contemporary Pakistan. The narrator says that Pakistan as a Muslim state is different from Iran: "Pakistan has never been a mullah-dominated society....

Islam and the Muslim state were, for him [Jinnah, the founder or Quaid-i-Azam], political and cultural ideas; the ideology was not the point" (277). He sees the revival of fundamentalism in Pakistan under Hyder as a disguised form of dictatorship rather than an indication of pure faith, since "it is imposed on them [people] from above" (278).

Rushdie seems to believe that a religious faith can be a form of dictatorship or tyranny when it is imposed upon people and driven by ardent zealots. His ambivalent attitude toward the "fundamentalism" or zealots can also be found in the episode of Ayesha Pilgrims in *The Satanic Verses* (1989). The power of faith makes whole villagers follow Ayesha relentlessly to pilgrimage despite other people's objections. The absolute faith is so rigid that it does not allow any other perspective in life. The suicidal death of the whole population of the village shown in the chapter, "The Parting of the Arabian Sea" illustrates ultimate submission to the power of faith. The narrator of *The Satanic Verses* maintains an ambivalent attitude in dealing with the meaning of this death; it could be both meaningless and sublime at the same time depending upon one's perspective. And yet Rushdie provides a tyrannical aspect of religious zealotism by showing how it manipulates the public consciousness.

Raza Hyder's use of the nation's myth for the basis of maintaining his political power creates its own vicious circle: the fall of the dictator only brings the disintegration of the myth or a new dictatorship. When "the ramming-down-the-throat point stands," "in the end you get sick of it, you lose faith in the faith, if not *qua* faith then certainly as the basis for a state" (278). If one does not want that to happen, the narrator suggests substituting the nation's old myth, Islam, with a new myth.

He offers three myths echoing the French Revolution: liberty; equality; fraternity. Here the inspirational echo of the French Revolution is again evident, after the analogy of political games in Pakistan between Raza Hyder and Iskander Harappa has been made. Rushdie makes clear his opinion of Third World politics through expressing his concern about the political situation in Pakistan; the replacement of dictatorship with democracy. As the French Revolution brought down the Regime Ancienne, the substitution of a nation's myth might lead to the fall of the current dictatorship.

Pakistan: "A Failure of the Dreaming Mind"

From the political duel between Hyders and Harappas, it is possible to sense a demythification of the Pakistani creation myth through satirical ridicule of its corrupted politics. And yet Rushdie once again tries to privatize history and to understand the failure of realizing one's dream in such a manner as to make a paralleled vision from Pakistan's shattered dream of being "the Land of Pure" and an artist's failure to create a perfect work.

> It is the true desire of every artist to impose his or her vision on the world; and Pakistan, the peeling, fragmenting palimpsest, increasingly at war with itself, may be described as a failure of the dreaming mind. Perhaps the pigments used were the wrong ones, impermanent, like Leonardo's; or perhaps the place was just *insufficiently imagined*, a picture full of irreconcilable elements, midriff baring immigrant saris versus demure, indigenous Sindhi shalwar-jurtas, Urdu versus Punjabi, now versus then: a miracle that went wrong. (92)

Like Saleem in *Midnight's Children*, the narrator is struggling to include everything in order to create an ultimate product and to impose his vision on the world. Like Saleem, he knows his desire is doomed to fail. The Pakistani dream to build a perfect nation is also doomed to fail because it contains too many unsolved conflicts. The miracle of "Birth" is fated to go awry, as manifested at the moment of the birth of Raza's still-born child.

Rushdie also connects successfully the idea of creating a new nation and the symbolism linked with the word like "immigrant." Pakistan was built by immigrants, uprooted from their history and past. They were hungry for stability. Among the characters, Raza's wife, Bilquis, is the epitome of the immigrants, the *Mohajirs*." The best thing about the migrant people is, according to the narrator, their hopefulness; the worst thing is the emptiness of their invisible luggage. Their situation is like a floating upward from history, or memory, or Time. He compares the sense of belonging to gravity. "Migration" is an "anti-myth of gravity and belonging" (90). When an individual seeks freedom and moves to a place away from his own "roots," he is called a "migrant." And when a nation does the same thing, the act is called "secession." The narrator describes himself as such a person, a migrant; Pakistan and Bangladesh are such seceded countries (92). To the immigrants, whether it is a nation or a person, the denial of their past is inevitable and their vision is altered as a result. A discussion of the sense of belonging seems to be a matter of gravity versus levity.

Since "anti-belonging is not accepted by modern science" (90) the narrator presents the myth of gravity in creating a vision of a new nation as follows:

> It is well known that the term "Pakistan," an acronym, was originally thought up in

> England by a group of Muslim intellectuals, P for Punjabis, A for the Afghans, K for the Kashmiris, S for Sind and the "tan," they say, for Baluchistan. . . . So it was a word born in exile which then went East, was borne-across or trans-lated, and imposed itself on history; a returning migrant, settling down on partitioned land, forming a palimpsest on the past. A palimpsest obscures what lies beneath. To build Pakistan it was necessary to cover up Indian history, to deny that Indian centuries lay just beneath the surface of Pakistani Standard Time. The past was rewritten; there was nothing else to be done. (91)

Pakistan is "borne-across or trans-lated" like the Persian poet Omar Khayyam. So is the shameless anti-hero of the story who shared the name of the famous poet. Besides, the narrator himself is this kind of "trans-lated" man.

> Omar Khayyam's position as a poet is curious. He was never very popular in his native Persia; and he exists in the West in a translation that is really a complete reworking of his verses, in many cases very different from the spirit (to say nothing of the content) of the original. I, too, am a translated man. I have been borne across. It is generally believed that something is always lost in translation; I cling to the notion—and use, in evidence, the success of Fitzgerald-Khayyam—that something can also be gained. (24)

Having been "borne across," the nation of Pakistan, Omar Khayyam the poet, the shameless hero of the story and the narrator all suffer from an improbable vertigo—the sense of being on the edge. In other words, Pakistan is a peripheral country on the map of international politics, and the others also can never be put into the center. They can only exist in the state of "Fitzgerald-Khayyam," as being "trans-lated" and "borne-across," losing something and gaining something. Their common marginality is also shared with Saleem in *Midnight's Children*. Both the narrator of *Shame* and Saleem have slightly "angle-poised" perspectives.

Above all, the Saleem of *Midnight's Children* and the "I" of *Shame* write about the Indian Subcontinent in English, a borrowed language. Pakistan and India are born again in fictional form created in the English language. To give Pakistan a new identity, Pakistanis have to rewrite its past and deny the whole Indian past. Ironically, as the narrator mentions, Pakistani history is rewritten in Urdu and English both borrowed languages. It is "borne-across."

> I, too, like all migrants, am a fantasist. I build imaginary countries and try to impose them on the ones that exist. I, too, face the problem of history: What to retain, what to dump, how to hold on to what memory insists on relinquishing, how to deal with change. (92)

Here the narrator as an artist tries to share the difficulty of rewriting history, since he, too, is dealing with the problems of history. The narrator, however, does not deal with the image of mass or the collective sense of history. Instead he makes Bilquis's experiences stand for those of other Pakistanis at the time of the Partition, and her marriage reflects the formation of the new nation. Bilquis is the epitome of immigrants, "the Mohajirs." And her daughter Sufiya Zinobia, "the miracle went wrong," represents situations which occurred after the building of the nation. Through their symbolic lives Rushdie demythifies the creation myth of Pakistan.

In the beginning, Pakistan has the geographical shape of a bird having two wings but no body. The wings are connected only through God, the power of Islamic faith. Pakistan's schizophrenic fear of separation comes true. Its two wings are finally separated as Pakistan and Bangladesh.

As an artist fails at the end because of his unattainable desire to create the perfect work, so the nation fails to remain intact and provide an ideal place to live. God is no longer to be found. Instead shame is rampant everywhere, whether revealed or hidden. The narrator's pessimistic remark—"perhaps the place was just insufficiently imagined" (92)—suggests that the failure of the nation is due to the failure of the dreaming mind; maybe they don't dream hard enough to create the perfect place.

Shame *as a Post-Modern Narrative*

The self-conscious narrator deliberately juxtaposes his fictional characters and the values they stand for with the contemporary reality of Pakistan. His personal narrative is episodic, separate and fragmented, and yet it functions like asides in a play. It explains, illuminates and connects each separate story and finally leads to a whole organic unity.

Shame is a story about two families, a love story between Omar Khayyam and Sufiya Zinobia, a political satire, a story of the birth of a natin and its aftermath, and, of course, a story about shame. And there are other plot devices, too. The narrator speaks of "male" and "female" plots in the story. He states in the middle of the story that he thought he was writing an excessively "masculine tale, a saga of sexual rivalry, ambition, power, patronage, betrayal, death, revenge" (189). But when he sees his "'male' plot refracted, so to speak, through the prisms of its reverse and 'female' side," he realizes that his "male' and 'female' plots are the same story, after all" (189).

The role of women in the story is rather ironic. Their place and role in the society are thoroughly ridiculed, but in the end they are the ones who show strength despite their repressed circumstances. Women are judged according to how well they marry and whether or not they give birth to male children. As Bilquis and Rani both fail to bear male children, their lives are significantly flawed, according to traditional norm. Naveed "Good News," however, has immense fertility. Yet she becomes a grotesque caricature mocking fertility and femininity, while at the same time, Arjumand the "Virgin Ironpants" is also ridiculed for denying her female identity and for building her own political career. No matter which way she chooses for her life, each woman faces repressive social norms. In the end, the final choice is either to free herself from the repression through death like Naveed, or to confine herself within invisible walls and cover herself with a veil like Bilquis.

> Repression is a seamless garment; a society which is authoritarian in its social and sexual codes, which crushes its women beneath the intolerable burdens of honour and propriety, breed repressions of other kinds as well. (189)

Male characters often use women as symbols of weakness and shame, as Raza says "How come the entire army turned into a bunch of blushing women overnight?" (222). Raza's dictatorship also falls "in improbability; in chaos; in women's clothing; in black" (290). Raza has to change his identity to that of a woman by wearing a black burqa in order to escape from his once powerful domain to the obscure periphery of town Q. Rushdie turns this symbolism of woman inside out. Instead of men, in the end, women are the final witnesses and preservers of history. Rani, for example, recaptures and preserves the real history of her husband's political era, which is quite different from Arjumand's idolized images of her father.

The name Iskander echoes that of Alexander the Great, but his real achievements are far from the popular image of him. Rani's eighteen shawls depicts the horror and terror of his shameful regime, as some of their titles suggest; the slapping shawl, the kicking shawl, the election shawl, the torture shawl, the white shawl of police state and the shawl of Hell, etc.

> An epitaph of wool. The eighteen shawls of memory. Every artist has the right to name her creation, and Rani would put a piece of paper inside the trunk before she sent it off to her newly powerful daughter. On this piece of paper she would write her chosen title: "The shamelessness of Iskander the Great." (210)

The narrator "I," who is living in London like the author himself, questions whether or not he has the right to write about the history of Pakistan. His imaginary voices accuse him of writing and criticizing Pakistan affairs. However, he asserts his right to deal with this history because history does not exclusively belong to the participants (23). But he knows he has to deal with the problem of fragmented visions, as if dealing with the images in a broken mirror.

> I think what I'm confessing is that, however I choose to write about over-there [Pakistan]. I am forced to reflect that world in fragments of broken mirrors, the way Farah Zoroaster saw her face at the bollarded frontier. I must reconcile myself to the inevitability of the missing bits. (71)

As in the case of India in *Midnight's Children*, the narrator poses "a slight angle to reality" in the creation of Pakistan in his mind and makes it exist "off-center" (24). Through the shifting of perspectives and language, he is "only telling a sort of modern fairy tale" (72).

Rushdie's narrative mode in the book is deconstructive in many ways. For example, he, as mentioned in the previous chapter, demythifies the creation myth of Pakistan through symbolic aspects in the lives of two women, Bilquis and her daughter Sufiya. Bilquis stands for the forming stage of the nation; Sufiya, the aftermath of its creation. The narrator also demythifies the Land of the Pure through Raza Hyder and Iskander Harappa's corrupted and dark political schemes. He skillfully and cynically reveals unspoken and hidden truth in modern Pakistani history, which makes this novel a kind of political satire.

Other distinctive post-modern aspects in Rushdie's narratives can be found in his treatment of tragic elements, such as revenge, death, love and fall of the privileged, etc. Even if death can be an element of tragedy, for example, too many killings and destructions without evoking a sense of justice or empathy can hardly be transcended to a level of ultimate aesthetics of tragedy. Whenever faced with death in the story, readers cannot feel any catharsis because there are so many meaningless deaths. No death carries a profound meaning. Instead, death reduces human life into a thing stripped of human dignity. Thus, the novel becomes an anti-tragedy or a parody of tragedy. For instance, the scene of Naveed's death does not evoke a sense of tragedy. The scene is rather disgusting and ridiculed as a scatology:

> There was jasmine in her hair and she had filled the room with the fragrance of Joy

by Jean Patou, the most expensive perfume in the world, imported from France to cover up the smell of her bowels opening in death. A suicide note had been attached to the obscene globularity of her midriff by a baby's safety-pin. It referred to her terror of the arithmetical progression of babies marching out of her womb. (251)

The description of the three mothers' killing of Raza Hyder illustrates how the narrator deliberately depicts the moment of death without any human emotion. Its effect seems to enhance the feeling of horror. The three mothers' cruelty explodes the conventional image of benign mother.

"We asked for these arrangements," Munnee Shakil said as the three sisters each placed a hand upon one of the levers, "thinking self-defence is no offence. But also, you must agree, revenge is sweet." The image of Sindbad Mengal flashed into Raza's mind as the three sisters pulled down the lever, acting in perfect unison, so that it was impossible to say who pulled first or hardest, ad the ancient spring-releases of Yakoob Balloch worked like treat, the secret panels sprang back and the eighteen-inch stiletto blades of death drove into Raza's body, cutting him pieces, their reddened points emerging, among other places, through his eyeballs, adam's-apple, navel, groin and mouth. His tongue, severed cleanly by a laterally spearing knife, fell out on to his lap. He made strange clicking noises; shivered; froze. (312)

Besides this kind of graphic description of death, numerous killings are too common to evoke any human emotion. The political duels between Raza and Isky are the main causes of such killings. Literally they get rid of anybody who interferes with their political game. This "shameless" act repeats itself, when the beast of shame, the transformed Sufiya Zinobia, gets loose and reenacts such killings.

The killings continued: farmers, pie-dogs, goats. The murders formed a death-ring round the house; they had reached the outskirts of the two cities, new capital and old town. Murders without rhyme or reason, done, it seemed, for the love of killing, or to satisfy some hideous need. (287)

Somehow, Rushdie ridicules the artificially glorified surface of Pakistani politics with many meaningless deaths, which paradoxically enhances a sense of injustice. The dehumanization of Pakistan's people is so severe that instead of accusing their politics directly, Rushdie rather indirectly reflects this sense into his narratives. The horror of dehumanization can be felt through insensitivity in narration toward human emotions. This makes the novel an anti-tragedy.

The narrator employs cynicism accompanied with foul language, symbolic metaphors and personal narratives like soliloquies or asides. In

Shame, however, there is not much sense of urgency in the narrator's voice unlike Saleem's narratives in *Midnight's Children*. It seems the author resolved how to formulate his ideas beforehand. The narrator of *Shame* does not suffer from self-doubt and suspicion. He says that he deliberately avoids realism because "realism can break a writer's heart" (71). Saleem in *Midnight's Children* depends on realism more than the "I" of *Shame*. Yet he knows the limits of realistic depiction through the failures of other realists. However, the "I" in *Shame* has other things on his mind than just the limits of realistic story-telling. He is more concerned with the messages of the novel. The improbability and limitation relying solely on realism in writing a historical and political novel are one reason to avoid such an undertaking; the censorship and protest from the countries realistically depicted in a political satire would be another reason. Thus, instead of applying various narrative devices to achieve equilibrium as in Saleem's rather realistic discourse, the "I" in *Shame* more heavily depends on fantasy for developing the plot and on narrative intervention for cementing the fantastic elements with the reality.

As for the use of English and Indian languages, Rushdie uses an approach similar to that of *Midnight's Children*. By writing Indian words side by side with English, he enriches and expands the text beyond the cultural boundaries of the English novel. It seems he consciously uses Indian words with the aim of "decolonizing" Indo-British English from the past. He mentions this aspect in his article, which appeared in *The Times* about Desani's English:

> Desani's triumph was to take *babu*-English, *chamcha*-English, and turn it against itself: the instrument of subservience became a weapon of liberation. It was the first great stroke of the decolonizing pen.[21]

Rushdie is well aware of the historicity of the language, which he calls "this peculiar language tainted by wrong concepts and the accumulated detritus of its owners' unrepented past, this Angrezi in which I am forced to write, and so for ever alter what is written . . ." (34).

The shifting nature of language is well symbolized by Sufiya's "favorite secret game." Through Sufiya's symbolic behavior of moving the furniture around, Rushdie justifies his employment of allegorical fantasy in recapturing the gloomy and dark side of reality. As Sufiya's rearrangement of the furniture does not change the substance but only the order of things and the overall look of the space, Rushdie shifts his materials through fantasy and metaphors: "God knows what you'll change with all this shifting shifting" (73).

The narrator as a psudo-author justifies his method of writing in this way, since he thinks realism hurts everybody and harbors the danger in the existence of the work. The shifting of truth does not fundamentally change anything. It merely disguises. After all, language is arbitrary and constantly shifting its relationship with the referent or the truth.

Through *Shame*, Rushdie ridicules Third World politics and the struggle of these developing countries to put their worlds in the center of global attention. Omar Khayyam's vertigo is the vertigo felt by the third world and his unstable and insatiable lust is their appetite and hunger for power. Every nation or every individual contains a sense of the marginality or insecurity expressed in Omar's vertigo or dizziness. However, that kind of vertigo or marginality can be a serious problem when it lacks autonomy. Omar Khayyam suffers from a sense of marginality because he lacks autonomy. To overcome this feeling, he denies his past, associates with powerful men such as Raza and Iskander, and marries a daughter of the powerful without considering its shameful outcome.

> Human beings have a remarkable talent for persuading themselves of the authenticity and nobility of aspects of themselves, which are in fact expedient, spurious, base. (218)

Like Omar, newly formed nations like Pakistan also lack essential autonomy. In order to hide or overcome its lack of identity, the society becomes repressive and breeds shame under a surface of order and false civility.

A more serious problem occurs when people refuse to see the reality or the truth of shame. Shame manifests itself in violence when people ignore its existence, as Sufiya Zinobia commits violent acts and turns into a beast. All the people around her refuse to see the truth, her hot blush or hidden shame. Rushdie criticizes this kind of passive attitude in dealing with "shame" in society by explaining, "humanity is more willfully blind than any flightless bird" (218). Shame, the origin of violence, dwells within civility, disguised in many forms.

> I [the narrator] repeat: there is no place for monsters in civilized society. If such creatures roam the earth, they do so out on its uttermost rim, consigned to peripheries by conventions of disbelief . . . but once in a blue moon something goes wrong. A

Beast is born, a "wrong miracle," within the citadel of propriety and decorum. This was the danger of Sufiya Zinobia: that she came to pass, not in any wilderness of basilisks and fiends, but in the heart of the respectable world. And as a result that world made a huge effort of the will to ignore the reality of her, to avoid bringing matters to the point at which she, disorder's avatar, would have to be dealt with, expelled—because her expulsion would have laid bare what-must-on-no-account-be-know, namely the impossible verity that barbarism could grow in cultured soil, that savagery could lie concealed beneath decency's well-pressed shirt. That she was, as her mother had said, the incarnation of their shame. (219)

Barbarism and savagery exist just beneath civility. The hidden shame turns into the beast of metamorphosed Sufiya and causes the eruption of violence. Nevertheless the people suffering from the vertigo of marginality or the nations eager to be called civilized do not want to acknowledge their shame. So the more powerful the beast of shame becomes, the greater are the efforts to deny its very being (220).

The denial of shame in a society creates cultural, sexual, political repressions "like a seamless garment" and traps its people in an inescapable web, until the repressed shame explodes. In the end, it all blows up and destroys everyone. "The power of the Beast of shame cannot be held for long within any one frame of flesh and blood, because grows, it feeds and swells, until the vessel bursts" (317). Both the existence of shame and the denial of its existence are responsible for this apocalyptic explosion. As for the world of *Shame*, the Rushdian vision is dark and pessimistic.

Apocalyptic Visions

Both *Midnight's Children* and *Shame* end with an explosion or imminent explosion. But *The Satanic Verses* starts with the explosion of an Air India jumbo jet. The explosion is the beginning of a "Fall." Like the Bible, *The Satanic Verses* begins with a fall of two characters: Gibreel Farishta and Saladin Chamcha. As is always the case that Rushdie's characters resemble gods/goddesses of Hinduism, real political figures, prophets in Christianity and Islam, each of the two characters resembles the archangel and the devil in Islam, popular actors of Indian film industry and partly the author himself in some ways.

Salman Rushdie suggested, in an interview with *India Today* after the publication of *The Satanic Verses*, that he somehow consider the work as a part of trilogy along with the two previous novels, *Midnight's Children* and

Shame. To the question on when he began the book, Rushdie answered "parts of the novel have been in my head since I first began to study Islamic history at the university 20 years ago."[22] As a writer from a Muslim family, it seems quite natural for Rushdie to use Islam in his literary creation as a means to express his view on religious fanaticism because the religion is what he knows most. He explained in the same interview that the nature of religious experience and the political implications of religious extremism were applicable to any religion.

Despite the author's defense on his use of Islamic background, the worldwide Islamic furor aroused by *The Satanic Verses* by no means is ready to "forgive" the author more than many years after the publication of the book. Salman Rushdie is still in hiding as the result of the late Ayatollah Khomeini's *fatwa*. Many doubted that it would ever be rescinded because of the late Imam's death. During the course of many years' "satanic" affair between the author and Islamic world, the involved two parties tried to send signals and gestures for the reconciliation and now the author is saved.

When I first read the book in the midst of the "Satanic Affair," I obviously felt that many elements of the book could be regarded as blasphemy, when one reads it only as a religious allegory or satire. Yet, I rather closely follow the theme of migration and displacement.

If one only looks at the theme of migration and displacement in modern society, both of Rushdie's previous novels, *Midnight's Children* and *Shame*, lack certain emotional strength and sincerity from the author's heart. In a way, *The Satanic Verses* complements such an emotional indifference by providing a certain quality of autobiographical reconciliation with his Indian past and tradition.

Saladin Chamcha's displacement is Rushdie's own, the former's experiences in England represent the latter's. Chamcha resembles the author in many ways. Like the author, Chamcha is an anglophile who has tried so hard to be an Englishman, more "English" than English. He has denounced his Indian past and has carefully built his new identity in new soil. Yet the fall destroys and uproots his rather successful life in London. Chamcha is transformed into a satanic creature, half goat and half man with terrible odor and an enormously enlarged phallus. Chamcha eventually grows out of his closed self and embraces his Indian past and reconciles with his father even if after his death. In a way, the book ironically ends on an optimistic note. He experiences his rebirth through emotional catharsis and ponders what his Indian past means to him.

As for religious elements in the book, I look at them as sorts of allegories for various difficulties in life of choosing or distinguishing between the angel (the good) and the devil (the bad). The two protagonists in the novel, Gibreel Farishta and Saladin Chamcha, are drawn to present such a difficulty. Despite his archangelic name and a halo around his head, Gibreel does not resemble exactly the angel in his characteristics. And Saladin, after his horrible metamorphosis to a devilish creature, does not incarnate absolute evil. Instead his plight suggests that of immigrants. Each of the characters has both the good and the bad. The religious theme in the novel, however, has gotten most attention from the world. Gibreel's transformation as the archangel after the "fall" and his love affair with Allie Cone—the climber of Everest—carry the explosive religious theme. Some scenes in one of Gibreel's dream have offended Muslim readers, since the characters name and allusions are drawn from Islamic history.

The narrative complexity in *The Satanic Verses*, where reality is mixed with dreams and fantasies, makes the novel difficult to read and its various thematic layers difficult to follow. The two characters' picaresque and confusing (to the characters themselves and to readers alike) adventures are mixed with dreamy and phantasmagoric sequences in the complex web of plots and themes. Many critics note that Rushdie's characters are not well developed and rounded but flat and two-dimensional. As Malise Ruthven writes in *A Satanic Affair: Salman Rushdie and the Rage of Islam*, however, it is themes rather than characters that hold *The Satanic Verses* together.[23] Often Rushdie's characterization lacks empathy so that his characters seem too cynical and too offensive to get readers' sympathy. Such lack of empathy may seem intentional on the author's part to create a magical realism and to strengthen his thematic concerns.

Malise Ruthven's *A Satanic Affair* informs the original story of the Satanic Verses and its controversies among Islamic commentators, and how Rushdie might have used his historical/fictional knowledge of them in his *The Satanic Verses*.[24] Ruthven acknowledges that Rushdie has transgressed the danger zone, and yet manages to remain sympathetic to Rushdie. About the structure of *The Satanic Verses*, Ruthven cites Timothy Brennan and states:

> The structure is as complex, and as confusing to many readers, as that of the Qur'an itself: indeed, *The Satanic Verses*, like its predecessor *Shame*, seems in ways to mirror the Muslim scripture. Like *The Thousand and One Nights*, it is a kind of 'anti-Qur'an'

which challenges the original by substituting for the latter's absolutist certainties a theology of doubt.[25]

Craig R. Whitney's article in *The New York Times*, of February 5, 1990, reports Rushdie's reaction to the "furor" of Muslim community:

> Mr. Rushdie, an immigrant to Britain from a Muslim family in Bombay, said he had not believed in any god since he was a young adolescent, was not a Muslim and therefore did not accept the charge that the novel was blasphemy or apostasy.
> Sequences in the book that described dreams of one of its characters, Gibreel Farishta—Gabriel Angel in translation—were not intended to vilify Islam, he wrote, but "to show how the loss of God can destroy a man's life."[26]

It seems a bitter irony that Rushdie, having been a victim of his own loss of faith in Islam, justified the novel as a way to "show how the loss of God can destroy a man's life" through his fictional characters.

On Christmas Eve of 1990, Rushdie tried to "mend his rift with Islam" by embracing the religion as a believer. He finally filled the "God-shaped hole" in his heart with Islam. Rushdie's public announcement of his conversion to Islam is a courageous act by an individual who has been sentenced to death by a leader of the religion. Rushdie states in his article, "Now I Can Say, I Am a Muslim," published in *The New York Times*:

> A man's spiritual choices are a matter of conscience, arrived at after deep reflection and in the privacy of his heart. They are not easy matters to speak of publicity. I should like, however, to say something about my decision to affirm the two central tenets of Islam—the oneness of God and the genuineness of the prophecy of the Prophet Muhammad—and thus to enter into the body of Islam after a lifetime spent outside it . . . In the past I described the furor over "The Satanic Verses" as a family quarrel. Well, I'm now inside the family, and now Muslims can talk to Muslims and continue the process of reconciliation that began with my Christmas Eve meeting with six Muslim scholars.[27]

It is a sad and forceful irony that Rushdie filled his lifetime "God-shaped hole" under the effects of *fatwa*. Regarding religious doubts displayed in Gibreel's dreams, he makes clear in the same article that he did not mean to insult Islam:

> For over two years I have tried to explain that "The Satanic Verses" was never intended as an insult; that the story of Gibreel is a parable of how a man can be destroyed by loss of faith; that the dreams in which all the so-called "insults" occur are portraits of his disintegration, and explicitly referred to in the novel as

punishments and retributions; that the dream figures who torment him with assaults on religion are representative of this process of ruination, and *not* representative of the point of view of the author. This is not a disavowal of my work, but the simple truth; to my great pleasure, it was accepted as such.[28]

However, a hard-line newspaper in Teheran, Iran, rejected Rushdie's such an attempt to belong to "the family."[29] The saddest part of the "Satanic Affair," is that the author is still hiding. The "Satanic" chapter in Rushdie's life seems yet unfinished. He has been sent into exile, to nowhere. Even Said's thoughtful essay, "The Mind of Winter: Reflections on Life in Exile," would not be enough to describe Rushdie's mind under such circumstances.

As noted earlier, one of the themes in *The Satanic Verses* is migration and/or displacement in modern society. The depictions of immigrant community in London illustrate how immigrants try to put down roots in an alien soil. The theme is also dealt in *Midnight's Children* and *Shame*. In *Midnight's Children*, the migration of Saleem's family from Kashmiri to Bombay and subsequently to Pakistan has its own consequences and has something to do with the modern history of India and Pakistan. In *Shame*, the narrator relates the subject of migration with more philosophical postulations and makes an analogy with the artist's creative process.

In a larger frame, Rushdie equates the subject such as migration, displacement, an "angle-poised" perspective, or "trans-lation" with the "translation" of his "Indianness" into "westness." His artistic ingenuity furthermore interweaves pure literary concepts and sociopolitical realities together, and creates something new. He creates a wide range of metaphors drawn from Hindu mythology, Islam and Christian religious traditions, contemporary political figures and situations, icons of popular cultures such as film stars, and actual events. The combination of Rushdie's erudition and artistic ingenuity in fiction provides readers with endless joy or it can make it very cumbersome for the reader to decode meanings in his texts. The power of Rushdian visions lies in his successful fusion of the concrete and the abstract, of reality and myth, of history and the present.

Chapter Five

Conclusion

After World War II, colonial discourse evolved into postcolonial discourse. Former colonies reclaimed their independent identity politically and culturally. Authors from Third World want their own voices to be heard. When read in the West, their works have created passages *to the west*, turning around the direction of the previous passages *from the west*. A *Passage to India* today might well become *A Passage from India*. With the decline of imperialism, the processes of unmasking the imperialist myth and of uncovering the falsity of that conception also take place through the analysis of colonial discourse. The fact that the West always has been the voice of the powerful, the oppressor, merely reflects the hegemonic nature of colonial discourse. Such a tendency is still the same in postcolonial era. The rise of neocolonialism and its strong economic structures continues the western or ex-colonial dominance over the world. Third World Countries are still struggling under the grip of neocolonialism, despite the fact that they have built their own national identities apart from the orbit of ex-colonial powers.

In western discourse, the colonized exists merely as a constructed object. By reading and studying works by the colonized, therefore, one can finally appreciate some of the ramifications of the colonial experience. There have been enough in-depth studies done from the colonizer's perspectives and too few, relatively speaking, from perspective of the colonized. It is time to change perspectives and direction in listening. Postcolonial studies devoted to the Other's voice, which could be literature, art, music and/or culture in general, also demythify "the Myth of the Other."[1]

A newly formed political identity of ex-colonies contributes to the formation of cultural pride through the process of rediscovering their past with dignity and confidence. Whether their voice is a cry of desperation and disillusionment or a yearning for hope, it is their own, not the projected. As if to reflect those cultural emergence, during 1980s many non-western writers western writers were among the recipients of the Nobel Prize in literature: first it went to Gabriel Garcia Marquez in 1982, later, to Wole Soynka for African literature in 1986, and to Naguib Mahfuz, an Egyptian writer, for capturing Arab experiences in 1988.

In general, non-western novels in the twentieth reflect struggles to comprehend their historical contextual reality as they face the West. Among non-western countries, the reception of the West differs from each other by the nature of their colonial experiences. Countries like Japan and China facing the western expansion, for example, reacted differently. However, colonized countries were forced to be inferiors. And new ways of life were imposed upon them. The invasion by foreign powers and their continued dominance deprived the native's autonomy to choose their path in life. Such conditions meant not only constant devaluation of their native cultures but also demoralization and dehumanization of the colonized. Thus the colonized suffered from a newly created inferiority complex and, at the same time, they had to face new imposed conflicts such as native versus foreign, self versus other, tradition versus modernity, new versus old. These contrasts reflect the split of the formerly intact whole; they reflect cultural schizophrenia. Again, the saddest part was that they were deprived of autonomy or freedom both/either political and/or cultural.

Despite such harsh colonial conditions, each of the three writers dealt in this study shows a remarkable clear sense of self identity in response to colonizer's discourse. Each of the three authors—Yŏm, Achebe and Rushdie — captures the colonial experience as a universal human experience of Imperialism; in doing so, each transcends those cultural, regional and temporal differences which suggest that this colonial experience is unique.

The Korean novelist Yŏm Sang-sŏp recreates middle class life under the Japanese occupation through a realistic description of both social and individual circumstances, unlike other contemporary Korean authors. Even though he didn't write about the stark reality of suffering, his works stretch to hold all aspects of life under the oppression by keeping a certain objective narrative distance. Though his protagonists are alienated intellectuals, the narrative voice of his works conveys a strong sense of national identity. Yet his depiction of the Japanese is somewhat negative and ambivalent—it is not a kind of direct attack on the Other but a restrained condemnation, since the times in which he lived imposed a severe and strict censorship on every form of writing and publication.

Yŏm's works also reflect the distinctiveness of Korean colonial experiences in comparison with those reflected in Achebe and Rushdie. The fact that Yŏm wrote his works during the colonial period makes quite a difference in terms of the rhetorical tone in his narratives and his employment of metaphors. They bring readers the immediacy of his colonial reality in fiction. However, the unpredictability of Korea's future to Yŏm and his contemporaries affects his approach to colonialism and Japan's presence in Korea. Instead of giving us a direct expression of his nationalistic or patriotic sentiment in narrative discourse, Yŏm created hidden structures in the plot showing an ambivalent attitude toward Japan. When compared to the original version published in 1923, for example, the 1948 edition of *Mansejŏn* contains much stronger and more explicit expressions of nationalistic sentiment. Works written in the later phases of colonialism or in the postcolonial era (here we find Achebe and Rushdie) are even more strongly critical of colonialism. Achebe and Rushdie have a certain freedom to be more critical than Yŏm does.

In terms of colonial experiences, those of Korea are not as diverse as those of Africa and India. Of these countries, Africa was the one considered in the most monolithic terms. Africa was, for long time, a vast blank slate to the West. Thus the tradition of western discourse on Africa perpetuated Africa as a backward, primitive, savage land as the Other's other. This kind of negative Conradian African discourse sets Africa apart from the so-called civilized world.

Even though Chinua Achebe writes in English, the colonizer's language, he creates a new type of African discourse by filling his literary works with the African spirit, traditional dignity and oral heritage. He presents to the world "true" images of Africa with an alien language, English. Africa has its own civilization and cultural heritage and tradition, has preserved its glory and even its own weakness in the face of other civilizations.

Achebe's *Things Fall Apart* and *Arrow of God* show the African past and its spirit in all its might and even imperfections and vulnerability. Okonkwo in *Things Fall Apart* embodies Igbo masculinity, just as Ezeulu in *Arrow of God* embodies Igbo spirituality. Both novels are tragic in the sense that the protagonists' downfall symbolizes the disintegration of traditional Africa and its spirit as the result of British colonial incursions. *No Longer at Ease* also deals, similarly, with the irrevocable and tragic disintegration of African society and soul. Its protagonist, Obi Okonkwo, a grandson of Okonkwo in *Things Fall Apart*, loses himself in the materialism of the dizzy modern metropolitan city of Lagos. His morality decays as he loses the ties with traditional Igbo values and spirit. Through Obi's downfall, Achebe tells us that Obi's moral decay and spiritual corruption are contemporary problems that modern Africa has to face as a colonial legacy.

Instead of remaining as a symbol of darkness and a projection of the white's fear—the extreme "otherness" of the black African to the West— Achebe presents an African life filled with cultural dignity and complex traditions. He has achieved this through the creation of an African discourse with an anthropological fusion of folklore and proverbs. Achebe's world is the antithesis of Joseph Conrad's, Joyce Cary's and even V. S. Naipaul's.

In Rushdie's world of the Indian subcontinent, an individual's life is strongly tied to the course of history. Through a symbolization of India, Rushdie presents the metaphorical essence of the Indian subcontinent observed with "angle-poised" perspectives. Like Achebe, Rushdie depicts a world with inward perspectives. Rushdie's heavy usage of symbolism both overwhelms and impresses readers.

Rushdie privatizes the history of India through his protagonist, Saleem, in *Midnight's Children*. His narrative devices, as discussed in earlier chapter, create a reciprocal dynamic in the relationship of the mass, the society, or history versus the individual. The individual's absolute subjectivity, individualism, is no longer allowed under the tyranny of the mass and the history, no matter how hard one tries to escape from t. Besides, the almost parodied political situations in Rushdie's both novels reflect Rushdie's concerns for centrality versus marginality.

The analysis of *Shame* focuses on Rushdian notion of "shame." Each of the main characters, Sufiya and Omar, stands for "shame" and "shamelessness." They are rather abstract and allegorical compared to the portrayal of two political figures, Raza Hyder and Iskander Harappa, whose resemblance to real political figures in Pakistan makes this novel a political satire. The distinctiveness of character portrayals leads us to ponder the question of periphery versus centrality in history. The idea is applicable not only to characters and their lives but also to nations like Pakistan and India, which can be expanded to all Third World nations. Omar Khayyam, for instance, represents an extreme marginality of an individual's existence in society and a loss of one's autonomy in relationships. Through his novels, Rushdie also emphasizes displacement or migration as a modern condition. He tries to illuminate such issues in light of their historical consequences.

By bringing out the dignity and complexity of Igbo tradition, Achebe presents a series of antitheses to European colonial discourse in order to combat the devaluation and primitivization of African culture. Yŏm does not have a nostalgic recapitulation of Korean tradition as Achebe does toward Africa in his novels. Instead, Yŏm's narration is naturally filled with sociopolitical signifiers. The jargoned expression like "*juŭija*" is a signifier which exemplifies the suppressive political mood in the society.

Rushdie's reification of the conflict between society and individual is effectively achieved by his use of psycho-somatic metaphors in the two novels. The shape and function of Saleem's nose, social and historical experiences inflicted on Saleem's body in form of mutation, the cracking of his body, for example, are the direct result of Rushdie's artistic employment of linguistic and philosophical concepts. As a result, the Rushdian world is a strange mixture of both reality and fantasy.

As far as colonial discourse is concerned, one of the major distinctions in the three writers can be found in their use of language. Each writer's choice of language reflects and determines the nature of his discourse in relation to colonialism.

Yŏm wrote in Korean, his mother tongue. And thus his writings were primarily meant for his compatriots, an advantage in a real sense, and a disadvantage in that he did not reach western readers. Thus certain elements of Korean literary identity remain unalloyed, closer to the Korean soul because it did not suffer from the mutilation of translation. However, the historical and ontological circumstances within which Yŏm was placed affected his narrative to reflect contemporary Korean colonial reality. Yŏm's narrative voice as an anti-colonial discourse is sometimes weak and ambivalent because in the midst of colonial occupation he was not able to make any historical and political judgment on what he wrote about or how he looked at his immediate reality.

Achebe writes in the language of the former colonizer. Since Nigeria did not have a written literature of its own at the beginning of colonialism, Achebe's choice was motivated both by his desire to preserve his cultural identity and to present dignity in being Igbo or African. He also might have been motivated to synthesize African civilization and the western elements, because he did not write for African audience only. Achebe refused to be a victim of colonial prejudices. Instead of being confined within projected negativity, he bounces back with a sense of aesthetic and cultural equality.

Salman Rushdie shares with Achebe in his choice of language in which to write. Rushdie tells us that he writes for privatization of history, seeing it through broken mirrors. He describes his imaginary self and imaginary lands with their myriad angles and gods, its hells and heavens, for his own understanding of "translated" residents in the West. Yet he is saddened and made restless by his creative visions. As if not to allow his western readers to smile with glee, he shows his western readers how in the garbs of civility there also exist shame and violence on every corner in the cesspool of modern civilizations.

These three authors—Yŏm Sang-sŏp, Chinua Achebe and Salman Rushdie—have a strong sense of history and cultural identity. They speak themselves through their fictions; Yŏm for Korea, Achebe for Nigeria and even for the African continent and Rushdie for the Indian subcontinent. Above all, they re-examine and re-define colonialism either as past experience or as present reality. Their works counter the Kiplingian colonial discourse of Imperialism. And this study in some ways vindicates their literary efforts, acknowledges their literary worth and importance.

Notes

Chapter One

Introduction

1 By the term colonial discourse, I take a position similar to that of Peter Hulme in his *Colonial Encounters: Europe and the Native Caribbean, 1492–1797* (London, 1986). He writes of colonial discourse as "an ensemble of linguistically-based practices unified by their common deployment in the management of colonial relationships" (2). Since my study of colonial discourse is through fiction, it is obvious that I analyze colonial attitudes reflected in language and literature. However, in general, I do not limit its meaning and usage only to "linguistically-based practices." Colonial discourse is shaped by the colonial attitude, which I also often call colonial rhetoric or colonialism as an ideology in my text; one can find its tropes in many other fields of study such as art (painting) or cartography. For example, one's psychological distance to a certain place or people or extent of one's knowledge about them can be reflected in one's painting or in contemporary maps. Looking at a map of African continent, Marlow in *Heart of Darkness* by Joseph Conrad is fascinated by the "unknown" area. The map of Africa is the psychological map of Europe's relation to Africa. Before Europe had an accurate and scientific knowledge of the world's geography, it had a false one somehow reflecting its subjective relations to the other parts of the world. This can be noted by looking at European world maps in the fifteenth and sixteenth centuries. The same holds true for Chinese and Korean; for example, Europe's view of China or Korea can be felt by looking at contemporary map and vice versa.

2 Christopher L. Miller, *Blank Darkness: Africanist Discourse in French* (Chicago: The University of Chicago Press, 1985) 23.

3 Joseph Conrad, *Heart of Darkness*, ed. Robert Kimbrough, 3rd. ed. (New York: Norton, 1988) 10.

4 Frantz Fanon, *Black Skin, White Masks*, trans. Charles Lam Markmann (New York: Grove Press Inc., 1967) 100.

5 Henry Louis Gates, Jr. ed., *"Race," Writing, and Difference* (The University of Chicago Press, 1985) 5.

6 Ngugi wa Thiong'o, *Homecoming* (New York: Lawrence Hill and Co., 1973) 145–50.

7 Salman Rushdie, "The Empire Writes Back with a Vengeance," *The Times* 3 July 1982: 8.

8 Bill Ashcroft, Gareth Griffiths and Helen Tiffin, *The Empire Writes Back: Theory and*

Practice in Post-Colonial Literatures (London: Routledge, 1989) 53.

9 Kim Tong-in, "Mundan Samsimnyŏnsa (A Thirty-Year History of Literary World)," *Tong-in Chŏnjip (Complete Collection of Kim Tong-in's Works)*, vol. 8 (Seoul: Honghak Ch'ulp'ansa, 1964) 476.

10 Paek Nak-ch'ŏng, "Sinsingminji Sidae wa Sŏyang Munhak Ilkki (Neocolonial Era and Readings in Western Literatures)," *Hanguk Minjok Minjung Undong Yŏn'gu (A Study of Korean People's Movement)*, eds. Paek Nak-ch'ŏng and Chŏng Ch'ang-ryŏl (Seoul: Ture, 1989) 352.

11 Henry Louis Gates, Jr., *Figures in Black: Words, Signs, and the "Racial" Self* (Oxford University Press, 1987) xv-xxii.

12 Charles R. Larson, *The Emergence of African Fiction* (Bloomington: Indiana University Press, 1972) 28.

13 Timothy Brennan, *Salman Rushdie and the Third World: Myths of the Nation* (New York: St. Martin Press, 1989) x.

14 Salman Rushdie, interview, "My Theme is Fanaticism," *India Today* 15 Sept. 1988, 98–99.

Chapter Two

Yŏm Sang-sŏp and Colonial Reality

1 The first issue of the magazine was dated July 25, 1920. After its second issue published six months after the previous one (January 1921), the coterie were not able to continue the magazine because of their financial trouble. A year later they published *After P'yehŏ* as an attempt to continue their coterie magazine, however, they were not successful. Yŏm Sang-sŏp wrote about his involvement in *P'yehŏ* and about other members in several essays: "Na wa P'yehŏ Sidae (Me and P'yehŏ era)," (*Sinch'ŏnji* 1954: 2); "P'yehŏ" (*Sasangkye* 1960: 1); "Hoengbo Mundan Hoesanggi (Hoengbo's Recollection of Literary Movements)," (*Sasanggye* 1962: 11–12), all reprinted in *Yŏm Sang-sŏp Chŏnjip* (Seoul: Minŭmsa, 1987), vol. 12.

2 For the text discussed here, I used *Yŏm Sang-sŏp Chŏnjip* (Seoul: Minŭmsa, 1987) 12 vols., the whole collection of Yŏm's works. Henceforth this collection shall be abbreviated as *YSC*.

3 Suh Du-su. *Korean Literary Reader* (Seoul: Dong-A Publishing Co., 1965) 34. The quote from the text is in Korean. Its English translation is mine.

4 For further details on this subject written in English, see Frank P. Baldwin, "The March First Movement: Korean Challenge and Japanese Response," diss., Columbia University, 1969.

5 Yŏm Mu-ung, "Kŭndae Sosŏl kwa Minjok Ŭisik (Modern Fiction and Nationalistic Awareness)," *Ilche Sidae ŭi Hang'il Munhak (Anti-Japanese Literature during the Japanese Occupation)*, (Seoul: Sin'gu Munwhasa, 1976), 179–80. Unless otherwise stated, all translations from Korean texts are mine.

6 Yŏm Mu-ung 180.

7 Kim Yun-sik, *Yŏm Sang-sŏp Yŏn'gu* (Seoul: Seoul University Press, 1987) 53–54.

8 Kim Yun-sik 33.

9 It is a "New Novel," a popular form of fiction in late nineteenth and early twentieth century Korea. Yi In-jik's *Hyŏl ŭi Nu (Bloody Tears)* in 1906 was the first of its kind.

10 The *sijo* is a fixed form of Korean poetry. It is a three-line poem, each consisting of four rhythmic phrases. The basic standard syllable counts are: First line; 3-4-3(4)-4, Second line; 3-4-3(4)-4, Third line; 3-5-4-3. The sijo form, however, is very elastic. There are many variations, except for the first 3 syllables in the last line.

11 The *waka* is a fixed form of Japanese poetry. The term *waka* (Japanese poem) is a synonym of *tanka* (short poem). The *tanka* consists of five phrases of lines of 5-7-5-7-7, 31 syllables respectively. *Haiku* is the shortest type in Japanese poetry, and consists of three lines or phrases, 5-7-5, all just 17 syllables.

12 Yŏm Sang-sŏp, "Munhak Sonyŏn Sidae ŭi Hoesang" *YSC* 12: 215.

13 Yŏm Sang-sŏp 215.

14 Edward Fowler, *The Rhetoric of Confession* (Berkeley: University of California Press, 1988) 193.

15 Kim Tong-in accused Yŏm of unjustly criticizing Kim Whan's personality in the criticism on Kin Whan's work, who was a member of the Ch'angjo Circle. Even though Kim Tong-in himself did not like Kim Whan's work, Kim Tong-in took the side of Kim Whan and criticized Yŏm's writing and stand as a critic. The main reason behind Kin Tong-in's accusation of Yŏm was not that Yŏm was wrong but that he belonged to the P'yehŏ. Kim Tong-in might have felt hurt and offended when he read Yŏm's criticism on a work done by a Ch'angjo member, and he meant to defend his group.

16 *YSC* 12:14.

17 Kim Tong-in, "Ch'angjo wa P'yehŏ," *Tong-in Chŏnjip*, vol. 8 (Seoul: Honghak Ch'ulp'ansa, 1964) 398.

18 Kim Tong-in, "Yŏm Sang-sŏp" in *Tong-in Chŏnjip*, 8:415.

19 Kim Yong-jik, "Ilje Sidae ŭi Hang'il Siga" in *Han'guk Munhak kwa Minjok Ŭisik* 34.

20 Kim Tong-in, "Manggugin Ki (Record of the People of the Lost Nation)" *Tong-in Chŏnjip*, 10:71–74. "Tong'inji ŭi Palgan (Publication of the Coterie Magazine)" *Tong-in Chŏnjip*, 8: 382-84.

21 Kim Yun-sik, *Yŏm Sang-sŏp Yŏn'gu* 164.

22 For the family background of Yŏm and the biographical approach to Yŏm's works, see both Kim Chong-kyun's *Yŏm Sang-sŏp ŭi Saeng'ae wa Munhak* (Seoul: Pagyŏngsa, 1981) and Kim Yun-sik's *Yŏm Sang-sŏp Yŏn'gu*.

23 Yŏm wrote in his essay, "Hoengbo Mundan Hoesang'gi," that he had her permission beforehand to take her as his literary model. *YSC* 12: 230.

24 In the interpretation of Yŏm's works in his *Yŏm Sang-sŏp Yŏn'gu*, Kim Yun-sik relates Yŏm's personal experiences very strongly and it makes Yŏm's early works highly autobiographical.

25 For the explanation of this sudden achievement by Yŏm, Kim Yun-sik turns to contemporary Japanese literature. Kim attributes Yŏm's new narratives to Japanese authors, such as Arishima Takeo and Shiga Naoya. According to Kim, Yŏm's new narratives are the exact translation of Japanese Taisho literature at that time. It seems, however, that Kim does not acknowledge much of Yŏm's originality in creating his own unique literary world. Instead Kim's interpretation of Yŏm's works relies too much upon the Japanese elements. The pitfall in Kim's argument on Yŏm is his overemphasis on the Japanese influence in Yŏm's life. Kim states that Yŏm would have not been able to create such good work without the contemporary Japanese literature (Kim Yun-sik, *Yŏm Sang-sŏp Yŏn'gu* 94–95). I agree that Yŏm owed much to the Japanese literature for his literary education. But he did not merely mimic the Japanese as Kim indicates; instead he reached beyond and created his own unique literary world. If Kim's logic is right, why didn't the other Korean writers, Yŏm's contemporaries, who were also familiar with the Japanese and Western literatures, take the same literary path as Yŏm did? Instead of emphasizing Yŏm's influence by Japanese authors and works, I would like to focus on Yŏm's personal sincerity and uniqueness in his attitude toward the literature and himself and in treatment of the reality into his works. At the same time, the background information about the Japanese literature has to be kept in mind as a partial condition for the great advance in modern Korean literature achieved through Yŏm's works.

26 Actually X goes to Nampo. Kim Yun-sik claims that this story is a record about Yŏm's actual and emotional journey right before he became a teacher at the Osan School in Chŏngju, where his famous brother was the vice principal at that time. Kim Yun-sik, *Yŏm Sang-sŏp Yŏn'gu* 133.

27 Kim Yun-sik, *Yŏm Sang-sŏp Yŏn'gu* 168–69.

28 Kim Yun-sik, *Yŏm Sang-sŏp Yŏn'gu* 166–67.

29 Here I quote the important dialogues between Helmer and Nora in the Act III:

Helmer: Your duties towards your husband, and your children.
Nora : I have another duty which is equally sacred.
Helmer: You have not. What on earth could that be?
Nora : My duty toward myself.
Helmer: First and foremost you are a wife and a mother.
Nora : I don't believe that any longer. I believe that I am first and foremost a human being, like you — or any way, I must try to become one.

As in china and Japan at the time, the play was widely read by many intellectuals in Korea. Yŏm mentioned the work in many of his early essays. It is obvious that *A Doll's House* influenced him a great deal in his intellectual growth. Compared to Kim Tong-in, Yŏm showed more empathy toward women's issues. The first Korean translation of Ibsen's *A Doll's House*, entitled as *Nora*, was done by Yang Paek-wha published in June, 1922. Kim Pyŏng-chŏl, *Han'guk Kŭndae Pŏnyŏkmunhaksa Yŏn'gu* (Seoul: Ulyumunwhasa, 1975) 950.

It is possible, however, that Yŏm might have already read a Japanese edition of the translated play and been influenced by it, not by the Korean edition.

30 The *yobo* was a derogatory term referring Koreans, and was used by the Japanese during the colonial period. It seems the word was derived from the Korean word, "Yŏboseyo" (means "Hello"). The *yobo* is no longer used either in Japanese or in Korean.

31 Ryusaku Tsunoda et al., compiled, *Sources of Japanese Tradition*, vol. II (New York: Columbia University Press, 1964) 147–55.

32 Kang Tong-jin, *Ilche ŭi Han'guk Ch'imnyak Chŏngchaek Sa* (*History of Japanese Imperial Policies in Invading Korea*) (Seoul: Han'gilsa, 1980). This book is very useful to know Japanese colonial policies especially after the March First Movement. The author's careful study of all the Japanese documents and newspapers at that time shows Japanese prudence and calculation in dealing with Koreans. Despite all of their efforts to rule Korea efficiently, they had faced with a lot of difficulties and strong reactions from Korean.

33 Frank P. Baldwin, *The March First Movement* 167.

34 Kim Yun-sik, *Yŏm Sang-sŏp Yŏn'gu* 30, 63–64.

35 *Han'guk Munhak Chŏnjip*, vol. 3 (Seoul: Minjungsŏgwan, 1959) 488.

36 Yŏm Sang-sŏp wrote a sequel to *Samdae* in 1931 to 1932, serialized in *Maeil Sinbo* (The Daily Newspaper), which was a government organ. Its title is *Muwhagwa* (*Figs*), which symbolizes the whole of Tŏk-ki's generation in *Samdae*. The author said in his introduction to this noel that this generation was born without the blossom of its flower like figs. Through this work, Yŏm presents the gradual downfall of the middle class headed by a young person like Tŏk-ki. The protagonist, Yi Wŏn-yŏng, inherits fortune from his grandfather. Because of his inexperience in life and the sociopolitical situations under the Japanese Rule Yŏm depicts, Yi's downfall seems inevitable. The irony in these two novels is a contradiction found in the ending. Tŏk-ki in *Samdae* appears so promising in his future, Yi's downfall in its sequel seems surprising. Yet, in some sense, Yŏm's

intention to describe accurate reality is obvious. As a novel, the sequel is not as good as *Samdae*. As the Japanese government tightened its repression during the 1930s, Yŏm's typical political tones were mitigated noticeably because of censorship and the pro-colonial nature of the *Mail Sinbo*.

Chapter Three

Chinua Achebe and the Creation of an African Discourse in English

1 At first Achebe spelled the word as "Ibo," but he changed it to "Igbo" by the time he published his collection of essays, *Morning Yet on Creation Day: Essays*, in 1975. According to Robert M. Wren, this change indicates that the orthography of Igbo words in general has become more precise. Currently, Igbo is widely accepted as the correct spelling. Thus in this book, in order to reduce confusion, I spell the word as Igbo except for quotations from texts, *Things Fall Apart*, *No Longer at Ease* and *Arrow of God*, in which Achebe spelled the word as Ibo. Presumable Ibo was used in the colonial period by the English.

2 Chinua Achebe, "Thoughts on the African Novels," *Morning Yet on Creation Day: Essays* (Garden City, N.Y.: Anchor Press, 1975) 90.

3 Abiola Irele, "The Tragic Conflict in the Novels of Chinua Achebe," in C. L. Innes and Bernth Lindfors eds. *Critical Perspectives on Chinua Achebe* (Washington, D.C.: Three Continents Press, 1978) 11.

4 Austin J. Shelton, ed., *The African Assertion: A Critical Anthology of African Literature* (New York: The Odyssey Press, 1968) 2–3.

5 Chinua Achebe, "Africa and Her Writers (1973)", *Morning Yet on Creation Day: Essays* 29.

6 Martin Tucker, *Africa in Modern Literature: A Survey of Contemporary Writing in English* (New York: Frederick Ungar Publishing Co., 1967) 3.

7 Tucker 3–4.

8 Chinua Achebe, "The African Writer and the English Language (1964)," *Morning Yet on Creation Day: Essays* 92. In this essay, however, the year when the conference was held in Makerere is printed as 1952. It seems to me it is a printing mistake of 1962. There was a conference held at Makerere University College, Uganda, in 1962, titled as "A Conference of African Writers of English Expression."

9 Chinua Achebe, "Thoughts on the African Novel," *Morning Yet on Creation Day: Essays* 83.

10 Chinweizu et al., ed., Toward the Decolonization of African Literature, vol. 1 (Washington, D.C.: Howard University Press, 1983) 14–15.

11 M. Keith Booker, *The African Novel in English: An Introduction* (Portsmouth, NH.: Heinemann, 1998) 29–64.

12 Eldred Jones, "The Decolonization of African Literature" Per Wästberg, ed., *The Writer in Modern Africa* (New York: Africana Publishing Corp., 1969) 71.

13 Lloyd W. Brown, "Cultural Norms and Modes of Perception in Achebe's Fiction," *Critical Perspectives on Chinua Achebe* 23.

14 Eldred Jones, "The Decolonization of African Literature," Per Wästberg, ed., *The Writer in Modern Africa* 71.

15 Jones 73.

16 Obiajunwa Wali, "The Dead End of African Literature?" (*Transition* 3.10: 1963), reprinted in *Ngugi wa Thiong'o: The Making of a Rebel* by Carol Sicherman (London: Hans Zell Publishers, 1990) 31.

17 Chinua Achebe, "The African Writer and the English Language (1964)," *Morning Yet on Creation Day: Essays* 95.

18 Ngugi wa Thiong'o, "Return to the Roots (1979)" in *Writers in Politics* (London: Heinemann, 1981) 57–58.

19 Carol Sicherman, *Ngugi wa Thiong'o: The Making of a Rebel* 29.

20 Ngugi wa Thiong'o, *Decolonising the Mind: The Politics of Language in African Literature* (London: James Currey Ltd., 1986) xii.

21 Chinua Achebe, "Thoughts on the African Novel (1973)," *Morning Yet on Creation Day: Essays* 81–90.

22 Chinua Achebe, "The African Writer and the English Language (1964)," *Morning Yet on Creation Day: Essays* 100.

23 Frantz Fanon, *Black Skin, White Masks* (New York: Grove Press, Inc., 1967) 18.

24 Fanon 32.

25 Wali reprinted in Sicherman 31.

26 Chinweizu, et al., *Toward the Decolonization of African Literature* 13.

27 Chinua Achebe, "Colonialist Criticism (1974)," *Morning Yet on Creation Day: Essays* 13.

28 Eldred Jones, "The Decolonization of African Literature," *The Writer in Modern Africa* 73.

29 Chinua Achebe, "Colonialist Criticism," *Morning Yet on Creation Day: Essays* 13.

30 Ernest Emenyonu, "African Literature: What Does It Take to be Its Critic?" in Eldred Durosimi Jones, ed., *African Literature Today: An Annual Review*, no.5 (New York: African Publishing Corp., 1971) 1–11.

31 Joseph Conrad, *Heart of Darkness*, Robert Kimbrough, ed., A Norton Critical Edition (1988) 11–12; emphasis mine.

32 Conrad 35–36; emphasis mine.

33 This kind of fear of the unknown is not uncommon. E. M. Forster's *A Passage to India* (1924) illustrates the feeling exquisitely through white characters. A young white woman's experience in the Marabar caves is the ultimate. Facing an unfamiliar sight, Miss Quested cannot appreciate and comprehend the surroundings. Having lost her reasoning ability in a western frame of perception dominant with certain rules and forms, she is overwhelmed by the fear of the unknown and experiences hallucinations. The cave expedition makes the white characters face their void in spirituality. After this Indian excursion, Mrs. Moore dies on the way home to England, Miss Quested faces reality and comes to grips with herself. Through the novel, Forster tries to build a bridge between the East and the West with its symbolic title. But he ends the novel pessimistic about the success of such an attempt here and now.

34 Conrad 37; emphasis mine.

35 Numbers in parentheses indicate pages in the same text of *Heart of Darkness*.

36 Conrad 37–38.

37 Chinua Achebe, "An Image of Africa," *Research in African Literature* (vol.9, no. 1, spring 1978) 4, which was reprinted from *The Massachusetts Review* (1977).

38 Achebe, "An Image of Africa" 9.

39 Achebe, "An Image of Africa" 13.

40 Achebe, "An Image of Africa" 13.

41 Wilson Harris, "The Frontier on Which *Heart of Darkness* Stands," *Research in African Literatures* (vol.12, no. 1, spring 1981) 86.

42 Harris 87.

43 Nancy Schmidt, "Nigerian Fiction and the African Oral Tradition," in Joseph Okpaku, ed., *New African Literature and the Arts*, vol. 2 (New York: Thomas Y. Crowell Co., 1968) 26.

Notes 193

44 Chinua Achebe, *Things Fall Apart* (1958; Heinemann; New York: Fawcett Crest, 1969) 10; For further reading of Achebe's use of proverbs in his fictions, Bernth Lindfors's "The Palm-Oil with Which Words are Eaten," is useful and illuminating, which is in *Critical Perspectives on Chinua Achebe* 47–66.

45 The paperback edition by Fawcett Crest Books, which contains the complete text of the original edition of Heinemann, is used: *Things Fall Apart* (New York: Fawcett Crest, 1969). All citations from the text will be indicated in my text with page numbers in parentheses.

46 An *egwugwu* is a masquerader who impersonates one of the ancestral spirits of the village.

47 Donald J. Weinstock, "Achebe's Christ-Figure," *New African Literature and the Arts*, vol. 2 (New York: Thomas Y. Crowell Co., 1968) 56-65.

48 Robert M. Wren, *Achebe's World: The Historical and Cultural Context of the Novels of Chinua Achebe* (Burnt Mill, Essex: Longman, 1980) 13.

49 Wren, *Achebe's World* 14.

50 M. M. Bakhtin, "Epic and Novel," *The Dialogic Imagination: Four Essays*, Caryl Emerson and M. Holquist, tr. (Austin: University of Texas Press, 1981) 15.

51 Lloyd W. Brown, "Cultural Norms and Modes of Perception in Achebe's Fiction," *Critical Perspectives on Chinua Achebe* 25–26.

52 Robert M. Wren, "*Mister Johnson* and the Complexity of *Arrow of God*," *Critical Perspectives on Chinua Achebe* 207.

53 Chinua Achebe, *Arrow of God* (1964; Heinemann; Garden City, N. Y.: Anchor Books, 1969). All citations from the text will be indicated in my text with page numbers in parentheses.

54 Emmanuel Obiechina, "The Human Dimension of History in *Arrow of God*," *Critical Perspectives on Chinua Achebe* 175.

55 M. J. Melamu, "The Quest for Power in Achebe's *Arrow of God*," *English Studies in Africa* 2 (1971):233.

56 A. M. Kemoli, "The Novels of Chinua Achebe: A Prophecy of Violence," *Joliso* 1 (1974): 51

57 M. M. Mahood, "Idols of the Den: Achebe's *Arrow of God*," *Critical Perspectives on Chinua Achebe* 182.

58 Robert M. Wren, *Achebe's World* 38.

59 Chinua Achebe, *No Longer at Ease* (1960; Heinemann; New York: Fawcett Premier Book,

1969).

60 Lloyd Brown, "Cultural Norms and Modes of Perception in Achebe's Fiction," *Critical Perspectives on Chinua Achebe* 26.

Chapter Four

"Pickling" History in Rushdie's Works

1 William Walsh, "India and the Novel." Boris Ford, ed., *The New Pelican Guide to English Literature*. vol. 8 (Penguin Books, 1983) 257.
 William Walsh mistakenly calls the protagonist Saleem Aziz instead of Saleem Sinai.

2 Salman Rushdie, *The Jaguar Smile: A Nicaraguan Journey* (New York: Elisabeth Sifton Books. Viking, 1987).
 When he mentions his keen awareness and involvement in the politics of and about Nicaragua, he also points out his tendency to connect different events together. According to his explaination, his Nicaraguan watch grew from the proximity of his son's birthday and the "Nicaragua Libre," which were exactly one month apart from each other.
 "I've always had a weakness for synchronicity, and I felt that the proximity of the birthdays forged a bond" (12–13).

3 Salman Rushdie, *Shame* (New York: Borzoi, 1983) 23–24.

4 Salman Rushdie, "Imaginary Homelands," *London Review of Books* 4. 18 (1982): 7.

5 Gamini Salgado, "V. S. Naipaul and the Politics of Fiction," *The New Pelican Guide to English Literature* 8: 326.

6 Salman Rushdie, *Midnight's Children* (1980; New York: Alfred A Knopf, Inc.: Bard Printing, 1982) 4.

7 George Orwell, *Burmese Days* (A Harvest/HBJ book, 1934) 17.

8 J. R. Hammond, A George Orwell Companion (London: The Macmillan Press Ltd., 1982) 93.

9 Abdul R. JanMohamed, "The Economy of Manichean Allegory: The Function of Racial Difference in Colonialist Literature," *"Race," Writing, and Difference*, ed. Henry Louis Gates, Jr. (Chicago and London: The U of Chicago Press, 1986) 81.

10 Salman Rushdie, "Imaginary Homelands," *London Review of Books* 4. 18 (1982): 18.

11 Rushdie, "Imaginary Homelands," 18.

Notes

12 Rushtom Bharucha, "Rushdie's Whale," *The Massachusetts Review* (Summer 1986) 223.

13 Bharucha 224.

14 Thakur Guruprasad, "The Secret of Rushdie's Charm," *Three Contemporary Novelists: Khushwant Singh, Chaman Nahal, Salman Rushdie* ed. R. K. Dhawan (New Delhi: Classical Publishing Co., 1986) 191–93.

15 Mario Cuoto, "Midnight's Children and Parents," *Encounter* 58.2 (1982): 61.

16 Cuoto 63.

17 Keith Wilson, "*Midnight's Children* and Reader Responsibility," *Critical Quarterly* 26.3 (1984): 30.

18 Wilson 33.

19 Salman Rushdie, *Shame* (New York: Vintage International, 1983); all further references to the novel will be included in the text, with page numbers in parentheses.

20 M. D. Fletcher wrote that *Shame* is essentially an apologue distinguishing it from satire in his essay, "Rushdie's Shame as Apologue," *The Journal of Commonwealth Literature* 21.1 (1986): 120–32.

21 Salman Rushdie, "The Empire Writes Back with a Vengeance," *The Times* 3 July 1983.

22 Salman Rushdie, interview, "My Theme is Fanaticism," *India Today* 15 Sept. 1988, 98–99.

23 Malise Ruthven, *A Satanic Affair: Salman Rushdie and the Rage of Islam* (London: Chatto & Windus, 1990) 20.

24 Ruthven 37–47.

25 Ruthven 17.

26 Craig R. Whitney, "Rushdie Appeals for Muslim Tolerance of 'Satanic Verses,'" *The New York Times* 5 Feb. 1990: C11.

27 Salman Rushdie, "Now I Can Say, I Am a Muslim," *The New York Times* 28 Dec. 1990.

28 Rushdie, "Now I Can Say, I Am a Muslim." *NYT*.

29 "Iranian Newspaper Rejects Rushdie's Conciliation Effort," *The New York Times* 26 Dec. 1990.

Chapter Five

Conclusion

1 I still have to call the oppressed the Other. I do so not because I identify my perspective to that of the colonizer but because I am trapped in the "prison house of language." For the convenience of communication, I have used the term, the Other, to indicate the colonized or the oppressed.

Bibliography

Theriories, Criticism and Other Related Works

Ahmad, Aijaz. *In Theory: Classes, Nations, Literatures.* New York: Verso, 1992.

Anderson, G. L. ed. *Masterpieces of the Orient.* New York: Norton, 1977.

Arendt, Hannah. *Imperialism: Part Two of The Origins of Totalitarianism.* New York: A Harvest/HBJ Book, 1968.

Ashcroft. Bill, Gareth Griffiths, and Helen Tiffin. *The Empire Writes Back: Theory and Practice in Post-Colonial Literatures.* London: Routledge, 1989.

———. *Key Concepts in Postcolonial Studies.* New York: Routledge, 1998.

———. *The Post-Colonial Studies Reader.* New York: Routeldge, 1995.

Bakhtin, M. M. The *Dialogic Imagination: Four Essays.* Ed. Michael Holquist. Trans. Caryl Emerson and Michael Holquist. Austin: University of Texas Press, 1981.

Barthes, Roland. *S/Z: An Essay.* Trans. Richard Miller. New York: Hill and Wang, 1974.

Bassnett, Susan and Harish Trivedi, eds. *Post-Colonial Translation: Theory and Practice.* Translation Studies Series. London, New York: Routledge, 1999.

Bhabha, Homi. *The Location of Culture.* New York: Routledge, 1994.

———. "The Other Question: Difference, Discrimination and the Discourse of Colonialism" in Baker, Houston and others, eds. *Black British Cultural Studies: A Reader.* Chicago: University of Chicago Press, 1996. 87–106.

Bharucha, Rustom. "Somebody's Other: Disorientations in the Cultural Politics of Our Times," *Third Text* 26 (1995): 3–10

Brantlinger, Patrick. *Rule of Darkness: British Literature and Imperialism, 1930–1914.* Ithaca: Cornell University Press, 1988.

Brinkler-Gabler, Gisela, ed. *Encountering the Other(s): Studies in Literature, History and Culture.* Albany: State University of New York Press, 1995.

Chatman, Seymour. *Story and Discourse: Narrative Structure in Fiction and Film.* Ithaca: Cornell University Press, 1978.

Conrad, Joseph. *Heart of Darkness.* Ed. Robert Kimbrough. 3rd ed. New York: W. W. Norton and Company, 1988.

Darby, Philip. *The Fiction of Imperialism: Readig Between International Relations and Postcolonialism.* London and Washington: Cassell, 1998.

Eagleton, Terry. *Marxism and Literary Criticism.* Berkeley and Los Angeles: University of California Press, 1976.

———. *Criticism and Ideology: A Study in Marxist Literary Theory.* London: Verso Editions,

1976.

———. *Literary Theory: An Introduction*. Minneapolis: University of Minnesota Press, 1983.

———. *The Ideology of the Aesthetic*. Oxford: Basil Blackwell Ltd., 1990.

Eliot, T. S. *The Complete Poems and Plays, 1909–1950*. New York: Harcourt, Brace and World, Inc., 1971.

Etienne, Mona and Eleanor Leacock, eds. *Women and Colonization: Anthropological Perspectives*. Preager: A. J. F. Bergin Publishers Book, 1980.

Fanon, Frantz. *The Wretched of the Earth*. Trans. Constance Farrington. New York: Grove Press, Inc. 1963.

———. *Black Skin, White Masks*. Trans. Charles Lam Markmann. New York: Grove Press, Inc., 1967.

Forster, E. M. *A Passage to India*. 1924. A Harvest/HBJ Book, 1984.

Gandhi, Leela. *Postcolonial Theory: A Critical Introduction*. New York: Columbia University Press, 1998.

Gates, Henry Louis, Jr. ed. *"Race," Writing, and Difference*. Chicago: The University of Chicago Press, 1985.

Genette, Gérard. *Narrative Discourse: An Essay in Method*. Trans. Jane E. Lewin. Ithaca: Cornell University Press, 1980.

Hammond, J. R. *A Geroge Orwell Companion*. London: The MacMillan Press Ltd., 1982.

Harasym. Sarah. ed. *Gayatri Chakravorty Spivak, The Post-Colonial Critic: Interviews, strategies, Dialoques*. New York: Routeldge, 1989.

Hassan, Ihab. "Beyond Exile: A Postcolonial Intellectual Abroad," *Southern Review* 29.3 (1993): 453–464.

Hulme, Peter. *Colonial Encounters: Europe and the Native Caribbean 1492–1797*. London: Methuen, 1986.

Hutcheon, Linda. "The Post Always Rings Twice: The Postmodern and the Postcolonial," *Textual Practice* 8.2 (1994): 205–38.

Jameson, Frederic. *The Political Unconscious: Narrative as a Socially Symbolic Act*. Ithaca: Cornell University Press, 1981.

Kabbani, Rana. *Europe's Myth of Orient: Desire and Rule*. London: MacMillan Press Ltd., 1986.

———. *Europe's Myth of Empire*. Bloomington: Indiana University Press, 1986.

Krishnaswamy, Revathi. "Mythologies of Migrancy: Postcolonialism, Postmodernism and the Politics of (Dis)location," *Ariel* 26.1 (1995): 125–146.

Loomba, Ania. *Colonialism/Postcolonialism*. London, New York: Routledge, 1998.

Loomba, Ania and Suvir Kaul. "Introduction: Location, Culture, Post-Coloniality," *Oxford Literary Review* 16.1(1994): 3–30

Lee, Kyung-Won. "Is the Glass Half-Empty or Half-Full?: Rethinking the Problems of Postcolonial Revisionism," *Cutural Critiue* 36.1 (1997): 89–117.

Mannoni, O. *Prospero and Caliban: The Psychology of Colonization.* Trans. Pamela Powesland. New York: Frederick A. Praeger, Publishers, 1964.

McClure, John A. *Kipling and Conrad: The Colonial Fiction.* Cambridge, Mass.: Harvard University Press, 1981.

Memmi, Albert. *The Colonizer and the Colonized.* New York: The Orion Press, 1965.

Meyers, Jeffry. *Fiction and the Colonial Experience.* Totowa, NJ.: Rowmann and Littlefield Inc., 1968.

Miller, Christopher. *Blank Darkness: Africanist Discourse in French.* Chicago: The University of Chicago Press, 1985.

Mongia, Padmini, ed. *Contemporary Postcolonial Theory: A Reader.* New York: Arnold, 1996.

Naficy, Himid and Gabriel, Teshome, eds. *Discourse of the Other: Postcoloniality, Positionality and Subjectivity.* Chur: Harwood Academic Publishers, 1991.

Olson, Gary A. and Lynn Worsham, eds. *Race, Rhetoric, and the Postcolonial.* Albany: State University of New York Press, 1999.

Orwell, George. *Burmese Days.* 1934. A Harvest/HBJ Book, 1988.

Parry, Benita. "The Postcolonial: Conceptual Category or Chimera?," *Yearbook of English Studies* 27 (1997): 3–21.

———. "Problems in Current Theories of Colonial Discourse" in Ashcroft, Bill and others, eds. *The Post-Colonial Reader.* New York: Routledge, 1995. 36–44.

Said, Edward W. *Culture and Imperialism.* New York: Knopf, 1993.

———. "The Mind of Winter: Reflections on Life in Exile." *Harper's Magazine* 269 (1984): 49–55.

———. *Orientalism.* New York: Pantheon Books, 1978.

Scholes, Robert and Robert Kellogg. *The Nature of Narrative.* London: Oxford University Press, 1966.

Spivak, Gayatri Chakravorty. "Can the Subaltern Speak?" *Marxism and the Interpretation of Culture.* Edited by Cary Nelson and Lawrence Grossberg. Urbana: University of Illinois Press, 1988. 271–313.

———. *A Critique of Postcolonial Reason: Toward a History of the Vanishing Present.* Cambridge, Mass.: Harvard University Press, 1999.

Tiffin, Chris and Lawson, Alan, eds. *De-Scribing Empire: Post-Colonialism and Textuality.* New York: Routledge, 1994.

Watt, Ian. *The Rise of the Novel: Studies in Defoe, Richardson and Fielding.* Berkeley and Los Angeles: Univerity of California Press, 1957.

Weber, Samuel. *Institution and Interpretation.* Theory and History of Literature 31. Minneapolis: University of Minnesota Press, 1987.

Williams, Raymond. *The Politics of Modernism: Against the New Conformists.* London: Verso, 1989.

Van Ghent, Dorothy. *The English Novel: Form and Function.* New York: Harper Torch Books,

Harper and Row, Publishers, 1953.

Yŏm Sang-sŏp and Korean Literature

Baldwin, Frank P., Jr. *The March First Movement: Korean Challenge and Japanese Response*. Diss. Columbia University 1969. Ann Arbor: UMI, 1982.

Cho Tong-il. *Han'guk Munhak Tongsa* [An Outline of Korean Literary History]. 2 vols. Seoul: Chisik Sanŏpsa, 1983.

Choe Jong-gil. "Yŏm Sang-sŏp ŭi *Samdae* wa Irony" [Yŏm Sang-sŏp's *Samdae* and Irony]. *Ŏmunnonjip* 42.1 (2000): 239–60.

Choe Ju-han. "Yŏm Sang-sŏp kwa Kŭndaejŏl Juche" [Yŏm Sang-sŏp and Modern Subjectivity]. *Sŏgang Ŏmun* 13.1 (1997): 225–55.

Choe Hye-sil. "Yŏm Sang-sŏp sosŏl e Natananŭn Kŭndaesŏng" [Modernity in Yŏm Sang-sŏp's Works]. *Sŏnchŏng'ŏmun* 21.1 (1993): 163–85.

Cummings, Bruce. *The Origins of the Korean War: Liberation and the Emergence of Separate Regimes 1945–1947*. Princeton: Princeton University Press, 1981.

De Bary, William Theodore, ed. *Sources of Japanese Tradition*. Vol. 2. Compiled by Ryusaku Tsunoda, William Theodore de Bary and Donald Keene. 1958. New York: Columbia University Press, 1964.

Fowler, Edward. *The Rhetorics of Confession: Shishosetsu in Early Twentieth-Century Japanese Fiction*. Berkeley and Los Angeles: University of California Press, 1988.

Han Woo-keun. *The History of Korea*. Seoul: The Eul-Yoo Publishing Co., 1970.

Hŏ Myŏng-suk. "Yŏm Sang-sŏp ŭi 'Sarang kwa Joe' Yŏn'gu" [A Study of Yŏm Sang-sŏp's "Love and Sin"]. *Sungsil Ŏmun* 15.1 (1999): 403–22.

Kang Tong-jin. *Ilche ŭi Han'guk Ch'imnyak Chŏngch'aeksa: 1920nyŏndae rŭl chungsimŭro* [History of Japanese Imperial Policies in Invading Korea: Focusing 1920s]. Onŭl ŭi Sasang Sinsŏ 14. Seoul: Han'gilsa, 1980.

Kim Byŏng-gu. "1930 nyŏndae Realism Janpyŏn Sosŏl ŭi Sikminsŏng Yŏn'gu." Dissertation, Sŏgang University, 2001.

Kim C. I. Eugene and Kim Han Kyo. *Korea and the Politics of Imperialism 1876–1910*. Berkeley and Los Angeles: University of California Press, 1967.

Kim Chong-kyun. *Yŏm Sang-sŏp ŭi Saeng'ae wa Munhak* [Yŏm Sang-sŏp's Life and Literature]. Pagyŏng Mun'go 231. 1981. Seoul: Pagyŏngsa, 1984.

———. *Yŏm Sang-sŏp: Hankuk Kŭndae Realism Munhak ŭi Kŏjang* [Yŏm Sang-sŏp: The Master of Realism in Korean Modern Literature]. Seoul: Dong-A Daily, 1995.

———, ed. *Yŏm Sang-sŏp sosŏl Yŏn'gu* [Studies of Yŏm Sang-sŏp's works]. Seoul: Kukhak Jaryo Won, 1999.

Kim Mi-ji. "1920–1930 nyŏndae Yŏm Sang-sŏp Sosŏl e Natanan 'Yŏnae' ŭi Ŭimi Yŏn'gu."

Dissertation, Seoul National University, 2001.

Kim Pyŏng-chŏl. *Han'guk Kŭndae Pŏnyŏk Munhaksa Yŏn'gu* [A Study of Modern Korean History of Translated Literature]. Seoul: Ŭlyu Munwhasa, 1975.

Kim Sŭng-jong. "Yŏm Sang-sŏp Danpyŏn Sosŏl Yŏn'gu" [A Study of Yŏm Sang-sŏp's Short Stories]. *Hyŏndae Munhak Iron Yŏn'gu* 6.1 (1966): 3–37.

Kim Tong-in. *Tong-in Chŏnjip* [A Complete Collection of Kim Tong-in's Works]. 10 vols. Seoul: Honghak Chulpansa, 1964.

Kim Yong-jik. *Hyŏndae Han'guk Chakka Yŏn'gu* [A Study of Modern Korean Writers]. 1976. Seoul: Minŭmsa, 1984.

Kim U-jong. *Hyŏndae Sosŏl ŭi Ehae* [Understanding of Modern Novels]. Seoul: Iu Chulpansa, 1980.

Kim Yŏl-kyu and Sin Tong-uk, eds. *Yŏm Sang-sŏp Yŏn'gu* [A Study of Yŏm Sang-sŏp]. 1982. Seoul: Saemunsa, 1987.

Kim Yun-sik. *Han'guk Kŭndae Chakka Non'gong* [A Critical Evaluation of Modern Korean Writers]. Seoul: Ilchisa, 1981.

———. *Yŏm Sang-sŏp Yŏn'gu* [A Study of Yŏm Sang-sŏp]. Seoul: Seoul Taehakkyo Chulpanbu [Seoul National University Press], 1987.

Kim Yun-su, Paek Nak-chŏng and Yŏm Mu-wung, eds. *Han'guk Munhak ŭi Hyŏndankye* [Present Phase of Korean Literature]. 2 vols. Seoul: Changjak kwa Pipyongsa, 1983.

Ku Dae-yeol. *Korea Under Colonization: The March First Movement and Anglo-Japanese Relations*. Seoul: Seoul Computer Press for the Royal Asiatic Society, 1985.

Kwŏn Yŏng-min, ed. *Yŏm Sang-sŏp Munhak Yŏn'gu* [Researches on Yŏm Sang-sŏp's Works]. Seoul: Minŭmsa, 1987.

Lee Bo-yŏng. *Yŏm Sang-sŏp Munhakron* [Critical Discourses in Yŏm Sang-sŏp's Literature]. Seoul: Kŭmmun Sŏjŏk, 2003.

———. "Yŏm Sang-sŏp Munhak kwa Chŏngchi ŭi Munje" [Questions in Yŏm Sang-sŏp's Works and Politics]. *Hyŏndae Munhak Iron Yŏn'gu* 9.1 (1998): 201–31.

Lee Jae-sŏn. *Han'guk Hyŏndae Sosŏlsa* [A History of Modern Korean Novel]. Seoul: Hongsŏngsa, 1979.

———. *Han'guk Kaewhagi Sosŏl Yŏn'gu* [A Study of Pre-modern Novels]. Seoul: Ilchogak, 1972.

Lee Ch'ŏl-bŏm, *Han'guk Sinmunhak Taekye* [An Outline of Modern Korean Literature]. 3 vols. Seoul: Kyŏnghaksa, 1970.

Lee Chŏng-sik. *The Politics of Koran Nationalism*. Berkeley and Los Angeles: University of California Press, 1963.

Lee Ho. "Yŏm Sang-sŏp ŭi Chogi Sambujak" [Trilogy in Yŏm Sang-sŏp's Early Works]. *Sŏgang Ŏmun* 11.1 (1995): 277–312.

Lee, Peter H. *Korean Literature: Topics and Themes*. Tucson: The University of Arizona Press, 1965.

Lim Yŏng-chŏn. "Yŏm Sang-sŏp ŭi *Samdae* Yŏn'gu" [A Study of Yŏm Sang-sŏp's *Samdae*]. *Munhak kwa Jongkyo* 2.1 (1997): 65–110.

Mitchell, Richard H. *Censorship in Imperial Japan*. Princeton: Princeton University Press, 1983.

Munhaksa wa Bipyŏng Yŏn'gu Hŏe. *Yŏm Sang-sŏp Munhak ŭi Jaejomyŏng* [Re-readings of Yŏm Sang-sŏp's works]. Seoul: Barobook dot com, 2001.

Munhak kwa Sasang Yŏn'gu Hŏe. *Yŏm Sang-sŏp Munhak ŭi Jaeinsik* [Re-interpretation of Yŏm Sang-sŏp's works]. Seoul: Kipŭnsaem, 1998.

Nahm, Andrew C., ed. *Korea under Japanese Colonial Rule: Studies of the Policy and Technique of Japanese Colonialism*. The 3rd Conference on Korea in Western Michigan University, 1970. The Center for Korean Studies and Institute of International and Area Studies, Western Michigan University, 1973.

———. *Korea: A History of the Korean People, Tradition and Transformation*. Elizabeth, NJ: Hollym Int'l Corp., 1988.

Park Dong-kyu. *Yŏm Sang-sŏp ŭi* Samdae *rŭl Chaja: Hankuk Munhak kwa Nonsul ŭi Silje* [In Search of Yŏm Sang-sŏp's *Samdae*: Practices in Korean Literature and Critical Discourse]. Seoul: Pŏmhan, 1994.

Park Jung-wu. "Yŏm Sang-sŏp Haebang'gi Sosŏl Yŏn'gu: Hyŏnsil Insik ŭi Banyŏng Yangsang kwa Byŏnmo Kwajŏng" [A Study on Yŏm Sang-sŏp's Novels in the Emancipation Period]. Dissertation, Jung Ang University, 2000.

Park Sang-jun. *1920 nyŏndae Munhak kwa Yŏm Sang-sŏp* [Literature of 1920s and Yŏm Sang-sŏp]. Seoul: Yŏkrak, 2000.

Paek Nak-chŏng. *Minjok Munhak kwa Sekye Munhak* [National Literature and World Literature]. Seoul: Changjak kwa Pipyŏngsa, 1978.

———. "Sinsikminji Sidae wa Sŏyang Munhak Ilkki" [Neocolonial Era and Readings in Western Literature]. *Han'guk Minjok Minjung Undong Yŏn'gu* [A Study of Korean People's Movement]. Edited by Paek Nak-chŏng and Chŏng Ch'ang-yŏl. Seoul: Ture, 1989.

Song Hyŏn-kyŏng. *Han'guk Sosŏl ŭi Kujo wa Silsang* [Structure and Form of Korean Novel]. Kyŏngnam University Press, 1981.

Song Kyŏng-a. "Yŏm Sang-sŏp Chogi Sosŏl ŭi Yŏsŏngsang Yŏn'gu" [A Study on the Images of Women in Yŏm Sang-sŏp's Early Novels]. Dissertation, Yŏnse University, 2001.

Suh Du-su. *Korean Literay Reader*. Seoul: Dong-A Publishing, 1965.

Yim Yong-taek and Choe Wŏn-sik, eds. *Han'guk Kŭndae Munhaksaron* [Essays on the History of Modern Korean Literature]. Seoul: Han'gilsa, 1982.

Yŏm Sang-sŏp. *Yŏm Sang-sŏp Chŏnjip* [A Complete Collection of Yŏm Sang-sŏp's Works]. Edited by Kwŏn Yŏng-min and others. Seoul: Minŭmsa, 1987.

Yu Si-wuk. "Yŏm Sang-sŏp ŭi *Samdae* Ron" [A Thesis on Yŏm Sang-sŏp's *Samdae*]. *Sŏgang Ŏmun* 15.1 (1999): 139-58.

Yun Pyŏng-ro. *Han'guk Hyŏndae Sosŏl ŭi Tamgu* [Researches on Modern Korean Novel]. Seoul: Pŏmusa, 1980.

Yun Pyŏng-sŏp and others, eds. *Han'guk Kŭndaesaron: Ilche Singminji Sidae ŭi Sahoemunwha Undong* [Essays on Modern Korean History: Social and Cultural Movements during Japanese Colonial Period]. Vol. 3. Seoul: Chisik Sanŏpsa, 1977.

Yun Pyŏng-sŏp. *Yŏm Sang-sŏp Chŏnban'gi Sosŏl Yŏn'gu* [A Study of Yŏm Sang-sŏp's Early Works]. Seoul: Asea Munwhasa, 1985.

Chinua Achebe

Achebe, Chinua. *Morning Yet on Creation Day: Essays*. Garden City, NY: Anchor Press/ Doubleday, 1975.

———. *No Longer at Ease*. 1960. Heinemann; New York: Fawcett Premier, 1969.

———. *Things Fall Apart*. 1958. Heinemann; New York: Fawcett Crest, 1969.

———. *Arrow of God*. 1964. Heinemann; New York: Anchor Books, 1969.

———. "An Image of Africa." *Research in African Literature* 9. 1 (1978): 1–15. reprinted by permission of *The Massachusetts Review*, 1977.

Adebayo, Tunji. "The Past and the Present in Chinua Achebe's Novels." *Ife African Studies* 1.1 (1974): 66–84.

Ball, John Clement. *Satire and the Postcolonial Novel: V. S. Naipaul, Chinua Achebe, Salman Rushdie*. New York and London: Routledge, 2003.

Bloom, Harold, ed. *Chinua Achebe's* Things Fall Apart. Modern Critical Interpretations. Philadelphia: Chelsea House Publishers, 2002.

Booker, M. Keith. *The African Novel in English: An Introduction*. Portsmouth, NH.: Heinemann, 1998.

Booth, James. *Writers and Politics in Nigeria*. London: Hodder and Stoughton, 1981.

Brown, Lloyd W. "Cultural Norms and Modes of Perception in Achebe's Fiction." *Critical Perspectives on Chinua Achebe*. Edited by C. L. Innes and Bernth Lindfors. Washington, D. C.: Three Continents Press, 1978. 22–36.

Chinweizu, and others, eds. *Toward the Decolonization of African Literature*. Vol. 1. Washington, D. C.: Howard University Press, 1983.

Egejuru, Phanuel Akubueze. *Towards African Literary Independence: A Dialogue with Contemporary African Writers*. Westport, Connecticut: Greenwood Press, 1980.

Emenyonu, Ernest. "African Literature: What Does It Take to be Its Critic?" *African Literature Today: The Novel in Africa*. An annual Review 5. Edited by Eldred Durosimi Jones. New York: Africana Publishing corp., 1971. 1–11.

Gikandi, Simon. *Reading Chinua Achebe: Language and Ideology in Fiction*. Studies in African Literature. Portsmouth, NH.: Heinemann, 1991.

Griffiths, Gareth. "Language and Action in the Novels of Chinua Achebe." *African Literature Today: The Novel in Africa*. Edited by Eldred Jones. An Annual Review 5. New York: Africana Publishing Corp., 1971.

Harris, Wilson. "The Frontier on Which Heart of Darkness Stands." *Research in African Literatures* 12. 1 (1981): 86–93.

Innes, C. L. and Bernth Lindfors, eds. *Critical Perspectives on Chinua Achebe*. Washington, D. C.: Three Continents Press, 1978.

Irele, Abiola. "The Tragic Conflict in the Novels of Chinua Achebe." *Critical Perspectives on Chinua Achebe*. Editied by C. L. Innes and Bernth Lindfors. Washington, D. C.: Three Continents Press, 1978. 10–21.

Jones, Eldred. "The Decolonization of African Literature." *The Writer in Modern Africa*. Edited by Per Wästberg. New York: Africana Publishing Corp., 1969.

Kemoli, A. M. "The Novels of Chinua Achebe: A Prophecy of Violence." *Joliso* 2.1 (1974): 47–66.

Khayyoom, S. A. *Chinua Achebe: A Study of His Novels*. New Delhi: Sangam, 1999.

Killam, G. D. *The Novels of Chinua Achebe*. New York: Africana Publishing Corp., 1969.

———. "Notions of Religion, Alienation and Achetype in *Arrow of God*." *Exile and Tradition: Studies in Africa and Caribbean Literature*. Ed. Rowland Smith. New York: African Publishing Co., 1976. 152–65.

Larson, Charles R. *The Emergence of African Fiction*. Bloomington: Indiana University Press, 1971.

Lindfors, Bernth. *Folklore in Nigerian Literature*. New York: Africana Publishing Co., 1973.

Melamu, M. J. "The Quest for Power in Achebe's *Arrow of God*." *English Studies in Africa* 14. 2 (1971): 225–42.

McDaniel, Richard Bryan. "The Python Episodes in Achebe's Novels." *The International Fiction Review*. 3.2 (1976): 100–06.

Moses, Michael Valdez. *The Novel and the Globalization of Culture*. New York, Oxford: Oxford University Press, 1995.

Ogede, Ode. *Achebe and The Politics of Representation*. Trenton, NJ.: Africa World Press, Inc., 2001.

Ogunbiyi, Yemi. *Perspectives on Nigerian Literature: 1700 to the Present*. Vol. 1. Lagos: Guardian Books Nigeria Ltd., 1988.

Okechukwu, Chinwe Christiana. *Achebe the Orator: The Art of Persuasion in Chinua Achebe's Novels*. Westport, Connecticut: Greenwod Press, 2001.

Okpaku, Joseph, ed. *New African Literature and the Arts*. Vol. 2. New York: Thomas Y. Crowell Co., 1968.

Oliver, Roland and J. D. Fage. *A Short History of Africa*. 1962. London: Penguin Books, 1988.

Schmidt, Nancy. "Nigerian Fiction and the African Oral Tradition." *New African Literature and the Arts*. Vol. 2. Edited by Joseph Okpaku. New York: Thomas Y. Crowell Co., 1968.

25–38.

Shelton, Austin J., ed. *Exile and Tradition: Studies in African and Caribbean Literatures.* New York: African Publishing Co., 1976.

Thiong'o, Ngugi wa. *Decolonising the Mind: The Politics of Language in African Literature.* London: James Currey Ltd., 1981.

———. *Writers in Politics: Essays.* London: Heinemann, 1981.

———. *Writing Against Neocolonialism.* Wembly, Middlesex, 1986.

Tucker, Martin. *Africa in Modern Literature: A Survey of Contemporary Writing in English.* New York: Frederick Ungar Publishing Co., 1967.

Wren, Robert M. *Achebe's World: The Historical and Cultural Context of the Novels of Chinua Achebe.* Harlow, Essex: Longman, 1981.

Weinstock, Donald. "Achebe's Christ-Figure." *New African Literature and the Arts.* Vol. 2. Edited by Joseph Okpaku. New York: Thomas Y. Crowell Co., 1968.

Salman Rushdie

Ball, John Clement. *Satire and the Postcolonial Novel: V. S. Naipaul, Chinua Achebe, Salman Rushdie.* New York and London: Routledge, 2003.

Bharucha, Rushtom. "Rushdie's Whale." *The Massachusetts Review* Summer (1986): 221–37.

Booker, M. Keith, ed. *Critical Essays on Salman Rushdie.* New York: G. K. Hall and Co., 1999.

Brennan, Timothy A. "India, Nationalism, and Other Failures." *The South Atlantic Quarterly* 87. 1 (1988): 131–46.

———. *Salman Rushdie and the Third World: Myths of the Nation.* New York: St. Martin Press, 1989.

Chaudhuri, Una. "Handcuffed to History." Review of *Midnight's Children* by Salman Rushdie. *Commonweal* 108 (1981): 533–34.

———. "Fiction, History, Tragedy." Review of *Shame* by Salman Rushdie. *Commonweal* 110 (1983): 590–91.

Cronin, Richard. "The Indian English Novel: *Kim* and *Midnight's Children.*" *Modern Fiction Studies* 33. 2 (1987): 201–13.

Cundy, Catherine. *Salman Rushdie.* Manchester and New York: Manchester University Press, 1996.

Cuoto, Maria. "Midnight's Children and Parents: The Search for Indo-British Identity." *Encounter* 58. 2 (1982): 61–66.

Dhawan, R. K. ed. *Three Contemporary Novelists: Khushwant Singh, Chaman Nahal, Salman Rushdie.* New Delhi: Classical Publishing Co., 1985.

Enright, D. J. "So, and Not So." Review of *The Satanic Verses* by Salman Rushdie. *The New*

York Review 2 Mar. 1989: 25–26.

Fletcher, M. D. "Rushdie's Shame as Apologue." *The Journal of commonwealth Literature* 21. 1 (1986): 120–32.

———. ed. *Reading Rushdie: Perspectives on the Fiction of Salman Rushdie.* Cross/Cultures 16. Amsterdam: Rodopi, 1994.

Ford, Boris, ed. *The New Pelican Guide to English Literature.* Vol. 8. Penguin Books, 1983.

Goonetilleke, D. C. R. A. *Salman Rushdie.* New York: St. Martin's Press, 1998.

Harrison, J. *Salman Rushdie.* New York: Twayne, 1992.

Hassumani, Sabrina. *Salman Rushdie: A Postmodern Reading of His Major Works.* London: Associated University Press, 2002.

Hedges, Chris. "Rushdie Seeks to Mend His Rift with Islam." *New York Times* 25 Dec. 1990.

Hitchens, Christopher. "Siding with Rushdie." Review of *The Rushdie File* edited by Lisa Appignanesi and Sara Maitland, *Counter Blasts No 4: Sacred Cows* by Fay Weldon and *Salman Rushdie and the Third World: Myths of the Nation* by Timothy Brennan. *London Review of Books* 26 Oct. 1989: 11–15.

Jain. Madhu. "An Irreverent Journey." Review of *The Satanic Verses* by Salman Rushdie. *India Today* 15 Sept. 1988: 98–99.

Jenkins, McKay. "Rushdie's *Midnight's Children*, Meditation, and the Postmodern Conception of History." *Postmodernity and Cross-Culturalism.* Edited by Yoshinobu Hakutani. London: Associated University Presses, Madison, Teaneck: Fairleigh Dickinson University Press, 2002. 62–75.

Kakutani, Michiko. "Telling Truth Through Fantasy: Rushdie's Magic Realism." *New York Times* 24 Feb. 1989: C30.

Mortimer, Edward. "Satanic Verses': The Aftermath." Review of *The Rushdie File* edited by Lisa Appignanesi and Maitland, *The Satanic Affair* by Daniel Pipes and *Salman Rushdie: Sentenced to Death* by W. J. Weatherby. *New York Times Book Review* 22 July 1990: 3, 25.

Price, D. W. "Salman Rushdie's 'Use and Abuse of History' in *Midnight's Children*." *Ariel* 25.2 (1994): 91–107.

Pritchett, V. S. "Books: Two Novels." Review of *Midnight's Children* by Salman Rushdie and "The Hangwoman" by Pavel Kohout. *The New Yorker* 27 July 1981: 84–86.

Rosenblatt, Roger. "Zealots with Fear in Their Eyes." *U. S. News and World Report* 27 Feb. 1989: 8–11.

Rushdie, Salman. *Midnight's Children.* 1980. New York: Alfred a. Knoph, Inc.; Bard Printing, 1982.

———. "Imaginary Homelands." London Review of Books 4 (1982): 18–19.

———. "The Empire Writes Back with a Vengeance." The Times 3 July 1982: 8.

———. *Shame.* 1983. New York: Alfred A. Knoph, Inc.; New York: Vintage International, 1989.

———. *The Jaguar Smile: A Nicaraguan Journey.* 1st American ed. New York: Viking, 1987.

———. "My Book Speaks for Itself." *New York Times* 17 Feb. 1989: A39.

———. "Now I Can Say, I Am a Muslim." *New York Times* 28 Dec. 1990.

Ruthven, Malise. "Islam and the Book." *Times Literary Suppliment* 4469 (1988).

———. *A Satanic Affair: Salman Rushdie and the Rage of Islam*. London: Chatto and Windus, 1990.

Sanga. Jaina. *Salman Rushdie's Postcolonial Metaphors: Migration, Translation, Hybridity, Blasphemy, and Globalization*. Wesport, Connecticut: Greenwood Press, 2001.

Smith, William E. "Hunted by an Angry Faith." *Time* 27 Feb. 1989: 28–29.

Watson, Russel. "A 'Satanic' Fury." *Newsweek* 27 Feb. 1989: 34–39.

Weatherby, W. J. *Salman Rushdie: Sentenced to Death*. New York: Caroll and Graf Publishers, Inc., 1990.

Whitney, Craig R. "Rushdie Appeals for Muslim Tolerance of 'Satanic Verses.'" *New York Times* 5 Feb. 1990: C11, C18.

Wieseltier, Leon. "Midnight's Other Children." Review of *Shame* by Salman Rushdie. *The New Republic* 189 (1983): 32–34.

Wilson, Keith. "*Midnight's Children* and Reader Responsibility." *Critical Quarterly* 26. 3 (1984): 23–37.

Index

Achebe, Chinua, 1, 6, 8–9, 13 17–18, 25, 71–119, 180, 181–82, 183, 184; and English, 77–79; and Colonialist Criticism, 79-81; and Conrad, 81–87; *Anthills of the Savannah*, 72; *Arrow of God*, 17, 18, 71, 72, 87, 98, 99–109, 118, 119, 181; *Man of People, A*, 72; *Morning Yet on Creation Day: Essays*, 77; *No Longer at Ease*, 17, 18, 71, 72, 87, 99, 109–18, 181; *Things Fall Apart*, 17, 18, 71, 72, 86, 87–99, 100, 105, 109, 113, 118, 119, 181
Africa in Modern Literature, 73
African Assertion, The, 73
Africanisme, 2
African literature, 13–14, 73–81; definition, 73–79; language issue,75–79; colonialist criticism, 79–81
Anand, Mulk Raj, 15, 19, 121, 122
Arabian Nights, 20, 143, 175
Arendt, Hanna, 6; *Origins of Totalitarianism, The*, 6
Arishima Takeo, 31, 43; *Birth Pangs*, 43
Austin, Jane, 20

Bakhtin, M. M., 96, 121
Baldwin, F., 55
Balzac, 20, 26; "Sarrasine," 26
Barthes, R., 26; *S/Z*, 26
Bende-Onitsha Hinterland Expedition, 96
Bereng, David C. T, 74
Bharucha, Rustom, 146

Bhutto, Ali, 160
Black Skin, White Masks, 7, 78
Blank Darkness: Africanist Discourse in French, 2
Booker, M. Keith, 75
Booker Prize, 121
Brennan, Timothy, 18–19, 175–76; *Salman Rushdie and the Third World*, 18–19
Brown, Lloyd W., 75, 98, 118
Buchholtz, Johannes, 74
Buchner, Georg, 160–161; *Danton's Death* 160
Burmese Days, 139

Caliban, 75
Carlyle, Thomas, 14
Cary, Joyce, 74, 75, 101, 182; *Mister Johnson*, 75, 101–2
centrality, 126, 130, 135–38. see also marginality
Cervantes, 20
Ch'ae Man-sik, 58; *T'angnyu*, 58; *T'aep'yŏng Ch'ŏ nha*, 58
chamcha, 10
Ch'angjo, 21, 30
Ch'iaksan, 28
Choe Nam-sŏn, 21, 23, 33
choice of language, 8–11
chokbo, 62
Ch'unhyangjŏn, 28
chungin, 34
Colonial discourse, 2–5

Colonizer and the Colonized, The, 7
Coleridge, S. T., 14
confessional narrative, 30–36
Conrad, Joseph, 4, 5, 20–30, 50, 74, 75, 81, 101, 182; *Heart of Darkness*, 5, 17, 29–30, 50, 58, 74, 81–86, 87, 101
Conradian discourse, 83–86, 98, 185
Cuoto, Mario, 147

Dadié, Bernard, 74
Dali, Salvador, 82
Dante, 31
Danton's Death, 160
Darstellung, 8
Decolonising the Mind, 9, 77
decolonization 6
dehumanization 105
Derrida, J., 8
Desani, G. V., 15, 124, 147, 171
Diop, Birago, 74
Diop, David, 74
Doll's House, A, 47
Donne, John, 79

Eagleton, Terry, 1
East India Company, 138
Ekwensi, Cyprian, 74
Eliot, T. S., 72, 118
Emenyonu, Ernest, 81
Emerson, R. W., 14
Empire Writes Back, The, 6, 10

Fanon, Frantz, 6–7, 54, 78, 104; *Black Skin, White Masks*, 7, 78; *Wretched of the Earth, The*, 7, 54, 104
fatwa, 25, 123, 174, 176

Faulkner, William, 158; *Sound and the Fury, The*, 158
Fielding, H., 20
Flaubert, 20
Forster, E. M., 4, 123; *Passage to India, A*, 179
Foucault, Michel, 8
French Revolution, 160, 164
Fula, Nuthall, 74

Gates, Henry Louis, Jr, 7, 17; *"Race," Writing, and Difference*, 7; *Figures in Black: Words, Signs, and the*, 7–8
gender discourse in postcolonialism, 8
Ghandi, Indira, 131, 133
Gide, André, 74
Goethe, 13, 31
Gordimer, Nadine, 74
Grass, Günter, 20
Green, Graham, 74; *Heart of the Matter*, 74
Guruprasad, Thakur, 147

han'gŭl, 11, 12, 33
hanmun, 33
Harris, Wilson, 85–86
Heart of Darkness, 5, 17, 29–30, 50, 58, 74, 81–86, 87
Heerden, Ernst van, 74
Hemingway, Ernest, 74
Heuser, Kurt, 74
Hinduism, 14, 123, 131
historicity, 122, 125, 128, 130, 132, 138
historicizing, 25, 48, 50, 96, 136–37, 147–48
Hototogisu, 28
Hughes, Langston, 74
Hugo, 31

Index

Hwang Sŏk-wu, 32

Ibsen, Henrik, 47; *Doll's House, A*, 47
Igbo tradition, 17, 88, 97–98, 99, 105–6, 111–12, 182; balance of masculinity and femininity, 87–91, 105; and Christianity, 92–96, 97, 98, 103–4, 112–14; and 'falling apart,' 92, 99; proverbs and folklore, 18, 86, 98; and rigidity, 89–90, 92–94
Imperialism: the Highest Stage of Capitalism, 6
Imperial lie, 5, 29
India: A Wounded Civilization, 125
infantalization, 105
I-novel. *see Shishosetsu*
Iqbal, Mohammad, 15
Irele, Abiola, 72
Islam, 13, 14, 15, 123, 163

Jahn, Janheinz, 74
Jameson, Frederic, 1
JanMohamed, Abul R, 141–42
Japanese Occupation of Korea, The, 10, 12, 16, 22, 53, 54
Jones, Eldred, 75–76, 80
'Journey of the Magi, The,' 72, 118
Ju Si-kyŏng, 33

Kabo Reformation, 32
Kalidasa, 14; *Shakuntala*, 14
Kaebyŏk, 21
Kafka, Franz, 158; *Trial, The*, 158
Kang Tong-jin, 54
kanji, 33
KAPF (Korea Artista Proleta Federatio), 16

Kemoli, A. M., 105
Kessel, Joseph, 74
Khomeini, Ayatolah, 121, 174
Kim Ch'an-yŏng, 32
Kim Nam-chŏn, 58; *Taeha*, 58
Kim Ŏk, 32
Kim Tan-sil, 32
Kim Tong-in, 11, 21, 30, 32, 33, 34, 35, 39, 56
Kim Yun-sik, 27, 28, 30, 34, 43, 56
Kipling, Rudyard, 4, 14, 123, 139, 140; *Kim*, 4; Short stories on India, 4, 139
Konjiki Yasha, 29
Korean literature, 11–13, 15–17, 21–25; and the annexation by Japan, 22–23; and Japanese censorship, 26
Korean War, The, 22

language issue in postcolonial literature, 8–11; *see also* language issue in African literature
Larson, Charles, 18
Lartéguy, Jean, 74
lingua franca, 75
linguistic criteria, 79

Macaulay, Thomas, 3, 124
Makerere Conference, 74, 76
Mahabharata, 14, 20
Mahfuz, Naguib, 180
Mahood, M. M., 108
Malonga, Jean, 74
Mannoni, O, 7; *Prospero and Caliban*, 7
Manse Undong, The. *see* March First Movement, The
Manyoshu, 13
March First Movement, The, 11, 23, 24, 27,

34, 36, 37, 38, 48, 49, 52, 55, 68, 69
marginality, 135–38, 153–54, 159, 166. *see also* centrality
Marquez, Gabriel Garcia, 20, 125, 180
Memmi, Albert, 6, 7; *Colonizer and the Colonized, The*, 7
Miller, Christopher L, 2; *Blank Darkness: Africanist Discourse in French*, 2
Millin, Sarah Gertrude, 74
Milton, John, 79
Mister Johnson, 75, 103
Mofolo, Thomas, 74
Montaigne, 3; "On Cannibals," 3
Moslem literature, 14, 15. *see also* Islam
Mphahlele, 77
Mudan Chŏngch'i, 24
Mudan T'ongch'i, 36
mundan, 23, 30, 33, 34
Munwha Chŏngch'i, 24
Munwha T'ongch'i, 36
Myth of the Other, The, 2, 179

Na Hye-sŏk, 35
Naipaul, V. S, 123, 182; *India: A Wounded Civilization*, 123
Narayan, R. K., 15, 121, 122
national criteria, 79
new novel, 33
new woman. *see sinyŏsŏng*
Ngugi wa Thiong'o, 9, 17, 76–77, 78; *Decolonising the Mind*, 9, 77
Ngugi wa Thiong'o: The Making of a Rebel, 76
Nobel Prize, 121, 179
noble savage, 3
Ntara, Samuel Yosia, 74

Occident, 3
Okubo, 54
"On Cannibals," 3
Orient, 2, 3
Orientalism, 2
Origins of Totalitarianism, The, 6
Orwell, Geroge, 4, 139; *Burmese Days*, 139
Other, The, 1–5
Oyono, Ferdinand, 74
Ozaki Koyo, 28; *Konjiki Yasha*, 28

Paek Nak-chŏng, 12
p'ansori, 12
pantheism, 14
Partition of India, 140, 150, 167
Passage to India, A, 179
Paton, Alan, 74
pidgin, 79
politicizing, 48
Prospero, 75
Postcolonial discourse, 6–10
Prospero and Caliban, 7
P'yehŏ, 21, 30, 31, 32

Rabéarivelo, Jean-Joseph, 74
race consciousness, 7
"Race," Writing, and Difference, 7
racism, 7, 14
Ramayana, 14, 20
Rao, Raja, 15, 19, 121, 122
readerly text, 27
Rushdie, Salman, 1, 6, 9–10, 15, 18–20, 25, 26, 121–177, 180, 181, 182, 183; and English, 124, 146–47; 'Imaginary Homeland,' 143, 145; *Jaguar Smile, The*, 122, 124; *Midnight's Children*, 19, 25, 121, 122, 124, 125–49, 151, 154,

Index

155, 159, 165, 166, 169, 171, 173, 174, 177, 186; *Satanic Verses, The*, 19, 25, 121, 164, 173–77; *Shame*, 19, 20, 25, 121, 122, 126, 128, 147, 149–73, 174, 177
Russian Revolution, 16, 27
Russo-Japanese War, The, 11
Ruthven, Malise, 175; *Satanic Affair, A*, 175

Said, Edward, 1, 2, 177; *Orientalism*, 2; 'Mind of Winter, The,' 177
Saigo, 54
Saito Makoto, 24
Salman Rushdie and the Third World, 19
Samil Manse Undong, The. see March First Movement, The
Sanskrit literature, 14
"Sarrasine," 26
Satanic Affair, A, 175
Scarlet Letter, 47
Scheherazade, 143, 147. see also Arabian Nights
Schmidt, Nancy, 86
'Second Coming, The,' 71, 98
Shakespeare, W., 13, 79
Shakuntala, 14
Shelley, P. B., 14
Shelton, Austin J, 73; *African Assertion, The*, 73
Shiga Naoya, 30, 31, 43
Shin Ch'ae-ho, 33
Shirakaba group (*Shirakabaha*), 30, 31, 43
Shishosetsu, 31
Sicherman, Carol, 76; *Ngugi wa Thiong'o: The Making of a Rebel*, 76
sijo, 29
Sin Ch'ae-ho, 33
Sino-Japanese War, The, 11

sinsosŏl, 33
sinyŏsŏng, 35, 47
sosŏl, 33
sosŏlga, 33
Soyinka, Wole, 8, 71, 74, 77, 180
Spivak, Gayatri Chakravorty, 1, 8
Social Darwinism, 2, 83
Sound and the Fury, The, 158
Spenser, E., 79
Stern, Laurence, 20
Stewart, J. F, 95–96
Suh Du-su, 22
S/Z, 26

Tagore, R, 15, 121
Tale of Genji, The, 13
Terauchi, 52
Third World, The, 2, 9, 149, 162, 164, 172, 179, 182
Thoreau, H. D., 14
Thousand and One Nights, The. see Arabian Nights
Tokutomi Roka, 28; *Hototogisu*, 28
Tolstoy, 13, 20, 31
Trial, The, 158
Tucker, Martin, 73–74; *Africa in Modern Literature*, 73

Ulhaq, Zia, 160, 162

Vedic hymns, 14
Vertretung, 8

waka, 29
Wali, Obiajunua (Obi), 76–77, 78–79
Walsh, William, 121

Waseda Bungaku, 29
Watakushi shosetsu. see *Shishosetsu*
"white man's burden," 4, 140
Whitney, Craig R., 176
Williams, Raymond, 1
Wilson, Keith, 148
Wordsworth, W., 14
Wren, Robert M., 95, 109
Wretched of the Earth, The, 7, 104
writerly text, 27

Yanagi Muneyoshi, 30, 31
yangban, 34, 62
Yang Chu-dong, 16
Yeats, W. B., 71, 98, 100
Yi In-jik, 28; *Ch'iaksan*, 28
Yi Kwang-su, 12, 21, 23, 33
Yŏm Sang-sŏp, 1, 6, 10, 12, 13, 15–17, 21–69, 94, 180–81, 183, 184; and ambivalence, 25–30; and "brother complex," 27–28; and censorship, 25–27, 30; and confessional narrative, 30–33; "Am-ya," 22, 35–36, 37, 42–43, 48; "Che-ya," 22, 35–36, 37, 44–48, 56, 58; "Chŏsuha esŏ," 30, 32; "Chukŭm kwa kŭ Kŭrim-ja," 37; "E Sŏnsaeng," 28, 34; *Hae-baragi*, 35, 56; *Kyŏnuwha*, 43; *Manse-jŏn*, 22, 26, 27, 36, 37, 38, 43, 48–58, 68; "P'yobonsil ŭi Ch'ŏng'-gaeguri," 21, 22, 30, 32, 35–36, 37, 38–42, 48; *Samdae*, 25, 58–69, 94; *Sarang kwa Choe*, 56; *Sinhon'gi*, 35; "Yŏ ŭi P'yŏngjajŏk Kach'i rŭl Nonham e Tapham," 31; "*Yisim*, 56

COMPARATIVE CULTURES AND LITERATURES

The books in this series compare and contrast two or more national, ethnic, religious, historical or social cultures, and/or literatures. The scope is open to encourage innovative studies of societies or literatures that have traditionally been compared, or that have traditionally not been compared. Analyses may address contrasts and comparisons not only across national boundaries, but also across time.

For additional information about the series or for the submission of manuscripts, please contact:

        Dr. Daniel Walden, Editor
        Comparative Cultures and Literatures Series
        English Department
        Penn State University
        117 Burrowes Building
        University Park, PA 16802

To order other books in this series, please contact our Customer Service Department:

        (800) 770-LANG (within the U.S.)
        (212) 647-7706 (outside the U.S.)
        (212) 647-7707 FAX

Or, browse online by series:
        www.peterlangusa.com